S0-BJH-382

A Garland Series

The English Stage
Attack and Defense 1577 - 1730

A collection of 90 important works
reprinted in photo-facsimile in 50 volumes

edited by
Arthur Freeman
Boston University

The Impartial Critick

by

John Dennis

Miscellaneous Letters and Essays

by

Charles Gildon

8 4 5 9 3

with a preface
for the Garland Edition by

Arthur Freeman

Garland Publishing, Inc., New York & London

1973

Copyright © 1973

by Garland Publishing, Inc.

All Rights Reserved

Library of Congress Cataloging in Publication Data

Dennis, John, 1657-1734.
  The impartial critick.

  (The English stage: attack and defense 1577-1730)
  Reprint of 2 works, the 1st originally printed in
1693 for R. Taylor, London; and the 2d printed in 1694
for B. Bragg, London.
  1. Rymer, Thomas, 1641-1713. A short view of
tragedy. 2. Shakespeare, William, 1564-1616--
Criticism and interpretation. I. Gildon, Charles,
1665-1724. Miscellaneous letters and essays. 1973.
II. Title. III. Series.
PN1891.D4 1973   822.3'3   72-170436
ISBN 0-8240-0604-6

Printed in the United States of America

PN
1891
D4
1973

Preface

The most important contemporary responses to Thomas Rymer's Short View of Tragedy *were those of John Dennis and Charles Gildon, comprised in the former's* The Impartial Critick *(1693) and the latter's* Miscellaneous Letters and Essays *(1694).* The Impartial Critick *is Dennis' earliest independent book, consisting of five dialogues between "Freeman" and "Beaumont" tending to the vindication of Shakespeare above all, and endorsing the scattered opinions of Dryden, which had opposed, in prologues and conversation, the strictures of Rymer. It is generally accounted one of Dennis' finest individual performances.*

At the conclusion of the tract Dennis implies that he will presently return to a further vindication of Shakespeare from Rymer's aspersions, and for this reason Charles Gildon, whose own protective instincts were aroused, deferred to his more skillful predecessor. But a year passed, and at last Gildon included "Some Reflections on Mr.

Rymer's Short View of Tragedy, and an Attempt at a Vindication of Shakespear" in his Miscellaneous Letters and Essays. *Hooker surmises (I, 435) that any leftover ideas or notes preserved by Dennis may have come to rest in his* Essay on the Genius and Writings of Shakespeare *(1711), a full and distinguished appraisal.*

The Impartial Critick *has been edited by Hooker (I, 11-41; notes, I, 434-445) and previously included by Spingarn (with errors signaled by Hooker) in volume three of his* Seventeenth-Century Critical Essays *(1908). It was advertised in the* London Gazette *of 27 February 1693, and listed in the Term Catalogues (II, 441) for February, 1693. Nonetheless Lowndes, and Jaggard, probably following Lowndes, list editions of 1692 (virtually impossible) and 1697, of which no copies have been otherwise recorded. We reprint the British Museum copy (641.e.51), collating A^4 [a] ^{4} B-G^4 H^2. Wing D 1030; Lowe-Arnott-Robinson 3706. Of Gildon's* Miscellaneous Letters and Essays *we reprint the first edition of 1694 (Wing G 732; Lowe-Arnott-Robinson 3707; advertised in the Term Catalogues [II, 512] for June). A second edition appeared in 1696, and a third, under the revised title* Letters and Essays, on

PREFACE

Several Subjects. *Our copy is from the British Museum (1088.e.17), collating A-P^8 Q^4.*

May, 1973   A.F.

THE

Impartial Critick:

OR, SOME

OBSERVATIONS

Upon a Late BOOK, Entituled,

A Short View of TRAGEDY,

Written by Mr. RYMER,

AND

Dedicated to the Right Honourable

CHARLES Earl of DORSET, &c.

By Mr. DENNIS.

Hanc etiam Mecœnas *aspice partem.*

Virgil.

LONDON:

Printed for R. *Taylor,* near *Stationers-Hall.* 1693.

A

Letter to a Friend:

Sent with the Following

DIALOGUES.

SIR,

UPon reading Mr. *Rymer's* late Book, I soon found that its Design was to make several Alterations in the Art of the Stage, which instead of reforming, would ruine the *English Drama.* For to set up the *Grecian* Method amongst us with success, it is absolutely necessary to restore not only their Religion and their Polity, but to transport us to the same Climate in which *Sophocles* and *Euripides* writ; or else by reason of those different Circum-

stances,

ſtances,ſeveral things which were graceful and
decent with them, muſt ſeem ridiculous and
abſurd to us , as ſeveral things which would
have appear'd highly extravagant to them,muſt
look proper and becoming with us.

For an Example of the firſt: The Chorus
had a good effect with the *Athenians*, becauſe
it was adapted to the Religion and Temper of
that People, as I have obſerv'd more at large
in the Fourth Dialogue. But we having nothing in our Religion or Manners, by which
we may be able to defend it, it ought certainly to be baniſhed from our Stage. For
Poetry in general, being an imitation of Nature, Tragedy muſt be ſo too. Now it is
neither probable, nor natural, that the Chorus, who repreſent the Intereſted Spectators
of a Tragical Action, ſhould Sing and Dance
upon ſuch terrible or moving Events , as neceſſarily arrive in every Tragedy. And I
wonder that Mr. *Rymer* ſhould cry up a Chorus, in the very ſame Book in which he cries
down the Opera : for no Man can give any
Reaſon, why an Opera is an extravagant
thing ; but I will, by retorting the ſame Reaſon, prove a Chorus extravagant too. But
to

to make the abfurdity of it the more apparent, let me defire you, *Sir,* a little to look
back to the *Spanish Invafion,* which Mr. *Raid*
fancies a proper Subject for a Tragedy : Sup-
pofe then, that an Exprefs gives Notice to
Queen *Elizabeth,* of the Landing of the *Spaniards* upon our Coaft, and of great Number
of Subjects revolting and running in to them.
The Queen upon the reception of this News,
falls a lamenting her Condition, with an Air becoming of a Sovereign Princefs, in whom Sorrow
and Majefty muft be united : fo far there is no
offence to Nature or Decency ; for this may
be call'd Tragedy upon the Stage of the
World. But then, *Sir,* fuppofe that as
foon as the Queen has left off lamenting, the
Ladies about her, in their Ruffs and Farthin-
gals, fell a dancing a *Saraband* to a doleful
Ditty : Do you think, *Sir,* that if this had
really happened at *White-Hall,* it would have
been poffible to have beheld it without laughing, tho' one had been never fo much concerned for his Country ? Now can any thing
that is incongruous and abfurd in the World,
be proper and decent on the Tragick
Stage.

I

A Letter *to a* Friend, *&c.*

I now beg leave, *Sir*, to give a particular instance of something that must needs have been very moving with the *Athenians*, which yet would have been but ill receiv'd amongst us : And that is a passage in the *Antigone of Sophocles*. That Story, as it is manag'd by that admirable Poet is one of the most moving that ever was : And there is no part of it that touches me more, than the Complaints of *Antigone*, upon her Condemnation by *Creon*. But there is one thing peculiar in it, which must needs have exerted Compassion in the *Athenians* in an extraordinary manner; for otherwise *Sophocles*, who perfectly understood his Audience, would never have made her repeat it, at least, four times in the same Act : For when she was condemn'd to the severest Punishment, which was to be buried alive, the thing that lay most heavy upon her Heart was, that she was to go to Hell with her Maiden-head. I think, *Sir*, I need not take pains to demonstrate, that this passage would have been laugh'd at with us. Now what reason can be given, why that should appear so contempti-

ble

ble to us, which mov'd the *Athenians* so
much? The only Reason that can be
assign'd, is the difference of Climate and
Customs. The *Athenians* by using their
Women, as the Modern *Italians* do theirs,
plainly declared their Opinion of them;
which was, that Passion was predominant
over Reason in them; and that they
were perpetually thinking, how they might
make some Improvement of the Talent
which N A T U R E had given their
Sex. The *Athenians* therefore having these
thoughts of their Women, the Complaint
that *Antigone* made, could not appear peculiar and surprizing to them. Now it is
evident, that every thing which is ridiculous must be both particular and surprizing;
for nothing which is general and expected
can excite a sensible Man to Laughter. But
we having quite contrary thoughts of our
Women; which is plain, by the Confidence which we so generously repose in
them, a Maid who had said, what *Antigone*
did, upon our Stage, would have said something that would have appear'd a frailty

par-

particular and furprizing, and would have been ridiculous.

Thus, *Sir*, have I given you two inftances of things which fucceeded very well with the Ancients, and would yet be very ill receiv'd amongft us, upon the account of the difference of our Religion, Climate, and Cuftoms. I fhall now give you fome account of a thing, which is very well receiv'd upon our Stage, but would have fucceeded but ill with the Ancient *Grecians*, by reafon of the fame difference of Climate and Cuftoms.

The thing that I mean, is Love; which could but rarely be brought upon the *Grecian* Stage, without the violation of probability, confidering that their Scene lay generally in their own, or a warmer Country: For two People in a Tragedy cannot make Love without being together, and being alone. Now when Lovers came together in *Greece*, they found fomething elfe to do, than to talk. Their Women under fo

warm

warmer Sun, melted much sooner than ours. Nor were they so fantastick as long to refuse what they eternally desire ; or to pretend a mortal displeasure, for being offer'd to be oblig'd in the most sensible part of them. Therefore most of the Love that appear'd upon the *Athenian* Stage, was between such People as their own Customs oblig'd to cohabit, as *Admetus* and *Alcestis*, who were Man and Wife ; *Hippolitus* and *Phedra*, who were Son and Mother-in-Law, and with which last, the only Obstacle to Enjoyment, was the Horrour which so Criminal a Passion inspir'd. Had the *Athenian* Poets introduc'd upon their Stage two passionate Lovers, who had not been related, and engag'd them in a Conversation both tender and delicate, an Audience would have been apt to ask, with the *Spanish Lady*, mentioned by Monsieur St. *Euremont* : *Que d' esprit mal employé! A quoy bon tous ces beaux discours quand ils sont ensemble ?* You know, *Sir*, that this Lady made this Reflection, which St. *Euremont* commends so much, upon the Reading

[a]   ing

ing a Conversation in *Cleopatra*, between two paſſionate Lovers. Upon which that ingenious Gentleman, with his uſual good Sence, takes occaſion to condemn *Calpre-nede*, for making no diſtinction betwixt the *Love* of a *Southern* Climate, and that of *England* or *France*.

By what I have ſaid, *Sir*, it may be eaſily gueſs'd, that it is in vain to think of ſetting up a Chorus upon the *Engliſh* Stage, becauſe it ſucceeded at *Athens* ; or to think of expelling *Love* from our Theatres, becauſe it was rarely in *Grecian Tragedies*.

But ſince I ſhall treat of this laſt hereafter, and I have already treſpaſſed upon your Patience, I ſhall only beg leave of you to make one Apology for my ſelf, and ſo for the preſent take leave of you.

A Letter *to a* Friend, *&c.*

Let then the Admirers of Mr. *Waller* know, (that is, all the ingenious Men in the Kingdom) that if I have in the following Dialogue rigorously examin'd some Verses which were writ by that Great Man, I have been far from doing it out of a motive of Malice or Vanity, or so much with a design to attack Mr. *Waller*, as to vindicate *Shakespear.*

For Mr. *Rymer*, who pretends that this last is without Excellency, affirming, that the fore-mention'd Verses of the first are without Fault, it appears to me to be very plain, that the Man who overlookt Mr. *Waller*'s Faults, might overlook *Shakespear*'s Excellencies. For it is much more easie to find Faults, than it is to discern Beauties. To do the first requires but common Sense, but to do the last a Man must have a Genius.

There is no Man who has a greater Veneration for Mr. *Waller* than I have: We

have

have all of us reafon to Honour the Man, who has been an Honour to *England* : And it is with an inexpreffible pleafure, that I find his Death lamented by two great *French* Wits , *viz.* *La Fontaine* , and Monfieur St. *Euremont.* A Man may in many places of Mr *Waller's* Works, fee not only Wit, Spirit, good Sence, but a happy and delicate turn of Thought, with clearnefs, boldnefs, juftnefs, fublimenefs, and gallantry. For the laft of thefe Qualities, I know not whither he has been furpafs'd by any Writer in any Language.

Voiture, indeed, is a very gallant Writer too ; but his Gallantry is of fuch a different Character from our *Englifh* Poets, that they will not admit of Comparifon. Mr. *Waller's* is more fprightly, more fhining, more bold, and more admirable. The *French*man's, by the Character of his Country, more fupple , more foft , more infinuating, and more bewitching : But befides thofe rare Qualities which are to be found in that Admirable Man , there are Two

for

for which we were in a peculiar manner
oblig'd to him. For he not only improv'd
the Language of our Verse considerably,
but was the first who us'd our Ears to the
Musick of a just Cadence. Yet if any one
is of Opinion, that either his Language or
Numbers are always perfect, he errs. For
as there are sometimes Improprieties in his
Expressions, so there is a great deal of
Prose in his Verse. Mr. *Dryden*, who had
the good luck to come after him, has the
Honour to have finish'd what the other so
happily begun. For as we have nothing to
shew, ev'n in Prose, which has a greater purity than some of his blank Verse, and particularly that of the *Spanish Fryar*, (tho at the
same time that it has the purity and easiness
of Prose, it has the dignity and strength of
Poetry) so I cannot imagine any thing
more perfect than his Equal Numbers in
Heroick Verse, where ever he design'd them
perfect; and in this he will never be exceeded by any Man, unless length of Time
makes some strange Alteration in the Tongue.
I do not believe that any sensible Man can
be-

believe I say this to flatter him : For what can be got by flattering a Poet ; especially a Poet in Mr. *Dryden*'s Circumstances ? But this we may be assur'd of, that as long as we are foolishly partial to the Dead, and unreasonably unjust to the Living, we must resolve to continue at a stand in Politer Learning, and must not think of making that Progress which the *French* have made. I know very well, that we have greater Geniuses than they, and that we can shew better Writers ; but that they can shew more good Writers than we, no Man who knows them can doubt. Since our Poets want the solid Encouragement that theirs have ; that is, the plentiful Pensions : It would be folly to deny them that fantastick Possession which they are contented and pleas'd with ; since Fame is a sort of an Airy Revenue, which they who unjustly detain from the Owners, cannot themselves enjoy ; it is a base Envy to put the Legal Owners off to a vain Reversion.

Thus

A Letter to a Friend, &c.

Thus, *Sir*, have I fent you my Thoughts, with a great deal more haft than ever I thought to have writ any thing which was defign'd to be publifhed. I defire you therefore to pardon the negligence of the expreffion, if you find never fo little good Sence to make fome amends for it. I am,

SIR,

Yours, &c.

——————————— ———————————

The

The First DIALOGUE.

BEAUMONT, FREEMAN.

Beaum. JACK *Freeman!* This is an unexpected, and a surprizing Visit : with what Impatience have I long'd for this happy Hour, and how have I regretted this tedious Absence ! Prithee, how long haft thou been in Town?

Freem. But just time enough to shift me ; yet time enough to receive two Affignations, the one from a Lawyer, and the other from a Wench, who, as the Devil would have it, saw me as I passed in the Stage-Coach thro' the *Hay-Market.* But I resolv'd to visit neither, till I had seen thee.

Beaum. Surprizingly kind ! especially in this infamous Town, where 'tis almost scandalous to be so much a Friend ; where Friendship is seen to give place, not only to Business and Pleasure, but sometimes too even to Vanity ; where I have known an old grave Rogue, who has had nothing to do , disappoint three or four honest Fellows, purely that he might be thought a Raskal of Business : and where I have known a young Fop baulk a Drinking Appointment, out of a longing desire to be thought more leud, and diverted by some wicked Adventure. But, prithee, how do all our Friends in *Hamp-shire* ?

Freem. Why, Faith, here of late, they have done fomething odly ; but by the help of the Bottle, they have ftill made a hard fhift : they have been as conftantly wet, as the Weather in this obftinate Seafon, and being forbid by the perpetual Rains to follow the daily Labour of their Country Sports, they have handed about their Brimmers within doors, as faft as if they had done it for Exercife. But I long to hear fome News from thee. What fay our Politick Grumblers now ?

Beaum. Doft not thou know, *Jack*, that I hate both Politicks and Politicians ; every Politician who is not in a Publick Station is an Afs, and the fevereft Satyr on fo fantaftick an Animal as Man ; s'death ! that a Creature fo very impotent, fhould yet be fo very bufie ; he has feldom either Wifdom to fore-fee, or Power to prevent the leaft Accidents that befal him, in his own little private Capacity, yet muft be infolently enquiring into Secrets of State, and medling with mighty Kingdoms. For my part, I very often feek leud Company a Nights, tho' I hate it, on purpofe to efcape the News-mongers, and *Dyer* is not at more expence and trouble to obtain his Intelligence, than I am to avoid the Clamour of it.

Freem. Well ! faid moral *Ned Beaumont*, Philofophy and Whimfie, I fee, are not inconfiftent, however the Schools would impofe upon us. This puts me in mind of a very odd Anfwer, from one whom I ask'd once, What a Clock it was by his Watch ? he reply'd, That he had never been fuch a Sott, as to throw away his Money on Watches ; that he, indeed, was as profufe as another ; but that the very defign of his Profufion, was to be ignorant how the time paft away ; that the very Sound of a Clock, or an Alarum, occafioned melancholy Reflections in him, and difturbed the

Tran-

Tranquility of his Mind. So that this Fellow had as firmly refolved not to perplex his Noddle with the Apprehenfions of Hell and Futurity, as thou haft determin'd not to trouble thy Head with the Fear of a *French* Invafion. But, prithee, what News from the Commonwealth of Learning? You ufe to be more inquifitive after what paffes there, and able to inform a Friend of it : What New Books have you now abroad.

Beaum. I fent you down Two by the Carrier, the *Juvenal,* and the *Account of Tragedy* ; and we have had none fince in the Politer Studies, that deferve any confideration.

Freem. I read them over with a great deal of pleafure, and fome application ; Dear *Ned!* How have I long'd to talk with thee of the latter.

Beaum. Aye, *Jack,* the latter : tell me truly, Hadft not thou difcovered, tho' there had been no Name to it, that it was written by the fame Gentleman, the fame Judicious and Learned Gentleman, who writ the Obfervations upon the Tragedie of the Laft Age? Does not the fame Spirit of Learning, and exquifite Sence, feem to be diffus'd throughout it ?

Freem. There is good Sence and Learning in both thofe Books ; but if I may have liberty to fpeak my Mind, *Ned,* before you, who are the Author's Friend, there feems to be more Learning in the latter Book, and more good Sence in the former.

Beaum. Pray, Sir, what Exceptions have you to the Sence of the latter?

Freem. Why, to ufe plain dealing with one who is fo much my Friend, I am neither fatisfied with the Defign of that Book, nor with the Method of carrying on that Defign, nor with the Stile in which it was written.

Beaum.

Beaum. But sure you cannot find fault with the Stile, *Jack* ; Canst thou have a Quarrel to Pleasantry ?

Freem. Pleasantry ! you may call it what you please, *Sir* ; but that pleasant way, is by no means fit for a Critick : a Critick, whose business it is to instruct, should keep to the Didactick Stile, as *Aristotle, Longinus*, and the *French* Criticks have done : for if a Man is eternally Laughing, how can I possibly fall into his Opinion, who know not if he speaks in good earnest ?

Beaum. Why surely, *Jack*, one of your Apprehension may easily discern when another rallies, and when he speaks what he means.

Freem. Your Servant, good Mr. *Beaumont :* But supposing that may be done, when a laughing Critick condemns an Author, how can I know whether he has convicted him by the advantage of his Wit, or the force of his Argumentation ? The best thing in the World is as liable to be ridicul'd as the silliest. Has not *Scarron* impudently diverted all *Europe* at the Expence of *Virgil*, the best of Poets, and the justest of Writers ? upon which an ingenious *French*-man has made this Observation, That as all Human Grandeur is but Folly, so Sublimeness and the Ridiculum are very nearly related.

Beaum. But what is it that you call the Didactick Stile, *Jack ?* for I have read so little of Criticism, or of Rhetorick, since I have enjoy'd the leisure of a Country Life, that I have great need to be inform'd.

Freem. The Didactick Stile, is a Stile that is fit for Instruction, and must be necessarily upon that account, pure, perspicuous, succinct, unaffected and grave.

Beaum. Every Stile ought to have three of these qualities ; for barbarity, obscurity, and affectation, must certainly be faults in all : But why, particularly, does the Didactick Stile demand succinctness and gravity.

Freem.

Freem. It requires Succinctnefs, that its Precepts may be more readily comprehended, and more eafily retain'd ; and it requires Gravity to give it an Air of Authority, and caufe it to make the deeper impreffion.

Beaum. For my part, I thought Gravity had been long fince laught out of the World.

Freem The falfe and affected Gravity has been juftly and defervedly laught at, but the true both is, and will always be venerable, being the genuine refult of Wifdom and Vertue ; that Gravity will be always laught at, that ftrives to impofe a Fool upon the World for a Man of Sence, or a Raskal for a Man of Honour ; for all Cheats, when they are found out, are defpicable.

Beaum. But have not I feen thee laughing at a Fellow, only for looking gravely, tho' you never had heard him fpeak ?

Freem. Yes ; but by that very Gravity I foon difcover'd the Blockhead in him ; for to a Man who underftands the World never fo little, a Fool never looks fo fillily, as when he attempts to look wifely ; which *Butler* had certainly in his Head, when he writ the following Couplet.

> *For Fools are known by looking wife,*
> *As Men find Woodcocks by their Eyes.*

'Tis, as it were, a Revenge which Nature takes of them, for forcing her by Affectation : for Gravity muft be always affected, when it accompanies Vice or Folly ; but it is natural to Wifdom and Vertue. Now Nature will always be held reverend, and Affectation contemptible.

Beaum. Pray, what do you take Gravity to be ? for I have never confider'd it yet with attention.

Freem.

Freem. I think I may venture to deſcribe it thus : Gravity is a compos'd and majeſtick aſſurance, which appears in a Man's looks, or his air or manner of ex-preſſion, and proceeds from the tranquility and great-neſs of a Mind, that is guided by the Dictates of right Reaſon.

Beaum. Very well : But are not we then as obnoxi-ous to be impos'd on by that Aſſurance and that Air of Authority, which always go along with Gravity, as much as we are on the other ſide, by the Sophiſtication of Pleaſantry, which ſtums, as it were, an Argument, if I may uſe that expreſſion, to render it agreeable to the taſte of thoſe who are ignorant.

Freem. Not one jot obnoxious on that ſcore : for Gravity can no more make a ſilly Notion paſs upon a Man of Sence, than it can ſet off a Blockhead. Plea-ſantry, indeed, may make Sophiſtry paſs upon us, be-cauſe it puts the Mind into agitation, and makes it un-fit for enquiry ; but Gravity never fails to make it ſe-rene, and diſpoſe it for the ſtricteſt Scrutiny.

Beaum. Well, you have here ſaid enough to make me wiſh, that Mr. *R:——* had made choice of another Stile. But you told me, that you diſlik'd the Deſign of his Book.

Freem. Yes ; but I have neither eat nor drunk ſince I came to Town, and——

Beaum. I have Wine in my Chamber.

Freem. But I have not been in a Tavern this Month : Therefore prithee let's to the *Old Devil,* and talk the reſt o're a Bottle.

Beaum. Since it is your inclination, it ſhall be ſo.

The End of the Firſt Dialogue.

The

DIALOGUE II.

Beaumont, Freeman, Drawer.

Beaum. SO Sirrah! What need we have come so near Heaven to be wicked?

Draw. I'll make you amends in your Wine, Master.

Beaum. Look you do, Sir. Let me see, it must be your best *Red*, I think. Well, we have at least got this advantage by mounting, that we are not like to be interrupted; which is as great a Plague to Criticks, as it is to Poets; not so much as a Drawer will come near us, without half an hour's ringing for him: so that I am in no danger of getting drunk to Night, tho' I am in wicked *Jack Freeman*'s Company.

Freem. Sir, you do me too much Honour, tho' I dare swear, no body will take me for a Saint, who knows I have been thy Friend these ten Years. But prithee, what sort of Men were those two, whom you spoke to in coming up Stairs?

Beaum. Why one of them was a Bookseller: Now pray guess what the other was.

Freem. Why, Faith, an Author.

Beaum. If ever thou art indicted for a Magician, I'll turn Evidence 'egad, it was an Author, Sir.

Freem. I have been often in terrible apprehension of Authors, but I never was afraid of my Carcase before, from one of them; but this indeed had like to have

faln

faln foul upon me; they were both in a sweet pickle

Beaum. I suppose that *Morecraft* has been treating
his Author with the Generosity of a true Bookseller;
that is, with intention to make him drunk, and so to
cheat him of his Copy.

Freem. If that was his design, the Author has turn'd
the Dice upon him, I gad; for *Morecraft* is by much
in the worse Condition of the two; and perhaps the
Dog drank till he grew generous in earnest.

Beaum. If it should prove so, to morrow he'll hang
for his Vertue; for such a true bred Raskal can never
forgive himself a good Action, especially if it has been
costly to him.

Freem. You seem to know him well, Sir: But see,
here comes the Wine: Sirrah, fill to this Gentleman.

Beaum. Come, *Jack*, remembring our *Hampshire*
Friends: Faith, 'tis good Wine; but a Pox of this *Port*,
it is not so well tasted as *Claret*, and it intoxicates
sooner.

Freem. Why Faith, the intention was good; but I
think in my Conscience, the Prohibition of *Claret* has
mainly promoted Drunkenness. Come, here's the fore-
said Health to you.

Beaum. I thank you; and now to our business: but
before we proceed to this Book again, I desire you to give
me some satisfaction, in relation to a passage in the
Dedication. For Mr. *Rymer* mentioning the *Greek
Oedipus*, says afterwards of the *French*, and the *English*, *Quantum mutatus*. Now I have always taken our
English Oedipus to be an admirable Play.

Freem. You have had a great deal of reason to do
so; and it would certainly have been much better, if
Mr. *Dryden* had had the sole management of it. If
Mr.

Mr. *Rymer*, by his *Quantum mutatus*, defigns to fix any mark of difefteem upon Mr. *Dryden*'s Tragedy, he is doubtlefs to blame ; but if he only means, that Mr. *Dryden* has alter'd the Character of *Oedipus*, and made it lefs fuitable to the defign of Tragedy, according to *Ariftotle*'s Rules , then Mr, *Rymer* is in the right of it.

Beaum. Pray fhew me that.

Freem. I fhall do it as fuccinctly as I can : The Defign of Tragedy, according to *Ariftotle*, is to excite compaffion and terrour : from whence it neceffarily fol-lows   we are not to make choice of a very vertu-ous   , to involve him in mifery ; nor yet on the other fide, of one who is very vicious.

Beaum. I defire to know how you draw that Confe-quence.

Freem. The Confequence is juft : For the making a very good Man miferable, can neither move compaf-fion nor terror ; no, that muft rather occafion hor-rour, and be detefted by all the World. On the other fide, by reprefenting a very bad Man miferable, a Poet may pleafe an Audience, but can neither move terrour nor pity in them : for terrour is caufed in us by a view of the Calamities of our Equals ; that is, of thofe who refembling us in their faults, make us, by feeing their Sufferings, apprehenfive of the like Misfortune. Now if at any time an Audience fees a very wicked Man punifhed, each Man who knows himfelf lefs guil-ty, is out of all fear of danger, and fo there can be no terrour : nor can the calamity of a very wicked Man raife compaffion, becaufe he has his defert.

Beaum. What fort of Perfon muft be made choice of then?

                                              Freem.

Freem. Why one who is neither vertuous in a sove-reign degree, nor excessively vicious; but who keep-ing the middle between those extreams, is afflicted with some terrible calamity, for some involuntary fault.

Beaum. Well, and just such a Man is Mr. *Dryden's* *Oedipus,* who cannot be said to be perfectly vertuous, when he is both Parricide and Incestuous; nor yet on the other side excessively vicious; when neither his Parricide nor Incest are voluntary, but caused by a fa-tal ignorance.

Freem. Aye, but says *Dacier,* to punish a Man for Crimes, that are caused by invincible ignorance, is in some measure unjust, especially if that Man has other ways extraordinary Vertues. Now Mr. *Dryden* makes his *Oedipus* just, generous, sincere, and brave; and in-deed a Heroe, without any Vices, but the foremen-tion'd two, which were unavoidable both. Now *So-phocles* represents *Oedipus* after another manner; the di-stinguishing Qualities which he gives him, are only Courage, Wit, and Success, Qualities which make a Man neither good nor vitious. The extraordinary things that he pretends to have done in *Sophocles,* are only to have kill'd four Men in his Rage, and to have have explain'd the Riddle of *Sphinx,* which the worst Man in the World that had Wit, might have done as well as *Oedipus.*

Beaum. Well, but does not *Sophocles* punish *Oedipus* for the very same Crimes that Mr. *Dryden* does, *vid.* for his Incest and Parricide? If not, for what invo-luntary faults, does the *Sophoclean Oedipus* suffer.

Freem. *Aristotle* by those Offences, which his Inter-preter *Dacier* calls involuntary, does not mean only such faults as are caus'd by invincible ignorance, but
such

such to which we are strongly inclin'd, either by the bent of our Constitutions, or by the force of prevailing Passions. The faults for which *Oedipus* suffers in *Sophocles*, are his vain Curiosity, in consulting the Oracle about his Birth, his Pride in refusing to yield the way, in his return from that Oracle, and his Fury and Violence in attacking four Men on the Road, the very day after he had been fore-warn'd by the Oracle, that he should kill his Father.

Beaum. But, pray, how were those involuntary Faults?

Freem. Dacier means here by involuntary faults, faults that have more of human frailty in them, than any thing of design, or of black malice. The Curiosity of *Oedipus* proceeded from a Vanity, from which no Man is wholly exempt ; and his Pride, and the Slaughter that it caused him to commit on the Road, were partly caused by his Constitution, and an unhappy and violent Temper. These are faults that both *Aristotle* and *Dacier* suppose, that he might have prevented, if he would have used all his diligence ; but being guilty of them thro' his neglect, they afterwards plunged him in those horrible Crimes, which were follow'd by his final Ruine." Thus you see the Character of the *Athenean Oedipus*, is according to these Rules of *Aristotle*, the fittest that can be imagin'd to give Compassion and Terrour to an Audience : For how can an Audience choose but tremble, when it sees a Man involv'd in the most deplorable Miseries, only for indulging those Passions and Frailties, which they are but too conscious that they neglect in themselves ? And how can they choose but melt with compassion, when they see a Man afflicted by the avenging Gods, with utmost severity, for Faults that were without malice,

C 2   and

and which being in some measure to be found in themselves, may make them apprehensive of like Catastrophes? For all our Passions, as *Dacier* observes, are grounded upon the Love of ourselves, and that Pity which seems to espouse our Neighbor's Interest, is founded still on our own.

Beaum. Why, will you perswade me, that because an Audience finds in itself the same vain Curiosity, and the same ungovern'd Passions, that drew *Oedipus* to Murder and Incest, that therefore each Spectator should be afraid of killing his Father, and committing Incest with his Mother?

Freem. No, you cannot mistake me so far ; but they may very well be afraid of being drawn in by the like neglected Passions to deplorable Crimes and horrid Mischiefs, which they never design'd.

Beaum. Well then, now I begin to see the reason, why, according to the Sence of *Aristotle*, the Character of Mr. *Dryden's Oedipus* is alter'd for the worse : For he, you'll say, being represented by Mr. *Dryden* Soveraignly Vertuous, and guilty of Parricide only by a fatal invincible Ignorance, must by the severity of his Sufferings, instead of compassion create horrour in us, and a murmuring, as it were, at Providence. Nor can those Sufferings raise terrour in us, for his Crimes of fatal invincible Ignorance, not being prepar'd, as they are in *Sophocles*, by some less faults, which led him to those Crimes, as it were, by so many degrees. I do not conceive how we can be concern'd at this ; for Terrour, you say, arises from the Sufferings of others, upon the account of Faults which are common to us with them. Now what Man can be afraid, because he sees *Oedipus* come down at two Leaps from the height of Vertue to Parricide, and to Incest, that

there.

therefore this may happen to him ? For a Man who is himself in Security, cannot be terrified with the Sufferings of others, if he is not conscious to himself of the Faults that caus'd them : but every Man who is disturb'd by unruly Passions, when he sees, how the giving way to the same Passions, drew *Sophocles*'s *Oedipus* into Tragical Crimes, which were never design'd, must by reflection necessarily be struck with Terrour, and the apprehension of dire Calamities. This, I suppose, is your Sence.

Freem. Exactly.

Beaum. Well, but the Authority of *Aristotle* avails little with me, against irrefutable Experience. I have seen our *English Oedipus* several times, and have constantly found, that it hath caus'd both Terrour and Pity in me.

Freem. I will not tell you, that possibly you may have mistaken Horrour for Terrour and Pity : for perhaps it is not absolutely true, that the Sufferings of those, who are Sovereignly Vertuous, cannot excite Compassion. But this is indubitable, that they cannot so effectually do it, as the Misfortunes of those, who having some Faults, do the more resemble ourselves : And I think, that I may venture to affirm two things : First, That if any one but so great a Master as Mr. *Dryden*, had had the management of that Character, and had made the same mistake with it, his Play would have been hiss'd off the Stage. And Secondly ——

Beaum. I must beg leave to interrupt you : Why should you believe that another Man's Play upon the same Subject, would have miscarried upon that mistake. when I never heard it yet taken Notice of ?

Freem.

Freem. It would have miscarried, tho' the mistake had ne're been found out : For a common Author proceeding upon such wrong Principles, could never have touch'd the Passions truly. But Mr. *Dryden* having done it by his extraordinary Address, the Minds of his Audience have been still troubled, and so the less able to find his Error.

Beaum. But what was that second thing, which you were going to observe?

Freem. It was this : That if Mr. *Dryden* had not alter'd the Character of *Sophocles*, the Terrour and Compassion had been yet much stronger.

Beaum. But how could so great a Man as Mr. *Dryden*, make such a mistake in his own Art?

Freem. How did *Corneille* do it before him, who was certainly a great Man too? And if you'll believe *Dacier*, *C'etoit le plus grand genie pour le Theatre qu'on avoit Jamais veu* : Great Men have their Errors, or else they would not be Men. Nay, they are mistaken in several things, in which Men of a lower Order may be in the right. This has been wisely order'd by Providence, that they may not be exalted too much ; for if it were not for this, they would look down upon the rest of Mankind, as upon Creatures of a lower Species.

Beaum. Do you believe then, that *Aristotle*, if he could rise again, would condemn our *English Oedipus*?

Freem. He would condemn it, or he would be forc'd to recede from his own Principles ; but at the same time that he passed Sentence on it, he would find it so beautiful, that he could not choose but love the Criminal ; and he would certainly crown the Poet, before he would damn the Play.

Beaum.

Beaum. But 'tis high time to return to Mr. *Rymer's* Book ; you were saying, you dislik'd the Design of it.

Freem. Yes ; but if you will come to morrow Morning to my Lodgings, there I shall give you my Reasons for it. We have criticiz'd sufficiently for one time ; besides, at my Chamber I have two or three Books, which I may have an occasion to cite.

Beaum. Well then, let us drink a Glass and be merry. Come, *Jack,* here's your Mistress to you.

Freem. Nay, Faith, *Ned,* I am resolv'd to be sober to Night.

Beaum. Prithee, canst thou be otherwise in my Company ? How many grave Lectures have I been forc'd to read to thee over a Bottle, in order to keep thee sober ?

Freem. But, as the Devil would have it, thou art seldom Philosophically given in Company, but at the same time thou art inclin'd to be damnable Drunk too. Have you forgot since you grew drunk in *Hampshire,* in extolling the Dogma's of *Seneca* ? When the Company laugh'd to see the Speculative *Stoick,* a Practical *Epicurean.*

Beaum. However, 'tis something to speak for Sobriety ; I never heard you do that, unless when we were in *Italy* together, once at *Florence,* for want of better Employment, you declaim'd in praise of the *Italian* Temperance ; but it was only in order to get a sober Seignior to sit out another Flask with you.

Freem. Faith, Rallery apart, I always esteem'd Drunkenness the most odious of Vices. There is something to be said for Whoring, Whoring is according to Nature, but Drunkenness is a Vice against Nature ; we go always with the Stream to Letchery, but we
often

often tug againſt it to arrive at Drunkenneſs. He who drinks five Brimmers in a hand, might certainly have perform'd a very good Action without half ſo much violence offer'd to his inclination. And he who out of his Love to Converſation, is often perſwaded to drink hard, might, if he has but never ſo little delicacy, be vertuous with leſs reluctancy.

Beaum. But ſince Drinking is ſo unnatural a Vice, how comes it ſo much in faſhion amongſt us ?

Freem. Why ſome witty Men, they ſay, introduced it upon the Reſtoration, and the Fools finding the imitation eaſie, immediately fell into the Dance.

Beaum. The Wits were horribly o'reſeen in beginning it, but the Fools were in the right in carrying it on.

Freem. How can that be ?

Beaum. Becauſe a Fool has as much reaſon to declare for Drunkenneſs, as a poor Dog has to declare for Levelling : for Death does not level Conditions more than Drunkenneſs equals Capacities. A Blockhead when he's drunk, may talk as well as a Man of Sence, if in the ſame Condition ; nay, better perhaps : for that quantity of Wine will make a witty Man mad, which will but juſt be ſufficient to animate the cold and flegmatick Maſs of a Sot. They who have cauſe to be aſham'd of themſelves, have reaſon to be fond of Diſguiſes ; now Drunkenneſs is a very convenient Mask to make a Blockhead paſs *Incognito*.

Freem. Thou art in the right of it, and upon this Remonſtrance I would have left it off, if I had been never ſo fond of it before. But 'tis now ſome time that I have had a mortal Quarrel to it.

Beaum.

Beaum. I fhrewdly fufpect, that Drunkennefs began the Quarrel : for if that had not maul'd you with your Rheumatifm, I fuppofe thefe Invectives might have been fpar'd.

Freem. Well, come, will you go ? We'll pay at the Bar.

Beaum. Thou art Seven Years older, and fhalt be my Governour. But my Lodgings are neareft, will you go lie with me ?

Freem. No, Faith, Sir, I hope for a better Bedfellow ; but to Morrow at Eleven I expect you. Till then, Adieu.

Beaum. Your Servant.

The End of the Second Dialogue.

D   DIA

DIALOGUE III.

Freeman in his Chamber, repeating.

Should Nature's Self invade the World again,
And o're the Center spread the Liquid Main,
Thy Power were safe ——·

(*Enter to him* Beaumont.

Beaum. WHY how now *Jack* ? At the scandalous Exercise of repeating this Morning ? Art thou in Debt ?

Freem. What makes you ask that ?

Beaum. Because if thou art, thou reckest to scare away Duns perhaps. But whose are those Verses ? If they are thine, I scamper immediately.

Freem. You are very merry, Sir.

Beaum. 'Sdeath ! I had rather be lampoon'd this Morning, than stay to hear a Critick's Verses.

Freem. Well, they are *Waller's*, Sir.

Beaum. Aye, now thou say'st something, *Jack.*

Waller by Nature for the Bays design'd,
With Spirit, Force, and Fancy unconfin'd
In Panegyricks is above Mankind.

At least *Jack*, thou canst not be so impudent as to dissent from Mr. *Rymer*, in his Judgment of those incomperable Verses upon the Fleet.   *Freem.*

Freem. I am that impudent Dog, I gad.

Beaum. Why, are not the Thoughts new there?

Freem. Yes.

Beaum. And Noble?

Freem. Yes, very Noble; but a Pox they are not all of them true tho'.

Beaum. You had beft fay too, that the Language is not clean and majeftick.

Freem. I need not fay fo, it fays enough of itfelf.

Beaum. This is down-right Spirit of Contradiction; I defire you to fhew me three faults in thofe Verfes, without being hypercritical.

Freem. Here, take the Book and repeat them then.

Beaumont reads.

> *Where e're thy Navy fpreads her Canvas Wings,*
> *Homage to thee, and Peace to all fhe brings.*

Have you any thing to fay to that Couplet?

Freem. Yes; if Mr. *Waller* had been to fay that in Profe, he would have expreffed himfelf otherwife: he would have faid thus: Where e're thy Fleet goes, fhe carries Peace to all, and caufes all to pay or do Homage to thee: For where e're fhe goes fhe brings Homage; would not be good *Englifh* in Profe.

Beaum. Why, will you allow nothing to be faid in Verfe, that may not be faid in Profe too.

Freem. Yes, an Expreffion may be too florid, or too bold for Profe, and yet be very becoming of Verfe. But every Expreffion that is falfe *Englifh* in Profe, is barbarous and abfurd in Verfe too. But, pray proceed.

Bean-

Beaumont reads.

The French *and* Spaniard, *when thy Flags appear,*
Forget their Hatred, and consent to Fear.

Freem. I have nothing to say to that Couplet : Go
on.

Beaumont reads.

So Jove *from* Ida, *did both Hosts survey,*
And when he plea'd to Thunder, part the Fray.

Is not that a Noble Similitude ?
Freem. Yes; but the word Fray is altogether unworthy
of the Greatness of the Thought, and the Dignity of Heroick Verse. Fray is fitter to express a Quarrel betwixt
drunken Bullies, than between the *Grecian* and *Trojan*
Heroes, and fitter to be parted by *Stokes,* than by thundring *Jove.* But go on.

Beaumont reads.

Ships heretofore on Seas, like Fishes sped,
The mightier still upon the smaller fed

Freem. That is to say, as a great Fish Breakfasts or
Dines upon a small one, so a great Ship chops up a little one. I have known several, who, to their sorrows,
have seen a Ship drink hard but I never met with any
who have seen one eat yet.
Beaum. P'shaw, Pox, this is down-right Banter. This
is to fall into the very same fault which you have con-
demned in others.

Freem.

Freem. I ſtand correcſted, Sir, without rallery then, this Metaphor *Feed*, is too groſs for a Ship, tho'I per-fectly know what Mr. *Waller* means by it. But what think you of the word *Sped ?* Is that an Heroical word ?

Beaum. No, I muſt confeſs, that *Sped* is ſomething too mean.

Freem. Too mean ! why it is fit for nothing but Burleſque, Man. Beſides, the word *heretofore* ſeems too obſolete, nor is *Fiſhes* very Heroical.

Beaum. Come, *Jack*, you had better let them two paſs, it will be an Error on the Right-hand :· for Good Nature makes ſome amends for Error ; but Error and Ill Nature is the Devil and all.

Freem. Let them paſs then. In the ſecond Verſe of this Couplet, we have *mightier* oppos'd to *ſmaller* ; whereas the word that is truly and naturally oppos'd to *ſmaller* is *greater.*

Beaum. Methinks too, that ſhould ſooner have oc-cur'd to Mr. *Waller.*

Freem. Doubtleſs it did ſo :· But Mr. *Waller* could not make uſe of that ; for if he had, he muſt directly and apparently have affirm'd a thing which is not true. For we know very well, that a ſmall Privatier will take a Merchant man bigger than itſelf. Tho' all that Mr *Waller* has got by avoiding that Rock, has been only to run himſelf on another : for by oppoſing *mightier* to *ſmal-ler*, he infers, that the *mightier* are ſtill *greater*, which is to imply a falſe thought, if not to expreſs one. But pray go on.

Beaumont reads.

> *Thou on the Deep impoſeſt nobler Laws,*
> *And by that Juſtice haſt remov'd the Cauſe*

Of

Of those rude Tempests, which for Rapine sent,
Too oft, alas, involv'd the Innocent.

Freem. I see you have taken Notice yourself, of the
want of a Pause at the end of the first Couplet, by proceeding to the second. But, pray, what is that Comparative *Nobler* referr'd to ? For *Laws* are neither mention'd before nor after. Now every Comparative, according to Grammar and good Sence, ought to be referr'd to a Positive : *Nobler Laws* than what ? Or
then there were when ?

Beaum Why then there were, when one Ship destroy'd another.

Freem. That is as much as to say, *Nobler Laws* than
there were when there were no Laws at all. But
what do you understand by removing the Cause of
those rude Tempests ? for that seems to me to be something obscure.

Beaum. Thou art a pleasant Fellow, faith ; What accuse Mr. *Waller* of obscurity ?

Freem. I have always admir'd Mr. *Waller*, for a
great Genius, and a gallant Man. Nor am I more
pleas'd with any of his Excellencies, than with the
clearness of his happy turns. But from his being generally clear, can you infer, that he was not once in his
Life obscure ? Pray what do you understand by removing the Cause of those Tempests ?

Beaum. Why, I understand the Pyrates ; for Mr.
Waller could not think, that our Fleet could remove the
Winds sure.

Freem. No ? we shall see that immediately. But
what do you understand by involving the Innocent ?

Beaum. Why, involving them in Ruine, in Destruction.

Freem.

Freem. To involve a Man in Ruine is intelligible e-
nough, but barely to involve a Man cannot be good
English, methinks, because it presents no clear Notion
of any thing to my Mind. But tell me truly, *Ned*,
If any one should talk to thee of a rude Tempest, which
sent upon the Ocean for Rapine, sometimes involves
a very honest Fellow, would'st not thou swear, that
that Man banter'd thee ? Are not these thoughts and
words ill suited ? ——But I see you have nothing to reply. and therefore proceed.

Beaumont reads.

> *Now shall the Ocean, as thy* Thames *be free,*
> *From both those Fates of Storms and Pyracy.*

Freem. That is as much as to say, Now your Majesty's Fleet's at Sea, *Boreas* has blown his last. Henceforward the poor Dog will not dare to peep out of his
hole, for fear of being serv'd as the *Persian* serv'd his
Brethren.

> *In Corum atque Eurum solitus sevire flagellis.*

And as there never was a Storm yet upon the *Thames*,
so there shall never be one henceforward upon the O-
cean.

Beaum. 'Slife ! thou banter'st me now indeed.

Freem. Yet this is the down-right meaning of the
Couplet, or there can be no meaning at all in it. But
pray go on.

Beaum.

Beaumont reads.

> *But we most happy who need fear no Force,*
> *But winged Troops, or* Pegasean *Horse.*

Freem. That *winged* should have been *wing'd* ; but that was the fault of the Age, and not of Mr. *Waller* ; who, to do him Justice, was the first who began to contract our Participles which end in *ed* ; which being not contracted, exceedingly weaken a Verse.

Beaum. But are all our Participles that end in *ed*, to be contracted?

Freem. No, you must except wounded, confounded, boasted, wasted, and the like, because we cannot express two *d's*, or *td*, without a Vowel between them ; and consequently we should not be able to distinguish the fore-mention'd Participles from their Verbs, if they should be contracted.

Beaum. But is not cursed to be excepted too?

Freem. That may be sometimes excepted too : because when that Participle is not contracted, it is not only liable to be mistaken for the Preterperfect Tense of its Verb, but for an Adjective of a different signification, *vid.* curst, which signifies the same with fierce.

> *No* Tygress *on* Hyrcanian *Mountains nurst,*
> *No* Lybian Lioness *is half so curst.*

Says Sir *Richard Fanshaw* in his Translation of *Pastor Fido.* But pray go on.

Beaumont reads.

> *'Tis not so hard for greedy Foes to spoil*
> *Another Nation, as to touch our Soil.*

Freem.

Freem. There is nothing to fay to that : Go on.

Beaumont reads.

> *Should, Nature's Self invade the World again,*
> *And o're the Center fpread the Liquid Main,*
> *Thy Power were fafe, and her deftructive hand,*
> *Would but enlarge the Bounds of thy Command.*
> *Thy* ——

Freem. Hold, you go on to faft, Mr. *Beaumont.*

Beaum. Why, can any thing be more Noble than this ?

Freem. This is truly fublime indeed ; but I have an exception to make to the fecond Verfe. For what does Mr. *Waller* mean, by fpreading the Liquid Main o're the Center ? The Center is either taken for an imaginary Point, which is Mathematically in the midft of the Globe, and fo to fpread any thing over the Center cannot be good Sence ; or the Center is taken for the whole Globe, confifting of Land and Sea, and then to fpread the Main over the Center, is to fpread the Center over itfelf.

Beaum. This Criticifm feems to be juft enough.

Freem. Nor am I fatisfied with the Epithet Liquid ; for every Epithet is to be look'd upon as a Botch, which does not add to the thought. Now it is impoffible to think of the Sea, without thinking that it is Liquid at the fame time.

Beaumont reads.

> *Thy Power were fafe, and her deftructive hand*
> *Would but enlarge the Bounds of thy Command.*

E

Freem.

Freem. Well, go on.

Beaumont reads.

> *Thy dreadful Fleet would ſtile thee Lord of All,*
> *And ride in Triumph o're the drowned Ball :*
> *Thoſe Towers of Oak o're fertile Plains might go,*
> *And viſit Mountains where they once did grow.*

Freem. This is a moſt noble paſſage indeed ; but the word drowned is not ſonorous, beſides it ſhould be contracted. Proceed.

Beaumont reads.

> *The World's Preſerver never could endure,*
> *That finiſh'd* Babel *ſhould thoſe Men ſecure,*
> *Whoſe Pride deſign'd that Fabrick to have ſtood*
> *Above the reach of any Second Flood.*

Freem. Come make an end.

Beaumont reads.

> *To thee his Choſen more indulgent,* He
> *Dares truſt ſuch Pow'r, with ſo much Piety.*

Freem. That *He* ſeems to be a Botch.   But methinks Mr. *Rymer* has a very odd Obſervation at the latter end of theſe Verſes ; for here, ſays he, is both *Homer* and *Virgil* ; here is the pious *Æneas*, and the *Fortis Achilles* : whereas Mr. *Waller* does not deſign to praiſe the King for his Valour here. There is a great deal of difference betwixt Power and Valour ; the laſt is Perſonal, the other in the reach of Fortune.

Beaum

Beaum. Well, but you declare then, that you are of too refin'd a taſt to reliſh *Waller*?

Freem. I thought I had declar'd the quite contrary. My deſign in making theſe Remarks on his Verſes upon the Fleet, was only to ſhew you, that Mr. *Rymer* has miſtaken the moſt incorrect Copy of Verſes that perhaps Mr. *Waller* has writ, for one of his rareſt Maſterpieces. Yet all incorrect as thoſe Verſes are, I have told you, that I perfectly admir'd ſome places in them; from whence any Man may reaſonably conclude, that I have an Opinion of Mr. *Waller* in the main, which is anſwerable to the Merit of that extraordinary Man.

Beaum. But methinks the very faults of a Great Man ought to be reſpected upon the account of his Excellencies.

Freem. The very contrary of which is true: Upon that account they ought to be the rather expos'd. His Faults are the more dangerous on the account of his Excellencies. For young Writers, before they have Judgment to diſtinguiſh, are ſometimes ſo far miſtaken, as to copy the very Faults of famous Poets for Beauties. One thing I will eaſily grant you, that to expoſe a Great Man's Faults, without owning his Excellencies, is altogether unjuſt and unworthy of an honeſt Man.

Beaum. Well: But ſince you will not allow theſe Verſes to be what Mr. *Rymer* affirms them to be, pray let me hear you name a Copy of Verſes, whoſe Thoughts or Language you have no exception to. But a Pox, a Caviller can never eſteem any thing perfect.

Freem. Then will I ſhew you, that I am no Caviller.

Beaum. Nay, I am certain, I can name one Author, whoſe Verſes you can have no exception to.

Freem. Pray, who may they be, Sir?

Beaum.

Beaum. Who may it be? why who the Devil fhould it be, but thy Self, Man? To whofe Verfes can a Critick have no exception, but his own? Come, prithee, *Jack*, let us hear one of thy finifh'd Pieces now. Come, do not I know, that thou wouldeft not have taken all this pains to pull down the Reputation of another, if it were not to fet up thy own.

Freem. Curfe of this unfeafonable Rallery: Can any thing be more infipid than an untimely Jeft?

Beaum. Why are you fo barbarous, as to rake into the Afhes of the Dead then? If Selfifh and Haughty were but here, what d'ye think they would fay?

Freem. Thofe are two fpecial Sparks indeed. Who will allow the Dead to have had no Faults, and the Living to have no good Qualities. When Mr. *Oldham* was alive, thofe two Gentlemen would allow him to have neither Wit nor Genius, which none but Sots could deny him; and they have the impudence to be angry now, if a Man will not allow him to have had both Delicacy, and a good Ear, which none but Blockheads can grant him. In *Horace*'s time, there were a fort of Gentlemen, who were juft the Reverfe of thefe two: they would allow none to be paft Cenfure, but thofe who had been dead a hundred Years. *Horace* to expofe them, made ufe of a peculiar addrefs. I may venture to fhew the folly of our Sparks, by the very fame addrefs, with a contrary application: Ours will allow none to be liable to Criticifm, but thofe who have been rotten long enough to have fecur'd an Author in *Horace*'s time. You take it then for granted, that an Author who has been dead this hundred Years, is obnoxious to Cenfure?

Beaum. Yes; or elfe it would be barbarity to attack *Shakefpear*, who has not been dead fo long.

Freem.

Freem. Well then, suppose our Author has been dead a hundred Years, wanting one?

Beaum. One Year can signifie nothing, and he is still obnoxious to Censure.

Freem. Very good, Sir.

Vtor permisso, caudq; pilos ut equine
Paulatim vello : & demo unum, demo etiam unum
Dum cadat elusus ratione ruentis acervi
Qui redit ad fastos, &c.

That is to say, Sir, I will do as if I were to pull off a Horses Tail, I will one by one substract the Years, till you confess your Errors; for I will oblige you to one of these two things, either to confess that the Dead are not to be attack'd at all (and so there can be scarce any Criticism); or else to fix upon the particular Year when they begin to be liable. And I think you'll own, that to fix upon that would be ridiculous enough in all Conscience.

Beaum. But pray, what should be the reason, that all Men exclaim so against arraigning those who have been lately dead, if they have any Opinion of them?

Freem. One reason may be, that the shewing them Faults which they could not find out themselves, upbraids them with want of discernment, and disturbs their good Opinion of themselves : And another which is stronger is this ; that they have a secret fear of being thus arraigned in their turns.

Beaum. But People can with some Patience hear of the Faults of those who have been long since dead. What should be the meaning of that?

Freem. The meaning is plain : For how few are those who think of being remembred a hundred Years after they are dead?

Beaum.

Beaum. Yet all ais while you have forgot to name a Copy of Verse., which may be allow'd to be more perfect than thofe which you have juft condemn'd. Come name them, Sir.

Freem. You muft excufe me, Sir.

Beaum. Nay, prithee let's hear.

Freem. *Then hear, O hear, in what exalted Strains*
Sicilian Mufes, thro' thefe happy Plains,
Proclaim Saturnian Times, our own Apollo Reigns.

Beaum. So, Mr. *Dryden,* I perceive, is oblig'd to you.

Freem. Not a jot oblig'd : For art thou fuch an Afs to think, that I commend another Man's Verfes for the Author's fake ?

Beaum. For whofe then pray ?

Freem. For my own moft certainly, that I may pafs for a Man of Judgment.

Beaum. Well, tho' thou art a vain Dog, yet every vain Dog would not have made this honeft Confeffion. But when fhall we come to the Main Point ? This has been a long Prelude : Faith, let us 'en Print this Conference, and give it the Title of *The Preamble,* as a worthy Author in King *Charles* the Second's time, entituled his Book, *The Preface.*

Freem. However, Chance has not fo unhappily thrown us upon this Method : for you being prepoffefs'd with the reafonablenefs of Mr. *Rymer's* Defign, the fhewing you his Errors in two or three things that are of lefs importance, may go fome way towards the removing your prejudices, and the preparing you to hear Truth when we come to the principal matter.

Enter

Enter Freeman's *Boy*

Boy. Sir, a Gentleman below would fpeak with you.

Freem. I beg your Pardon for a moment. There lies *Dacier* upon the Table, you may divert yourfelf with him, till I return

The End of the Third Dialogue.

DIALOGUE IV

BEAUMONT FREEMAN

Freem. SO, I have now got loofe, and have fecur'd us against more interruption.

Beaum. Now then, let me hear your Objections to Mr. *Rymer*'s Defign ; for nothing can feem more commendable to me, than his intention, which is to reftore Tragedy to its primitive purity, by re-eftablifhing the Ancient Method, and reviving the Rules of *Ariftotle.*

Freem. I am for obferving the Rules of *Ariftotle,* as much as any Man living, as far as it can be done without re-eftablifhing the Ancient Method. But becaufe the Ancients Tragedies had little Love in them, that therefore ours muft have little too ; becaufe the Ancient Tragedies had a Chorus, that therefore we muft ridiculoufly ape them ; this is what I cannot endure to hear of.

Beaum.

Beaum. But why ridiculoufly ape them ? Mr. *Rymer* pretends that the Chorus is neceffary ; nay, hat it is always the moft neceffary part of a Tragedy ; that the *French* have lately feen the neceffity of it, and that the fuccefs of their laft Plays has fufficiently juftified the Wifdom of their late Reformation.

Freem. 'Tis very inexcufable in a Man of Sence, to make any conclufion from fuccefs. The *French* before now have damn'd a very good Play, and confequently may like an ill one. *Jay veu* (fays St. *Euremont*) *Corneille perdre fa Reputation* (*s'il eft poffible qu'il la perdit*) *a la reprefentation d'une de fes meilleurs pieces. I have feen,* fays he, Corneille *lofe his Reputation* (*if it had been poffible for him to lofe it*) *at the acting of own of his beft Plays.* Which he fpeaks to condemn the changable Relifh of the *Parifians.* Nor is it true, that the *French* faw any neceffity for the reftoring the Chorus. Monfieur *Recine,* in his Preface to *Efther,* which was the firft Tragedy that has been lately writ with a Chorus, fays, That he was put upon the handling that Subject in that Method, by thofe who had the Superintendency of the Houfe of St. *Cyr* ; that is, by Madam *de Maintenon.* So thatwhat Mr. *R* — calls a neceffity, was but at the beft a conveniency.

Beaum. A conveniency !

Freem. Aye ; for upon the Writing this Religious Play with a Chorus, the cloifter'd Beauties of that blooming Society, had a favourable occafion of fhewing their Parts in a Religious way, to the *French* Court.

Beaum. Let me die, if thou haft not been reading the fcandalous Chronicle.

Freem. Many an honeft well-meaning Text has met with a wicked Comment.

Beaum. But what does it fignifie, whether the *French* found

found the Chorus neceſſary, or only found it convenient. Mr. *Rymer*, whom all the World allows to be
a competent Judge of theſe matters, not only affirms
it to be neceſſary, but the moſt neceſſary part of a
Tragedy.

Freem. That it is not the moſt neceſſary part of a
Tragedy, I ſhall prove by an Argument, which, if Mr.
Rymer admits of *Ariſtotle*'s Rules, will amount to a de-
monſtration. For Tragedy, according to *Ariſtotle*, is
the imitation of an Important Action. Now an Action may be imitated without the Chorus, but not without the Epiſode.

Beaum. What is it that you call Epiſode.:

Freem. All that was between the ſinging of the Chorus, which is all our Modern Tragedy. But further,
Fable is the very Soul of Tragedy, according to Mr.
Rymer himſelf. Now nothing is more plain than this,
that the Fable in Tragedy may ſubſiſt without the
Chorus, but not without the Epiſode: From whence
it neceſſarily follows, that the Epiſode is always the
moſt neceſſary part of a Tragedy; for without it,
Tragedy can have no Soul, and conſequently can have
no Being.

Beaum. This, I muſt confeſs, is ſomething.

Freem. Something? Well, to compleat your Con-
viction, I ſhall add the Authority of *Dacier*, who has
theſe words in his Comment upon *Ariſtotle*'s Treatiſe
of Poetry, *Chap.* 12. *Sect.* 6.

*Le Tragedie n'etoit dans ſon origine q un chœur ſans
acteurs Enſuite on ajouta les acteurs, pour delaſſer le
chœur, & tout ce que ces acteurs diſoient entre deux
chants du chœur, s'appelloit Epiſode, comme qui diroit
parte ajouteé; parce que ces recits etoient pieces etran-*

geres

*geres & surajouteés à une ceremonie dont elles ne faiso-
rent point partie ; mais quand la Tragedie eut commen-
cé à se former , & que les recits qui n'etoient que les partie accessoire furent devenues les principal alors, &c.*

So that it is plain, according to the Sence of *Dacier*,
that tho' the Chorus was at first the Foundation of Tra-
dy, it is now the least necessary part of it.

Beaum. Well, you seem to have prov'd, that the
Chorus is not the most necessary part of a Tragedy,
however it may be necessary, and therefore ought to
be restor'd. Mr. *Rymer* affirms particularly, that it is
necessary to confine a Poet to unity of place.

Freem. There he is so far mistaken, that Monsieur
Racine, who in several of his former Tragedies, has
with Religion, observ'd that unity, has not tied himself
to it so scrupulously in the very first Tragedy which
he writ with a Chorus, which he owns himself in his
Preface to *Esther*, and is plain to any one who reads
that Tragedy. And whereas Mr. *R* — affirms, that
the Chorus is not to be lost out of sight, let him but
consult the First Scene of the Second Act of *Esther*, and
the Seventh Scene of the Third Act of *Athaliah* (which
is the Second Play that *Racine* writ with a Chorus) and
he will find, that in those Scenes the Stage is without
a Chorus.

Beaum. But has not *Racine* in that deviated from the
ways of the Ancients ?

Freem. I must confess, I believe he has ; for having
lately read over the *Oedipus* and *Antigone* of *Sophocles*,
I find, that in those two Plays, the Chorus is always
in sight. However, this may serve as an Argument to
prove two things: First, That if a Poet will be irregular, he may as well break the unity of place with a Chorus,

rus, as without it. Secondly, It may prove, that *Racine* undertook to write his *Esther*, purely out of compliance with Madam *de Maintenon*. For if he had done it with a design of conforming to the Ancients, he would doubtless have conformed in every thing : but he has been so far from doing that, that his *Esther*, you know, has but Three Acts ; which is directly contrary to the Precept of *Horace*.

Neve minor quinto neu fit productior actu Fabula—

And to the Practice of the Ancients.

Beaum. Why, as far as I can remember, *Sophocles* and *Euripides* never distinguish'd their Plays by A

Freem. They did not make use of the word Act to denote their Distinctions, as the *Romans* afterwards did ; but however, the Chorus sung four times in the intervals of the Episode, as the Musick plays four times in the Intervals of the Acts with us.

Beaum. You affirm then, that the Chorus is necessary upon no account.

Freem. I cannot conceive how the Chorus can be necessary, if Tragedy can attain its end without it. Now the end of Tragedy, according to *Aristotle*, is to excite Compassion and Terrour, in order to the purging of those, and the like Passions. And Terrour and Compassion may be excited without a Chorus, perhaps better than with it.

Beaum. Pray, why so ?

Freem.

Freem. Becaufe the Chorus in fome meafure muft calm an Audience which the Epifode difturb'd by its Sublimity, and by its Pathetick ; and therefore he who makes ufe of a Chorus in Tragedy, feems to me, to do like a Phyfitian, who prefcribing a Dofe for the evacuation of Peccant Humors, fhould afterwards order Reftringents to be taken in the midft of its kind Operation. The Song of the Chorus muft be forreign from the matter, or pertinent : If forreign from the matter, it muft not only calm the Mind in fome meafure, but take it off from the fubject. But if it is never fo pertinent, it muft very much cool a Reader, if not a Spectator ; tho' I make no queftion, but it muft have the fame effect upon both.

Beaum. But you ought to prove, that it muft have the fame effect upon both.

Freem. If it has not, it muft be wholly unprofitable : for the defign of the Chorus is to give good Advice, to preach up Morality, to extol Vertue, to praife or pray to the Gods.

Ille bonis faveatq; & confilietur amici
Et regat eratos, & amet peccare timentes ;
Ille dapes laudet menfæ brevis : ille falubrem
Juftitiam legefq; & apertis otia portu.
Ille tegat commiffa, deofq; precetur & oret
Ut redeat miferis abeat fortuna fuperbis.

Horat. Art. Poet.

Now I would fain know, how an Audience that is ex-treamly difturbed with Terrour, or with Compaffion, can be capable of harkning to good Advice, of appre-hending the reafonablenefs of good Inftruction, or of performing Religious Duties.

Beaum.

Beaum. But pray, if Terrour and Compaſſion muſt be rais'd to ſuch a height without receiving any check, how can they be ſaid to be purg'd ?

Freem. *Dacier* has given us a very ſenſible account of that. For as the Humors in ſome diſtemper'd Body are rais'd, in order to the evacuating that which is redundant or peccant in them ; ſo Tragedy excites Compaſſion and Terrour to the ſame end : For the Play being over, an Audience becomes ſerene again, and is leſs apt to be mov'd at the common Accidents of Life, after it has ſeen the deplorable Calamities of Hero's and Sovereign Princes.

Beaum. Now here have I an Objection to make, which muſt be confeſs'd to be of ſome importance. *Ariſtotle* has given Rules for the Chorus, which he would not have done, unleſs he had believ'd it neceſſary. *Horace* has follow'd his ſteps. *Dacier*, who is *Ariſtotle*'s beſt Interpreter, has endeavour'd its reſtoration : He has declar'd the neceſſity of it, for teaching Morality to the People ; he has told us, that *Racine* was convinc'd that there was a neceſſity for it ; and he has commended him for reviving it in his laſt Tragedies.

Freem. But pray, Sir, how came you to know what *Dacier* ſays ? I thought you had told me, you had not convers'd with the Criticks lately.

Beaum. I read this in *Dacier*'s Preface, but now, when you left me alone.

Freem. Indeed, it muſt be confeſs'd, that *Ariſtotle* has mention'd the Chorus, and diſcours'd of the different parts of it. But then, conſider how large a ſpace the Chorus took up in the ancient Tragedy, and how little *Ariſtotle* has ſaid of it, and you will be oblig'd to own that he ſlighted it, and would have made no

men-

mention of it, if he could have avoided it ; but he could not do that, being engaged to treat of the whole Art of the Stage. Nor could he in prudence condemn the use of it, if you consider that it was Religious in its Office and Institution. The same Answer will serve for *Horace*; because his Religion and Design were the same with *Aristotle*'s. *Dacier* shall answer himself: For if he declares a Chorus to be necessary in his Preface, he tells you in his Comment upon the Sixth Chapter of *Aristotle*, that he scarce believes it to be natural, and that having several times wonder'd, how so delicate and so ingenious a People as the *Athenians* must be allow'd to be, could think it agreeable to Nature, or Probability, that a Chorus who represented the Spectators of a Tragical Action, should sing and dance upon such extraordinary and moving Events ; he was oblig'd to attribute it to the Inclinations and Superstition of the *Greeks* ; who, as they were the People of the World, the most inclin'd to Singing and Dancing, (which natural bent of theirs was fortified by Education) so were they the most bigotted of all Nations ; and Singing and Dancing, which help'd to constitute the Ceremonials of their Religion, were held as Sacred by them, and of Divine Institution : So that when *Dacier*, who tells us in his Comment upon the Sixth Chapter, that he could not have believ'd the Chorus natural, if it had not been so adapted to the Superstition and Musical Temper of the *Greeks* ; declares it to be necessary in his Preface , he must do it out of belief, that his own Country-men were as airy Bigots as the *Greeks*.

Beaum.

Beaum. And, Faith, he was very much in the right of it; How many *French*-men have we seen, who between the First and Second Courses have risen from Table, and danc'd to their own damn'd Voices? I must confess, they do not dance at Church, but they have several apish Gesticulations there, which one may easily mistake for Dancing, and which are as entertaining to the full. But for Singing, in is both their Diversion and Duty.

Freem. Well then, all this considered, it is no wonder that *Dacier* should tell us, That *Racine* being to write upon a Religious Subject, saw a necessity for a Chorus; that is, for a great deal of Singing and Dancing; for without it there had been two inconveniences: First, The Religion of the Stage had been more free from Superstition, than that of the Altar. And, Secondly, a Play had been more insipid than High Mass.

Beaum. Yet *Dacier* has given us two Reasons for the necessity of a Chorus, that have nothing to do with *Racine* : For a Chorus, says he, is necessary, First, To deliver Moral Sentiments to the People. And, Secondly, To reflect upon what is vicious and commendable in the Characters of the primary Actors; in which he is certainly in the right. Now, the Chorus being retrench'd from our Modern Tragedy, Morality must be retrench'd at the same time. For the principal Actors being shaken by violent Passions, cannot be made sentencious ; for Sentences require Reflection, and that requires Serenity ; at least some degree of Serenity. How then can our Theatre, the Chorus being retrench'd, be said to be the School of Virtue ? Or how can any one be the better for Modern Tragedy ?

Freem.

Freem. Our Theatre may be said to be the School of Vertue, upon two accounts. First, because it removes the greatest Obstructions to Vertue, by reducing the Passions to a just mediocrity, from their violence and irregularity. And Secondly, because it teaches some Moral Doctrine by the Fable, which must always be allegorical and universal.

Beaum. This Answer is something satisfactory. But what can you answer to the Second pretended necessity for restoring the Chorus ? which is, that the Stage may be furnish'd with Persons, who may commend or blame any thing that may be vicious or excellent in the Characters of the primary Actors ? For there may be a necessity sometimes for their speaking prophanely and impiously ; which may be of dangerous consequence, without the Reflections of the Chorus.

Freem. Nothing that is said, can be of pernicious consequence in a Tragedy, if it is writ as it ought to be. That is, if it is what *Horace* calls, *Fabula recte morata.*

Beaum. Pray what may that be ?

Freem. A Tragedy is *Fabula recte morata,* in which the Manners are well painted : So that every Actor discovers immediately by what he says, his Inclinations, his Designs, and the very Bottom of his Character ; then if any thing is said impiously, an Audience not only knows that it is spoken by an impious Man, but by one that is upon the Point of being punish'd for his Impiety.

Beaum.

Beaum. This feems to be fenfible enough : But now good Sence requires that we fhould think of our Dinner : for a hungry Sophifter, who difputes at the time he may eat, does but defraud his own Genius, to put a cheat upon another Man's Reafon : Therefore, let's to the Cock, and I'll fend for *Jack Wild* to make a third Man ; who fhall very dogmatically tell you, that there can be no Tragedy without a Chorus.

Freem. But can he prove it ?

Beaum. That you fhall judge when you have heard him.

Freem. Well : I'll follow you.

The End of the Fourth Dialogue.

DIALOGUE V.

BEAUMONT, FREEMAN.

Scene, Freeman's *Chamber, after Dinner.*

Beaum. WAS ever any Man mawl'd as thou haft been! *Jack Wild* has handled you as you deferv'd, I'faith: Thou wert quite bafled, quite run down, Man!

Freem. Bafled and run down, Good! Are we in *Bow-ftreet,* or on the *Bank-fide?* Your Mr. *Wild* has an admirable Talent for running People down, I confefs. But doft not thou know, that the filliest thing that a Man can do, is to fpeak Sence in fome Company? Is it not a greater fign of Judgment to hold one's Tongue, than to talk Reafon to People who cannot hear it?

Beaum. Then you do not believe he was in the right, it feems?

Freem. I am not quite fo credulous. I muft confefs Mr. *Wild* had got *Dacier* without Book perfectly; nay, and that very place in *Dacier* which pleads moft ftrongly for a Chorus. But then he would admit of no Anfwer. I would advife Mr. *Wild* to take Orders; a
                                                        Pulpit

Pulpit fure is the only place where Impertinence has priviledge to be tedious, without interruption. But thou wert as attentive as any Fanatical Bigot at a Conventicle : therefore, if you can recollect his Reafons, I dare undertake, to convince you of their infufficiency.

Beaum. Faith, I'll try ; but then you fhall engage, that if I happen to fhew fuch a plaguy Memory, I fhall not lofe my Reputation of a Wit with you.

Freem. That I do readily engage for, I'faith.

Beaum. So then; his firft Argument was this : Tragedy is the imitation of a Publick and Vifible Action ; therefore there ought to be a Chorus.

Freem. I muft confefs, *Dacier* affirms, That Tragedy muft be the Reprefentation of a Publick and Vifible Action ; but *Ariftotle* fays no fuch thing, that I know of.

Beaum. But common Sence tho' fays fo : For if an Action is not publickly vifible, how can it be feen by fuch a numerous multitude ?

Freem. How can an Action, the Scene of which is in *Greece*, be feen by us here in *England* ?

Beaum. Nay, I will grant you, that there is an occafion for us to give way to a wholfome delufion, if we defign to receive either delight or profit from the *Drama*. But however, a Poet is ftill to endeavour, that his Reprefentation be attended with as much probability as it is capable of : And it is much eafier for a thoufand Spectators to imagine themfelves in fome open place, either at *Mycenæ* or *Thebes*, than to imagine themfelves in a King's Cabinet, in either of thofe two places.

Freem. I muſt confeſs what you ſay appears to be reaſonable, but how do yon infer from hence, that there ought to be a Chorus?

Beaum. The Action of a Tragedy being publickly viſible, and acted by Perſons of the moſt exalted Ranks, it is impoſſible but that there muſt be People beſides the Actors, intereſted in the principal Action, upon which Action the Fortune of thoſe People muſt in ſome meaſure depend.

Freem. And thoſe People you'll tell me, are to conſtitute the Chorus.

Beaum. Right.

Freem. This, I muſt confeſs, is according to *Dacier* ; but his Doctrine is neither warranted by *Ariſtotle*, nor always by the Practice of the Ancients ; for it does not appear to me, for example, what dependance, as to their Fortunes, the Chorus in the *Electra* of *Sophocles*, has upon the principal Actors. But ſuppoſe we had Charity to grant, that it is impoſſible for a grave and important Action to be acted in publick by great Men, but others muſt intermeddle in it : Can *Dacier* infer from hence, that theſe People thus concerned, ought to ſing and dance at their Princes Sufferings : I will grant it probable, that at the Sufferings of Kings ſeveral ſhould be concern'd ; at the ſame time you muſt grant it abſurd, that they ſhould ſing and dance at their Sufferings. Now would you have a Poet ſhew a thing that's abſurd, to ſhew ſomething elſe that is probable, when the probability may be ſuppos'd as well as ſhewn, or ſhewn without an abſurdity?

Beaum. How can that be?

Freem. In our modern Tragedies, as well as the ancient, there are ſeveral concern'd beſides the Actors ;

I mean, besides the primary Actors (for the Chorus was an Actor in the old Tragedy, and spoke like a Jury by its Fore-man) but they have some better reason for their being concern'd, than purely their itch of medling ; nor do they express their concern in a way which is contrary to all Decorum : But I could give you an example of a Chorus, where the singing is not only absurd and unnatural, but destructive of the Poet's design.

Beaum. That example I should be glad to hear.

Freem. 'Tis the Chorus at the end of the First Act in the *Electra* of *Sophocles*.

Beaum. How does that which is sung by the Chorus there, run counter to the design of the Poet?

Freem. I will, in as few words as I can, give you the Fable of that Tragedy : *Clytemnestra*, with her A-dulterer *Ægystus*, assassinates her Husband *Agamemnon* ; but her Son *Orestes*, by means of his Sister *Electra*, escapes : after a long absence from *Mycenæ*, he arrives secretly with *Pylades* and his Governour, surprizes *Clytemnestra* and her Adulterer, and revenges the Death of his Father. The Scene opens with the Arrival of *Orestes* before the Royal Palace of *Mycenæ*, at Break of Day, where they find *Electra* lamenting her sad Condition. The Chorus advise her not to be so loud, least she should be heard by *Ægystus* : yet as soon as ever she is gone, they grow infinitely louder, and in a Consort of Fifteen Voices, threaten Ruine to *Clytemnestra* and her Adulterer. 'Tis true, they were told that *Ægystus* was not in the Palace ; but they knew very well, that *Clytemnestra* was there, and that *Ægystus* would be with her that very day. Now this coming after an unlucky Dream, which *Clytemnestra* look'd on as ominous ;

rious ; which Dream is mentioned by this very Chorus : This Song muſt in all reaſon alarm *Clytemneſtra*, and prevent the ſurprize which is deſign'd by the Poet. Beſides, how did this Chorus dare thus loudly and publickly to contemn *Clytemneſtra* before her own Palace, at the very time that ſhe had the Sovereign Power in her hands ?

Beaum. I muſt confeſs, I am not able to give any Anſwer to this.

Freem. I could ſhew you another groſs abſurdity in that very Tragedy, which is purely occaſion'd by the Chorus. But pray go on to the next Argument.

Beaum. I would fain know firſt, what that other abſurdity is : a digreſſion ſometimes is as much worth the while as the main matter ; and I have always been pleas'd to hear of the Errors of any extraordinary Man, becauſe it has ſtill been the beſt ſupport to me, under the mortifying Sence, which I have of my own Infirmities.

Freem. The abſurdity which I ſpeak of, is, the diſcovery that *Oreſtes* makes of himſelf and his deſign, to *Electra*, in the Fourth Act of that Tragedy (which he does in the preſence of the Chorus); ſo that he entruſts a Secret upon which his Empire and Life depends, in the hands of Sixteen Women : For *Oreſtes* had no Friends, on whoſe aſſiſtance he might rely, unleſs it were his Friend and his Governour, and conſequently he had nothing to depend upon, but Secreſie and Surprize, and a ſwift Execution.

Beaum. Has *Dacier* in his late Comment upon *Electra*, taken no notice of thoſe two miſtakes :

Freem. He has taken no notice at all of the firſt; which I was extremely ſurpriz'd at : For that Error ſeems to me apparently to ſhock common Sence. I muſt confeſs, he has taken notice of the laſt, becauſe he thought he could make a defence for it. But he has done it after ſuch a manner, that I am ſorry that a Man of Monſieur *Dacier's* Merit ſhould talk at ſo poor a rate.

Beaum. At how poor a rate?

Freem. I have conſidered that paſſage enough to give you the *Engliſh* of it *Verbatim.* There are ſeveral Perſons, ſays he, of extraordinary Merit, who cannot endure to ſee Plots and Contrivances againſt the Lives of Princes, in the preſence of a Chorus, pretending that this cannot be probable ; nay, that it cannot be natural. But theſe People, ſays he, ought to reflect upon the Conditions that are neceſſary to qualifie a Chorus rightly. The Chorus ought to be intereſted in the Action, as much as the principal Perſons, they ought to be animated by the ſame Spirit , and all their Happineſs ought to depend upon their Secrecy and their Fidelity. And when a Chorus is thus qualify'd, there is nothing which may not be ſaid before it, without any violation to probability. And then it is as natural to ſee a Conſpiracy concerted before it, as it is to behold a number of Conſpirators cloſely conſulting in ſome ſecure Retirement. The Chorus of *Electra* is of this nature, ſays he.

Beaum. And is It ?

Freem. Monſieur *Dacier* may imagine what he pleaſes, but there is nothing that the Chorus or Electra ſays, that may induce a Man to believe, that the fortune of the firſt depends upon the ſucceſs of the laſt.

laft. But fuppofing it did, can any Man who has common Sence believe, that a Prince, as difcreet as *Oreftes* is reprefented by *Sophocles*, fhould entruft a Secret, upon which his Empire and Life depended, with fifteen Women, only upon the recommendation of his Sifter, whofe difcretion he had no reafon to have any mighty Opinion of? But this has been a long digreffion, therefore pray proceed to the next Argument, which Mr. *Wild* brought for a Chorus.

Beaum. A Tragedy, faid he, is the imitation of an Action, which muft be one and entire ; and therefore there muft be a Chorus : For without it the Acts can never be joyn'd, there will be a folution of continuity, and Tragedy can never be one entire Body. Pray, what can you anfwer to this ?

Freem. This, I muft confefs, is the Bugbear Argument ; but we fhall do well enough with it. Then Mr. *Wild* and you fancy, that the Action breaks off every time that the Mufick plays between the Acts ?

Beaum. That is Mr. *Wild*'s Opinion.

Freem. But then I could tell you, that the Action is fuppos'd to be continued behind the Scenes.

Beaum. How can an Audience be fure of that ? Or when the Stage is left empty upon the end of the Firft Act, what grounds has a Company to believe the Actors will return ? What grounds, I fay, can they have, but Cuftom, which is but a ridiculous Security at the beft, and can be none at all, to one who fees a Tragedy acted the firft time. Whereas a Chorus naturally keeps the Company together, till the return of the principal Actors.

Freem.

Freem. But sure, I should think, that an Audience between the Acts should have a much better Security for the return of the Actors than Custom, and that is from the nature of Tragedy, which is the imitation of an entire action ; that is, of an Action which has a beginning, a middle, and an end. Now this beginning and middle, are, according to *Aristotle*, Things that necessarily suppose something to follow.

Beaum. When you talk at this rate, you suppose that every one who sees a Tragedy, understands the Rules of *Aristotle.*

Freem. The Rules of *Aristotle* are nothing but Nature and Good Sence reduc'd to a Method : I may very well suppose, that every one who goes to see a Tragedy acted, goes with a hope, that he shall not see something absurd; and that he has common Sence to know, that a Tragedy would be very absurd, which should conclude abruptly, before the just end of the Action ; that is to say, before that part of it, which necessarily supposes nothing to follow it.

Beaum. You say the Song of the Chorus is very absurd and unnatural ; but are not the Fiddles between the Acts a great deal more absurd and unnatural. A Poet in a Tragick Imitation, is always to have an eye to probability. But is it probable, that *Oedipus*, or any other Prince, should four times in the height and fury of his Passion, leave the Scene of Action, purely to give leave to a Company of Musitians to divert the Spectators four times, least they should be too much shaken by the progress of the terrible Action ? Would not such a one be a merry Monarch, a very complaisant Wretch ?

H

Freem.

Freem. Has not *Dacier* reason to be asham'd of this empty Sophistry, which may so easily be retorted upon himself? For would it not be as ridiculous to make a King leave the Scene of the Action four times, only to give way to the People who compose the Chorus? Any Man knows, that in Plays which have a Chorus, and in Plays which have none, 'tis the necessity of the Action, which makes the Actors leave the Stage. For an Actor never leaves the Stage in a Tragedy which is writ as it should be; but when he has business in another place. But suppose I should grant you, that the Fiddles are more absurd than a Chorus, we do not pretend that our Musick makes a part of Tragedy, as you pretend that the Chorus does, and if there must be an absurdity, it had better been in Ornament than in Essentials.

Beaum. But if your Musick does not make a part of the Modern Tragedy, how can it be said to be one body, when the parts of it are not united?

Freem. 'Tis not the tagging of the Acts with a Chorus, that properly makes a Tragedy one Body, but the Unity of the Action; and for my part, I cannot conceive, but that the Parts are sufficiently united, when the Action has a Beginning, a Middle, and an End, which have a mutual necessary and immediate dependance. But if it should be granted to *Dacier,* that the Fiddles between the Acts are absolutely destructive of the Unity of the Poem, he could never infer from it, that there ought to be a Chorus, when the mischief may be prevented another way.

Beaum. What way is that?

Freem. Why, by not dividing Tragedy into Acts at all.

Beaum.

Beaum. But several Inconveniences would follow from thence.

Freem. I will eafily grant it ; but any inconvenience ought to be admitted, rather than that grand abfurdity a Chorus. For Poetry being an imitation of Nature, any thing which is unnatural ftrikes at the very Root and Being of it, and ought to be avoided like Ruine.

Beaum. Well, thou haft here taken a great deal of pains to prove, that we ought not to re-eftablifh the Chorus ; but you promis'd to fhew me, that we ought not to banifh Love neither.

Freem. I have now an appointment which I am ob-lig'd to keep touch with. But when we next meet, I will not only engage to demonftrate that to you, but to fhew you, that contrary to Mr. *Rymer*'s affertion, *Shakefpear* was a great Genius.

Beaum. I fhall be very glad, if you perform what you fay. But prithee tell me before we part, your Opinion of Mr. *Rymer*'s Judgment of our *Englifh* Comedies.

Freem. Never was there a more righteous Decree. We have particularly a Comedy which was writ by a Gentleman now living, that has more Wit and Spirit than *Plautus*, without any of his little contemptible Affectations ; and which, with the Urbanity of *Terence*, has the Comick force which the Great *Cæfar* requir'd in him.

Beaum. What Comedy can that be ?

Freem. What indeed can it be, but the *Plain Dealer* ?

Beaum. I find then, that you do not diffent from Mr. R —— in every thing.

Freem.

Freem. No, I should be very sorry if I should do that; for his Censures of *Shakespear* in most of the particulars, are very sensible and very just. But it does not follow, because *Shakespear* has Faults, that therefore he has no Beauties, as the next time we meet I shall shew you.

Beaum. Well, till then, your Servant.

Freem. Honest *Ned*, Adieu.

THE END.

ERRATA

In the LETTER to a Friend.

FOR *exerted Compassion.* read *excited Compassion.* For *wanner Sun* r. *warm a Sun.* for *desire* r. *desired.* for *following Dialogue* r. *following Dialogues:* for *is a base Envy* r. *it shews a base Envy.* for *greater Geniusses than they* r. *greater Geniusses (in* England, *than they have in* France.

Dialogue the Third.

PAge 18. for *Punegyricks* r. *Panegyrick.* p. 19. for *I desire you* r. *I desie you.* p. 22. for *gallant Man* r. *gallant Writer.* for *Sevigue* r. *Sevigné.* p. 29. for *caudæ &c.* r. *caudæq; pilos ut equinæ,* | Dialogue IV, p. 32. for *Recine* r. *Racine.* p. 34. for *parties accessoire* r. *les parties accessoires furent devenuer les principales.* p. 36. for *amici* r. *amicis,* for *eratos* r. *iratos.*

ADVERTISEMENT

MIscellany Poems, &c. By Mr. *Dennis*, will be Publish'd this next Week. Printed for *James Knapton*, at the *Crown* in St. *Paul's* Church-yard.

Miscellaneous
LETTERS
AND
ESSAYS,

On several

SUBJECTS.

Philosophical, Moral, Historical, Critical, Amorous, &c. in *Prose* and *Verse.*

DIRECTED TO
John Dryden, Esq; } { *Walter Moile,* Esq;
The Honourable } { Mr. *Dennis,*
Geo. Granvill, Esq; } { Mr. *Congreve,*
And other Eminent Men of th'Age.

By several Gentlemen and Ladies.

LONDON: Printed for Benjamin Bragg, at the *White-Hart*, over against *Water-Lane* in *Fleetstreet,* 1 6 9 4.

TO THE
HONOURABLE

Sir *JOHN TRENCHARD*,

Their Majesties Principal Secretary of State. And one of the Lords of their Majesties most Honourable Privy Council.

Honour'd Sir;

I am so far from being Apprehensive of the Censure of any *thinking* Man, for Dedicating a Book of this Nature to a Man of your *Station*, that I'm satisfyed I shou'd have injur'd your Merit in choosing any o-

ther

ther Patron for That, in which the Glory of the ENGLISH NATION is in some Degree defended: for tho' I confess the *States Man* (according to our Modern Notion) has little to do with the ensuing Discourses; yet I'm very sure the TRUE ENGLISH MAN (a Name I know you far more value) must extreamly interest you in them; for the *Patriots* Zeal ought to extend to the *Glory*, as well as *Happyness* of his Country: so that you must be *pleas'd* to shelter with your Protection, a Piece that aims at a Vindication of our known RIGHT and HONOUR, which are impiously invaded, and as *weakly*, as *ignobly* betray'd to a *Foreign People*, by a *biggotted* Veneration for a former Age. But *Poetry*, Sir, will appear from the following *Essays*, to be a Prize we ought no more to surrender to *Foreign* Nati-

Nations than our *Courage* or *Liberty.*
For *Greece* and *Rome*, who have given us the noblest Examples of the
Latter, have been the most famous
for the Former. And as we are not
inferior to either of those *Common-
Wealths*, in the Honor of *Arms*,
or the Wisdom of our Laws, so I
can never yield them the precedence
in *Poetry.*

Nor is this *Glory* I plead for, a meer
Noitionary Fantom, which affords no
Benefit to the *Public*, as is evident
from its very *Nature* and *Design*, as
well as the Authority of the Wisest
Nations, who have Esteem'd POETS
very necessary, as well as very Honourable Members of the *Common-
Wealth.* This *Athens* thought, when
on the loss of *Eupolis* in a Sea Fight,
she decreed that no *Poet* shou'd for the
future, ever venture himself in the

A 3   War,

The Epistle Dedicatory.

War, least by one Fatal Blow, a Treasure should be lost, an Age cou'd not repair, for POETS *were not born ev'ry Day.*

But this Veneration which *Greece* paid the Poets, is built on the innate Excellence of their Art. *Pleasure* is the Sovereign Aim of all Men, 'tis that which the *Soul* naturally and justly desires, and for which 'tis made, and what the greatest *Stoic* persues; for 'tis impossible for any Man to desire *Pain.* Now *Poetry* do's not only make *Pleasure*, its *Medium* but its *Aim*, and so employs the surest Means to obtain the noblest *End.* Majestic and delightful Numbers, surprizing and noble Thoughts, and Charming Expressions, awake all the Faculties of the Soul, to receive the *Mighty Lessons* it imparts, which all terminate in the most *Solid*, and *Rational Pleasure.*

For

For they either establish some Virtue by a great *Example*, or by the same, punish some *Vice*, or redicule, and lash some *Folly*, that may be injurious to our *Happyness*; the Establishment of which on the Basis of *Virtue* and *Wisdom*, fixes us in the sweet *Enjoyment* of the *Greatest* and most lasting of Pleasures.

As a farther *Proof* of *Poetry's*, being a Friend to, and promoter of *Virtue*; and an Enemy to *Vice*, 'tis observable, that all the *Heroes* and Men of *Virtue* of Antiquity lov'd and encourag'd *Poetry*, and that the worst of *Princes*, and greatest TYRANTS always persecuted, and hated the *Poets*, as their known and most dangerous Enemies, for they wou'd spare no *Vice* in the most powerful Offenders. *Lucan* fear'd not in the time of the greatest Tyrant of the *Cæsars*, to extoll *Cato*

A 4   the

the most obstinate Stickler for his Countrys Liberty against the first of em ; and he chooses rather to condemn *Providence* for the success, the destroyers of the Liberty of *Rome* met with, than not praise *Cato* for dying with his falling Country. *Victrix causa dijs placuit, sed Victa Catoni.* The POETS indeed have been the bold Persecutors of *Vice* in all Ages, and have ever rewarded *Virtue* with *Immortality.* They are beneficial to *Posterity,* by conveying to it the most prevailing Motives Illustrious Examples, so that he that is a generous Patron of the MUSES, is a Benefactor to Ages to come, as well as to the Present.

Carmen amat quisquis, Carmine Digna gerit. is a certain Truth ; For the very Motives for performing Vertuous Actions, hold for the care of those that make them eternal, *viz. the good of Others,* the

The Epistle Dedicatory.

the *public Benefit*. To which Sir, your whole Life and Endeavours having been zealously applyed, I cannot doubt but you will by your patronizing *Poetry*, compleat the noble end of your *Honourable Ambition*. Then may Posterity see in YOU, Sir, such a pattern of *Fortitude*, *Temperance*, *Wisdom*, *Justice*, *Bounty*, and all other Virtues that make a Man truly Great, that copying You alone, wou'd make 'em all *Happy* and *Good*. I'm too unskilful a Dawber to dare to venture on drawing so noble an Image, as both your private and public Life compose. I can never reach up to that Generous Constancy to your Friends in the midst of your *Sufferings*, which has to my knowledge rais'd some to Wealth, if not Content. How can I ever hope to give the least Idea of your present Character, when your Love for the Public Good transports you from private Repose to Business

The Epistle Dedicatory.

Bufinefs, and the fatigues of *State*, that more, than thofe only, whom you know, may fhare in the Bleffings of your Adminiftration.

An ungenerous Self-intereft, feparate from the *Public Good*, has been obferv'd to prevail over moft *Statefmen*, which made the World put fuch a vaft diftinction betwixt the *Statefman* and the *Patriot*, as to make 'em irreconcileable; but You, Sir, contradict fo general an Obfervation, fince we all agree, that in you the *Patriot* and *Statefman* are eminently united. *Your Soul* is too *Large*, too *Noble*, to be wretchedly confin'd to fo narrow a Game, as the Chafe of your own private *Happinefs*, without regard to the public; or rather you are fo *True* an *Englifh-man*, that you cannot be *Happy*, unlefs your Country be fo too; and 'tis not your own private Stores, but the Public that gives you Content; for your Goodnefs is

exalted

exalted so near to Perfection, that it *cannot but be communicative*; we are so sensible of this, that we *unanimously* wish your *Power* to do Good, were as boundless, as we know your *Will*. We might then hope a long wish'd Union in those Minds, whose Variance with each other has produc'd a common Misery; and till that be effected, we have alass! but little Hopes of any *settl'd Happiness*. But what is worst, there is but small prospect of that, till Men have learn'd your *Virtue*, Sir, of sacrificing all private *Designs* and *Int'rests* to the *public Good*.

But I have unawares faln into a Contemplation of your Virtues, which I dare not persue; but as the Painter, who after he had given to the several Figures of his Picture, the various forms and expressions of Grief, drew a Veil over the Father's Face, as unable to express his: So, Sir, ought I, having given

ven

The Epistle Dedicatory.

ven a View of some part of your Merits, to leave the rest to the Imagination of the *Reader*, better inform'd by your *known Reputation.* I have said enough to make all Men admire, and love you, that do not know you; and it must be the Defect of my Abilities, if they stop on this side the highest and most Awful Veneration. However I have this Comfort, that I have rais'd the *first* Pyramid (tho' a very poor one) to your desert, to which greater Artists will in time build up more Glorious Monuments, when you shall declare your self, the Patron of the *Poetic Glory* of *England*, as you have been of her Int'rest. And these Hopes makes me presume to Dedicate not only this small Book to you, but also my self, and all the Endeavours of, Sir,

Your most Humble,

And most Obedient Servant,

CHARLES GILDON,

THE
PREFACE.

THere is no Man, I think, doubts but that 'tis Variety that composes the Regale of the Mind, as well as that of the Body, which has made me have a regard to that in the following Book; for I have intermixt things Historical, Moral, Amorous and Gallant, with the rougher Critical Discourses. Some will gratifie the Fancy, others the Judgment, or at least I design'd they shou'd. I shall not say much for that part of the Book which is none of mine, because that need no Defence; and I cannot urge much for the other, if the Reasons it contains be insufficient for its Justification.

In

The Preface.

In the hurry of writing **1** *forgot one very good Defence of a Paſſage in the Othello of* Shakeſpear, *which Mr. Ry-mer has loudly exclaim'd againſt, and which a very good Friend of mine adviſ'd me to inſert in the* Preface; *'tis this,*

Awake what hoa! Brabantio, &c.
An old black Ram is tupping your white Ewe, &c.

"Mr. Rymer *will have it, that a rap*
"at the Door *wou'd better expreſs* Jago's
"*Meaning, than all that noiſe; but if*
"Mr. Rymer *wou'd conſult the Reaſon*
"*of the thing he'll find, that the noiſe*
"Roderigo *and* Jago *made, contributed*
"*very much to their deſign of ſurpriz-*
"*ing and alarming* Brabantio, *by*
"*that, to tranſport him from Conſidera-*
"*tion to a violent Paſſion.*

I am ſorry, that a Man of Mr. Rymer's
Learning ſhou'd be ſo bigotted to the An-tients, as to become an Enemy to the
Honor

The Preface.

Honor of his own Country in that thing, which is perhaps the only we can truly pretend to excel all others in, viz. Poetry Courage, Virtue *and* Wisdom, Greece *and* ROME *will never be out-Rival'd in, but I am apt to think they have both been out-done in* Poetry *by the* English; *and tho' the latter once subdu'd this Island, yet were she now in all her Glory, with all the Encouragements she gave her* Poets, *she wou'd confess her self conquer'd in* Poetry.

For notwithstanding all those Encouragements Poets *met with there, and the want of 'em here in* England, *we have the Honor to have more and better* Poets *than ever* Greece *or* Rome *saw. So that* Poetry *like a Tree, Transplanted to a foreign Clime, grew not, with all their Care and Cultivation, so kindly, as here without any.* Poetry, *being therefore our Native Right, I hope the moderate*

The Preface.

moderate Reader will excuse the Heat I sometimes run into in the Defence of it.

I hope too the Graver Gentlemen, the Precisians, will not be scandaliz'd at my Zeal for the Promotion of Poetry, because the Reason of it is, that 'tis observable from History, that the Decay and Neglect of that, always was a fatal Symptom of the Loss of Antient Virtue, Power and Glory

A

COLLECTION

OF

Miscellaneous Essays
and Letters.

To *JOHN DRYDEN* Esq;

May the 10th. 1693.

I Hope, Sir, you'l not meaſure my Love and
Value for you by the Viſits I make you, for
then you wou'd extreamly injure me ; for
I cannot be ſo impudent with a Man I have
an aweful Eſteem for, as to intrude too often into
his Company, for I'm ſenſible I can in no meaſure attone for the loſs of that time, my Viſits
wou'd rob from your better Thoughts ; and I
rather ſatisfie my ſelf with the expreſſion of my
Zeal and Love in abſence, than, at the expence
of my Friend, gratifie my own deſire of his frequent Company. But yet, I confeſs, this long

B   default

default of my Duty, can be excus'd by nothing, but the unavoidable business about my Concerns in the Country, which has divorc'd me as long from, what I value next you, my Books.

Mistake me not, Sir, I mean not my *Scribling*, which I'm far enough from valuing, and only comply with, by the compelling Obligation that taught the Parrot, *suum* XAIPE. Nay, I have so little of an Author, that I have not *Arrogance*, and want all *Self-Esteem*, which some ev'n as dull as my self abound with beyond bearing; and which is, indeed, like a Wife, tho' an *Evil*, yet such a one that is necessary. For a *Diffidence* of one's self in Writing, as well as in Addresses to the *Fair* and the *Great*, is seldom any advantage to a Man, at least in this Age, where the highest Impudence passes for a handsom Assurance, and *Noise* and *much Talk* for *Wit*, and *Repartée*: It dispirits a Man, and as he can't please himself with what he Writes, so he very hardly can rise to the taft of any that are not duller. But when I was forc'd to this Curse of Scribling, I furnish'd my self with as much of a *Stoic*, as I cou'd, to fortifie my self against publick Censure; and in my own defence soon believ'd *Reputation* but a *Whim*, since the Worst had their Admirers, as well as the Best, at least in our Age; nor cou'd I perswade my self that the next wou'd be one jot better in its Judgment. And to say truth, there is nothing cou'd make me have any tolerable Opinion of my self, but the *Love* and *Esteem* I have for you; whom (give me leave to contradict

dict my self, and shew such *Arrogance*) I do pretend to value, as much as any Man can : and I defie my greatest Enemies to do me Justice, and contradict me by any word or discourse ev'n where I had a Moral Certainty, you cou'd never hear of it again.

This, Sir, I urge, as a Praise of my self; for next to being a good Poet, is to know how to value one ; the first has given *Immortality*, the latter (when in a Man of Quality) gain'd it. But lest the length of my Letter shou'd do, what I apprehend from my Visits I'll

Subscribe my self,

Your Friend and humble Servant

Charles Gildon.

To his Ingenious Friend Mr. George Isaacson, in defence of Personal Reflections.

London, May the 6th. 1693.

YOU tell me you have read Mr.——'s Book, and are extreamly pleas'd with the *Wit*, and *fine Sense* of it ; but that you cannot allow of his Personal Reflections. I wish you had subjoyn'd your Reason for your Opinion, because I know

you

you guide your self extreamly by Reason in all
things, and also because you know I'm very fond
of a Reason to strengthen an Assertion that is
brought against one I do esteem, as I do Mr.——
But since you have not sent your Reason against
him in this particular, I'll give you mine for
him.

Not to justifie him by the daily Example of
other Authors, which wou'd be tedious, and to
little purpose, the very Reason of the thing its
self (supposing all the Reflections Just and True)
shou'd Vindicate his Practice in that particular:
For if Men must not be told their Faults, they'l
never mend 'em ; and *general Reflections* will never
do the Business, because the Devilish good Opinion ev'ry Man has of himself, furnishes him with
an Evasion from the lash of general Characters.
Aristophanes kept many of the *Athenians* in awe,
and within moderate bounds by this means ; and
so regulated the City better than the Philosophers, with their empty Sophisms, or the Laws,
with their blunted Edge. But after the Thirty
Tyrants had put down this Liberty with their
Chorus, the Profitable was lost in Comedy, and
Menander cou'd do nothing but Delight. I know
Horace says, That this Liberty deserv'd a Curb ,
but that was, because it deviated from Truth, and
like other of the best Institutions, was perverted
by Passion or Int'rest to serve a turn. *Satire* a-
mong the *Romans* took this course where the Poets durst : and *Catullus*, that was no Satirist, told
Cæsar of his Vices, and that publickly in Verse ;

yet

yet *Cæsar* had that Temperance to Careſs him, tho' he had committed his Infamy to as long a Life, as he cou'd do his Noble Acts. But if the Fops, Fools, and Scriblers of our Age, are over-run with Vices more troubleſom to the Public, than *Cæsar's* venereal Sallies, without his Mode-ration, and Modeſty, Muſt they go unmark'd? Muſt the Town be always peſter'd with their in-ſufferable Impertinences, becauſe, tho' they have been ridicul'd in general Characters a Thouſand times, will yet by no means believe themſelves touch'd? There is no Remedy for theſe Public Grievances, but particular Reflections, and tho', as you ſay, No Man is free from Follies that may be expos'd, yet they will be much diminiſh'd in them that have any ſence, by this means, or at leaſt be made leſs viſible; and then 'tis not much more pains to be Wiſe, than to play the fool with Secreſie, and one might as weil ſhake hands with Vice for good and all, as to be at the fatigue to Sin with diſcretion.

You wonder, you ſay, That *Ariſtophanes* had not his Throat cut for the Perſonal Abuſes he gave his Countrymen: But I muſt tell you, That Vice and Folly then, tho' common enough, had not that lewd tye upon Mankind, as they have now. A *Fop* or *Knave*, that was then expos'd, had all the Audience againſt him, and to redeem his reputation, aſham'd of his Folly or Vice re-form'd. Men came then from a Play full of as many good Reſolutions, as a very Penitent Sin-ner from a ſenſible Pulpit Harangue of Death,

and

and Judgment, but now they come away no more affected, than a hardned Usurer from a Sermon of the Revelations. The World's extreamly alter'd since *Aristophanes* his days. we can't endure to be thought guilty of what we fondle and caress; Nay, now to touch upon a Vice that's grown a Public Grievance, this Fop; or that Whore, that's hit, shall engage a whole Party against you. To expose a Man by a particular, that's incorrigible by all general Characters, reforms him not; but makes him preposterously fonder of Vindicating his Error, than of mending it; and he had rather continue the Publick *Jest*, with the additional Scandal of having committed new Follies in Defence of the Old, than come into the common rank of Mankind, and cease to be singular, and troublesome. Men heretofore did with their Follies, and Vices, as some of our Modern Sparks do with their Mistresses, fondle them till they come to be known, but then turn 'em off, to avoid the Scandal of a keeping Cully: But now Men are Wedded to 'em, they take 'em with *Damn'd* for *better for worse, till Death doth them part*; and think themselves, as much bound to fight a Man for exposing them, as for attacquing the Honor of their House, tho' in reality they are no more oblig'd to do so, than a Man is to Vindicate the Honor of a Wife not only he himself, but the whole Town know to be a Whore, and have contributed to the making her so.

After

After all this, you'll ask me, perhaps, if I have not my fhare of Follies and Vices, that I am for falling fo foul upon thofe of my Neighbours? Why, 'faith to deal fincerely with you, I have abundantly more than my fhare, which makes me the feverer in my Obfervation of other Mens to keep my felf in Countenance. But this advantage I have made of it, I have leffen'd the incredible number, my Mind was over-run with, and fhall endeavour to perfue the courfe till I've brought 'em, within a more confcionable compafs, for I never hope to clear my felf entirely.

I am, Sir,

Your Friend and Servant

Char. Gildon.

An Apology for Poetry, in an Effay directed to Walter Moil Efq;

IN an Age when e'ery ignorant *Scribler* fets up for a Man of Authority; and as many as can but tell their Syllables on their Fingers, without Genius, without Learning, or any Excufe for Writing, arrogate the Glorious Name of *Poets*, and, by their Scandalous Pretenfions to it, bring the *Pride of Conquerors, and the Envy of Philofophers*, into an unjuft and fhameful Neglect; 'Tis the Duty of an humble and zealous Admirer of

B 4   thofe

those God-like *Few*, whom Art, Nature, and Heav'n have evidently exalted to that Supream Dignity, to make an Apology for them, who ought not to sink under the Crimes of this contemptible Race of wretched Poetasters, who ought to be avoided by all that have the least Regard to their own Repose. For this infamous Generation, these Bullies of *Parnassus*, forsaking the humble, and quiet *Call* of their own Fortune, with a Sacrilegious Ambition, to make a Noise in the World, endervour a Rape on the Sacred *Nine*: and having as little *Modesty* as *Poetry*, continually boast the Favours and Enjoyment of *Calliope* at least, tho' like *Ixion* they caress nothing but a Cloud, the Harmonious Goddess vanishing from their Prophane Embrace. These are Sparks, who, by perpetually repeating them, talk themselves into so good an Opinion of their own Performances, that they can never be brought to think ill enough of themselves to be discourag'd from their Poetical Vanity, in which they are confirm'd by the ignorant Applause of some, and the Unaccountable Diversion of others, who have a Vanity in pleasing themselves with caressing and indulging their Folly; tho' this is something pardonable, since the Admonition given by an old Poet to one of these Gentlemen's Inclinations wou'd be almost fruitless,

Quod mihi Celsus *agit monitus multumq; monendus Privatas ut quærant opes, & tangere vitet Scripta* Palatinus *quæcunq; recepit* Apollo.

They

They are not to be reclaim'd, nay, the Fate of *Thamyras* wou'd scarce effect it, the Breaking their Lute wou'd not hinder their Writing, nor the loss of their Eyes their Repeating, tho' perhaps Blindness might be some Advantage to their Acquaintance, by giving them a possibility of avoiding them; for a Seeing Poetaster has an Hawk's Eye at one he intends to recite too, he spies him at a distance, and swoops upon him before he can make his Escape.

These are the Banes of Society, and have brought an Odium on that admirable Science they pretend to, with some People; who, tho' they have Wit, want Judgment to distinguish betwixt *Pretence* and *Reality*. Others, who ought to have regard to the Protection of the *Muses*, and are sensible of the difference of Merit, and Impudence, are yet too fond of more ungenerous Pleasures, to Sacrifice them to the Care of the Poets. There are a Sort of Men, that love Pleasure, but are Sordid in their Choice of it; beyond measure preferring those of the Body to those of the Mind. They value not what Expence they are at in keeping a Whore for the use of half the Town, yet are sordidly Penurious in their Gratifications of a Poet; a look, a sigh, a senseless word of the first, can melt 'em into Profuseness, and Poverty, when the Noblest Thoughts, dress'd in the most Charming Numbers and Language, shall not move them to consider the Necessity of the Author of them. Nay, tho' they value themselves as Men of Sense as well as Fortune, their

Dogs,

Dogs, and their Bottle are more their Care, than the Darlings of Heav'n the Poets.

Mæcenas, and *Augustus*, were the only Keeping Patrons; the Poets were their Mistresses, and never were they so happy, or wanton'd so much in Pleasure, as in heir Intimacy with *Virgil*, *Horace*, *Gallus*, &c. Their Company was their Regale, tho' *Virgil* (if we measure the Excellence of it by our Tests, Facetiousness and Buffoonry) was none of the best. I'm extreamly pleas'd with *Augustus*; and cou'd almost Sacrifice to his Memory when I read this charming Expostulation to *Horace* —— *Iratum me tibi scito quod non in plerisq; Ejusmodi scriptis mecum potissimum loquaris. An vereris ne apud Posteros tibi infame sit, quod videaris familiaris nobis esse* You see he was ambitious that Posterity by often reading his Name in *Horace's* Writings, shou'd know how he valu'd him. Had our Poets this Encouragement, they wou'd surpass the *Romans* and *Greeks* too, and *England* wou'd have her greater *Horace* and *Virgil*; for as *Martial* says,

Sint Mæcenates non deerunt Flacce Marones.

And

Carmina proveniunt animo deducta Sereno.

But where there must be a care of Subsistence, the Mind can never have that Sereneness it ought for so Noble and Sacred an Office. What therefore

fore might we not expect, shou'd a *Richelieu* or
Mæcenas arise, from such who under all these dis-
advantages have performed so well? I hope this
Apology may remove some prejudices that may
oppose that Happiness, and provoke some better
Pen to do Poetry more Justice than my Time or
Ability wou'd permit.

If we regard the Antiquity of its *Origine*, the Nobleness of its Subject, or the Beauty of its Aim,
or Design (which three Things are the Test of
the Excellence of Arts and Sciences, in reference
to each other) we shall easily find *Poesie* most
ancient in its Rise, most honorable in the Subjects
and Matters it adorns, and most transcendently
excellent in its Usefulness and End.

First, To say nothing of other Authors, *Polydore,
Virgil* proves from the Second Book of *Eusebius's
Evangel. Prep.* that it is of a very early Date;
and from hence 'tis also evident, That it flourish'd
among the most ancient of the *Hebrews*, who were
by several Ages of greater Antiquity, than the
Grecian Poets. For *Moses*, their Leader, having
pass'd the Red Sea, inspir'd by a Divine Fury,
sung Praise and Thanks to his Omnipotent De-
liverer in Hexameter Verse, according to *Josephus* in the Second Book of his *Antiquity of the
Jews.* Thus the Royal *David* too, compos'd
Hymns to God, in various Numbers, as *Josephus*
in the Seventh Book of the *Antiquities of the Jews,*
in these words confirms. David *therefore (says he)
after he was deliver'd from War and Danger, in the
Enjoyment of full Tranquility, and Peace, compos'd
Songs.*

Songs and Hymns to God in various and different Numbers, as Trimeters, Quinquimeters : with whom St. *Jerome* in his Preface to the Chronicles of *Eusebius* agrees, where he writes in this manner. *Laſtly,* (ſays he) *What is more ſonorous than the Book of Pſalms? Which like the Works of our Ho*race, *or the* Greek Pindar, *now runs on Iambick Feet, now ſounds with Alcaic's, now ſwells with the Saphic Numbers,* &c.

But to come to the Gentils, we find Poetry ſo very Ancient that they know not its Riſe, but attribute it to their God *Apollo,* and the *Muſes;* as *Apollo,* in *Ovid,* himſelf aſſures us.

Juppiter eſt genitor : per me quod eritq; fuitq;
Eſtq; patet, per me concordant Carmina nervis.

Apollo reciev'd the Harp from *Mercury,* and then was made Preſident of the Muſes. By which attributing the Original of Poetry to the Gods, 'tis evident that the Gentiles themſelves look'd upon it as a Sacred and venerable Thing, above Humane Invention. From this Spring it deſcended, as it were by Succeſſion to *Linus,* (the Son of *Apollo* and *Urania.*) And *Orpheus,* (the Son of *Apollo* and *Calliope*) and *Thamyras;* Theſe two laſt with *Hercules,* were the Scholars to *Linus.* We need not inſtance *Arion, Amphion,* and *Muſæus,* who are Poets of a very ancient Date. Their uncommon Praiſes, are celebrated in ſo extraordinary a manner, that there can nothing be added to their Eternal Glory, their Encomiums, indeed,

indeed, tranſcending all Belief and Underſtanding: ſo much did ſucceeding Ages think was due to the firſt Fathers of Poëtry, as to make their Performances more, than Mortal.

The Divine *Orpheus*, the Wonder of *Better Nature*, with the Muſic of his Lyre and Song, drew Trees, Stones, and Beaſts to be his liſt'ning Audience, which is not ſo impoſſible, ſince *Campanella* proves that all things have Senſe. But the charming of Rocks, Stones and Trees, the taming Wild Beaſts, and the ſtopping the courſe of rapid Torrents, were the leaſt of his Performances. Hell loſt its Terror, and put on a more agreeable Face, the tortur'd Ghoſts forgot their paſt ſuff'rings in the Heav'n of their preſent Eaſe, and the very *Furies*, grew Mild and Calm at the ſound of his Melodious Verſe, and Lyre; all which is admirably deſcrib'd by *Ovid*, in his *Metamorphoſis*. Theſe Powers did Antiquity give to *Orpheus*, of the Sweetneſs of whoſe Poeſie, 'twou'd be ſuperfluous to produce the Teſtimony of the moſt ancient Authors. *Arion* and *Amphion* want not their Miracles, of the Dolphin and the Walls of *Thebes*. Of the latter, *Horace*, Art. Poetic.

Dictus & Amphion Thebanæ condior Arcis
Saxa movere ſono Teſtudinis, & prece blandâ
Ducere quo vellet. ———

Tho' there be nothing more vulgar, and common, than theſe Fables of the Ancient Poets, and Muſicians; yet do they evidently demonſtrate, that

that even from those Primitive Times, down to our Iron Age, these extraordinary Praises and Encomiums were only bestow'd on this divine Power of Poetry ; that Poets alone seem'd worthy by this most Sacred Art to have the next place to the Gods themselves. So that this Universal Applause (if there were no other Motive) ought to recommend it to our Admiration and Esteem.

But 'tis agreed by the universal, and unanimous consent of almost all Nations, and Authors, that *Poetry* not only contains all other Arts and Sciences, but has this Prerogative peculiar to it self, That no Rules, no Masters with the best Instructions, can teach it ; unless those who apply themselves to this divine Science, are destin'd to the Sacred Function, by *Nature*, and a *Genius*. Whence arose that Maxim, allow'd of by all Men of Sense, *Poeta Nascitur non Fit, That a Poet is Born not Made*. And from hence it follows in my Opinion, That a Poet derives the honor of that Name from his *Nature* and *Genius*, not from his *Art ;* *This* e'ery Scholar has, *That* none but the Darlings of Heav'n and Nature. This may be acquir'd by a Studious Pedant, That must be born, and grow up with the *auspicious Babe*, for *Poeta nascitur non fit.*

I'm much mistaken if *Polidore Virgil*, do not comment on this Axiom in his first Book *De Rer: Inventor. Cap.* 8. where he says, *'Tis certain that Poetry for many Reasons excels the other Arts and Sciences, either because no other Art is to be acquir'd but by a long Application to it , or because, as* Strabo

in the beginning of his Geography, against Eratosthe-
*nes, eloquently demonstrates, it contains all others;
because of all the Arts that Humane Wit has produc'd
Poetry alone, is taught by a Divine Inspiration,* &c.

Cicero in his Oration for *Archias* the Poet, has
left us the Praise of Poets (of which Name himself had been extreamly Ambitious) in these
words, *Atqui sic* (says he) *à summis hominibus,
eruditissimisq; accepimus, cæterarum rerum studia, &
Doctrinâ, & Præceptis, & Arte constare; Poetam Naturâ
ipsâ valere, & mentis viribus excitari, & quasi di-
vino quodam spiritu afflari; quare suo Jure* noster
Ennius *Sanctos appellat Poetas, quod quasi deorum
aliquo dono, & Munere commendati nobis esse vi-
deantur.*

You see, Sir, that *Cicero* confesses that divine
Fire in Poets which himself desir'd in vain, and
that Poets seem to be recommended by the
Gift, and Benefit of the Gods, to our reception.
If he that felt not this Sacred Fury was sensible
of this, we may credit *Ovid,* who by his own
Experience says, *De Fastis,* lib. 6.

*Facta Canam, sed erunt, qui me finxisse loquentur.
    Nullaq; Mortali numina visa putent.
Est Deus in Nobis, agitante Calescimus illo,
    Impetus hic sacræ semina mentis habet.*

And *Socrates* in *Plato* affirms this Poetical Fury
to be divinely inspir'd. *Plato* in his Second Book
of the Common-wealth, calls Poets the *Sons* of
the Gods, and in *Lysis* termis them, the Parents
                                                    and

and Guides of Wisdom ; and elsewhere he calls *Homer* the Father of all Wisdom and Philosophy, in these Words : Ὅμηρ‌Θ‌ πρῶτος διδάσκαλος, κ̀ ἡγεμὼν ἁπάντων τῶς κͅαλῶν τρωγικῶν, *Homer was the Guide and Master of the Tragical Beauties and Virtues.* And *Petronius Arbiter* tells us, that the Mind can neither conceive, or bring forth its Poetical Births, unless it be impregnated with great and boundless stores of Learning ; and for this reason he says in his *Satyricon*, that *Eumolpus* spoke oft'ner divinely, that is, Poetically, than like a Man.

Those who endeavour to draw the Original of Poetry from Singing, are not in my Opinion much mistaken. For when the Ancients endeavour'd to declare the Affections or Passions of the Mind in Song by the Sound, and peculiar Variation of the Voice, as it were in a more Polite and Elaborate Speech ; this rude and unpollish'd Sound by degrees refin'd into an Art. Which, when it became (where-ever it was) so improv'd, that with it the Praises of the Gods or Heroes, was celebrated into certain Verses or Rhimes, gave Birth to *Poetry*; which indeed seems truly, & really to be deriv'd from Singing, since with the Learned ev'n now, a Poet is not said, to *Speak*, but *Sing.* The antient *Germans*, a Warlike People, had no other History of the Acts of the Kings and Leaders, but certain Songs or Verses, by which they either extoll'd their Warlike Exploits or rous'd the Minds of the Soldiers to fight, as we find

find in *Polyænus*, *Solon*, annimated the *Athenians*, to Battle. And the *Lacedæmonians* Sacrific'd to the *Muses* before they began a Fight; that we read that the noble Heroe, *Matthias*, King of *Hungary*, us'd to be so touch'd with the Acts of the antient Heroes, as he sung 'em to his Lute, that the force with which it affected his Mind, was apparent in his Body; imitating *Achilles*, who sung the Praises of great Commanders to his Harp.

Another Proof of the Antiquity of *Poesie*, are the *Sibyls*, the Oracles of the *Pythian Apollo*, many of which are in *Herodotus*; Inscriptions, Monuments of Victories, Pillars, and Obelisc's, all which afford cause to believe Verse to have a very early Original. With these the Writings of the greatest and most antient Authors strow their Works by their Authorities and Sentences, to render them the more palatable and efficacious. Nay, St. *Paul* is said to have convinc'd the *Athenians* of the madness of their Idolatry, by part only of a Verse of the Poet *Aratus*; and to have us'd that Verse of *Menander* to the Christian *Corinthians*.

Evil Discourses corrupt good Manners

Thus much for the Divine, and very antient Origin of *Poesie*, and now we are come to the Subject of it, according to our former Division.

Tho' other Arts and Sciences afford abundant matter, and a large Field for our Thoughts and Consideration, yet none can stand in com-

petition

petition with *Poesie* ; for what is there in all the
wond'rous Variety, and vast extent of Nature
that falls not under the consideration of a Poet?
All the Wonders, Mercies, and Favours of the
highest God, can in nothing be more gloriously
exprefs'd than in Verse : Who can describe the
Beauty of his Providence, the Bounty of his
Gifts, the Sacredness of his Mysteries, with such
Charms, such Force, such Excellence, as the
Poet in his Melodious Numbers, Majestic Language, and Divine Thoughts. Hence it was that
the Royal Psalmist *David*, chose to appeafe the
Anger of an offended God, with the foothing
Sacrifice of this Penitential Verfes. To this we
add the Hymns of the antient *Hebrews*, of the old
Church, and of the Poetical and holy Fathers
of the New ; who to make their Ejaculations
and Jubilees of Seraphic Love, reach late Posterity,
put them into Verfe, as the moft agreeable, and Kin-
dred Repofitory of things fo Sacred. Hence alfo
(if with thefe Books we may mingle the
Prophane) flow'd all thofe Hymns, Odes, Secu-
lar Poems, and *Io Pæans* to *Jove, Mercury, Apollo*,
and the reft of the Imaginary Gods of *Heathens*.
So Sacred has *Poetry* been efteem'd in all Ages,
fo *Charming*, and fo *Comprehenfive*, that they always judg'd what-ever was defign'd for the
Praifes of Gods, Kings and Heroes, or for the
common and univerfal Ufe, Profit and Pleafure
of all Men, ought to be delivered in numbers, in
Verfe , as deftin'd to all that was Sublime and
Great. To this we owe the Geneology, and
noble

noble Deeds of the Kings and Commanders in *Homer*, the common Father of all Poets, and in *Virgil* his Competitor of Glory; these being wrote in noble Verse, fill our Minds with fresh and wonderful pleasure, e'ry time we peruse them.

To proceed to the several Institutes of our Life, particularly the spurs to Virtues, and flight from Vice, the purgation of the manners, &c. The Funeral Griefs, and Lamentations on the Dead, and finally all those particulars that the Accidents of humane Life produce, desirable or pleasant, all which are, and have been the subjects of Poems: Whence the antient Greek Authors reduc'd all things divine and humane, to five Heads.

The first they termed ποεανικὸν, under which they seem compendiously to have plac'd all that was referr'd to the *Praises* of the *Gods*, the Rights of *Religion*, and the Victories of the *Heroes*, and the Celebration of noble Acts. The second ἐγκωμιαστικὸν, in which the Virtues of great and extraordinary Men, were prais'd, as *Elogium* and *Panegyrics*. The third σωφρονιτικὸν, the use of which was to express the Virtues that tended to the purging and probity of the Manners. The forth θρηνητικὸν, which performed the Funeral Sorrows and Lamentations. The fifth they call'd ὀρχηματικὸν, under which was contain'd all that could be conducive to the Delight and Pleasures of Mankind.

Poetry

Poetry having been always generously imploy'd none can call in question the Nobility and Excellence of its Subject and Matter. Tho' some perhaps may object, that Phylosophy, Law, and History, *&c.* treat of other things of a higher Nature, whilst they discover things from their Causes, or by Arguments, prove to others those that are already discover'd : But they are but very raw Novices in the Academy of *Poetry*, who are ignorant that the Elements or first Foundation of most, if not all Arts, as well as their progress, are deriv'd from Poetry, and the best Authors of all times have granted the Poets the first Philosophers.

For from this Treasure, or Ocean of Arts and Sciences, are all the Rivulets of Learning sprung, and have lifted up their Heads ; nay, they have abundantly drawn whatever they contain of Pleasure or Artifice, from *Poetry*, as from the vast and Mother Receptacle of all the Mellifluous Waters of Eloquence. To this we may add, what *Strabo* says, *viz. Poeticem Antiqui vocant Primariam quandam Philosophiam, quæ nos a pueris ad vitam instituat, & cum Voluptate doceat, cujusmodi Mores & affectus, & Actiones nostras esse conveniat. Quin nostri homines Poetam vel solum sapientem esse perbribuerunt ; ob eamq; rem civitates Greciæ pueros primum omnium Poeticis erudiunt : non utiq; meræ oblectationis gratiâ, sed ut prudentiæ modestiæq; præceptis imbuantur,* i. e. The Antients term'd Poesie *a more excellent kind of Philosophy, which shou'd from our Childhood inform our Lives, and teach us with*
Pleasure,

Pleasure, *what our Manners, our Passions, and our Actions ought to be. Nay, our Countrymen wou'd scarce admit any into the Number of Wise Men, but Poets ; and for this Reason, the Cities of* Greece *ground Boys first of all in Poetry : not meerly for their Delight, but that they may be instructed in the Precepts of* Modesty, *and Prudence, or Wisdom.*

And justly too did the Ancients tearm *Poetry*, a more excellent Philosophy; for if the Excellence of a thing depend on its more or less aptness to obtain the End 'tis design'd for, this Prerogative is justly given to Poetry : The End of Philosophy is to form in the Mind Idea's, and habits of Virtue, and they are fixt there better by Pleasure than Pain, because the Mind is naturally averse to Pain, and propense to Pleasure. But the stiff and difficult Method of those who are *Simply* Philosophers, perplexes us too much with Metaphysical Notions, Logical Distinctions, and a long train of Arguments, which gives the Mind a fatigue to gain the Knowledge it aims at ; whereas the Poetic Philosopher proposes fairer, more adequate, compendious and comprehensive Instruction, which the Mind is so far from labouring to Unriddle, and Understand, that it at first sight perceives it, is in Love with its Beauty, and greedily takes the charming Impressions it gives, whilst convey'd into it by Melodious Numbers, betwitching Expression, Mighty Thoughts, and Illustrious Examples. That Great Poet and Critic *Horace* declares how fit he thinks Poetry for the Instruction of Youth in the First Epistle of the Second Book. C 3 Os

Os tenerum pueri balbumq; Poëta figurat ;
Torquet ab obſcænis jam nunc ſermonibus aurem:
Mox etiam Pectus præceptis format amicis
Aſperitatis, & Invidiæ, corrector & Iræ, &c.

The other admirable Verſes that follow theſe, you
are, Sir, extreamly well acquainted with, which
ſo beautifully ſet off the ſeveral Advantages of Poetry. And *Hieronimus Vida* (one of the beſt Italian Poets that have writ in Latin as *Rapin* aſſures
us) in the Firſt Book of his Poetics is of the ſame
Mind —

Poſtquam igitur primas fundi puer hauſerit artes ;
Jam nunc incipiat riguos accedere fontes
Et Phæbum, & Dulces Muſas aſſueſcat Amare.

Add to this what *Horace* ſays in his *de Arte Poetica,*

——— *Fuit hæc Sapientia quondam*
Publica privatis ſecernere, ſacra Prophanis, &c:

and the Ten following Verſe which I have not
room here to quote. *Eraſmus,* that wanted no
Wit, calls it a Banquet compos'd of all the Deli-
cacies, and Quinteſſence of all other Arts, and
Sciences. And *Melancthon* places the Excellence
of Poetry for the penetration into Mens Minds,
next to the Sacred Scriptures, eſpecially Tragedy.

Poets being, as you ſee, the Darling Sons of
the Gods, born to great and ſublime things, and
the

the Correctors and Guides of Common Life, they have not, without Reason, been esteem'd by the greatest Monarchs, and Potentates of the World, and made Instructors and Tutors to Kings, and Princes: I speak of true Poets, not of of the little Mushromes of *Parnassus*, the Street-repeating Poetasters. Thus *Linus* was the Tutor to *Hercules*, the tamer of Monsters, and Tyrants: And *Alexander* the Great, with veneration, respected *Homer*, as the Guide, and Director of his Life, reading his Works daily, in the heat and hurry of the Conquest of the World, and slept with them under his Pillow: *Ennius* instructed that great General *Scipio Africanus* in Poetry, which he judg'd so advantageous to him, that he took him with him in his most weighty Expeditions, and chose to be Bury'd in the same Tomb with the Poet. Nothing has to me given a greater instance of *Cæsar's* value for Poets, than the Welcome he gave *Catullus* to his Table, the same day he had fix'd such a Brand of Infamy upon him as remains in *Catullus* his Works to this day. *Augustus*, both the Patron, and Judge of the Muses, Caress'd that Noble Pair of Poets, *Horace* and *Virgil*, as his most intimate and bosom Friends, honor'd them as his Masters, and shower'd his Beneficent Favours on them, who, without doubt in return, introduc'd him to the Sacred *Penetralia* of the *Muses*, the divine Retreats of *Apollo*: which made this Emperor keep the Birth-day of *Virgil* e'ery Year, as if 'twere the auspicious Feast of his own Success. The Emperor *Julian* made the

Greek

Creek Lyric Poet *Bacchylides* his Master, or Director; and *Gratian* after he had made a great progress in the most generous of Learning, he honour'd and advanc'd his Master *Ausonius* ev'n to
the Consulship. And *Arcadius* and *Honorius* erected a Monument to the Memory of *Claudian*, in
the *forum* of *Trajan*.

But nothing, in my opinion, challenges the
Esteem of the World more for this Art, than that
it Corrects thus the Barbarity, and Sordidness
that so generally rules Mankind, and destroys,
that Happiness we falsly aim at by other means,

Emollit Mores (as *Ovid* has it) *nec finit esse feras.*

A Man may be a *Divine*, and yet be Covetous,
and Deceitful, two Banes of Piety, Religion, and
Morality; but a Poet cannot be guilty either of
Avarice or Deceit, I mean a True Poet, a *Virgil*,
a *Horace*, A *Dryden*, a *Waller*. And,

——— *Si carmina condes*
Nunquam te fallant animi sub vulpe latentes.

Hor. Art. Poet.

And,

——— *Vatis avarus,* (num:
Non temere est animus: Versus amat hoc studet u-
Detrimenta, fugas servorum, Incendia ridet:
Non fraudem Socio, Puerove incogitat ullam
Pupillo: Vivit siliquis, & pane secundo
Militiæ quanquam piger & Malus, utilis Urbi.

There

There is no need of profecuting the point of Efteem the Poets have been in, in the better Ages of the World, I will not therefore infiſt on the Seven Cities of *Greece*, that ſtrove for the Glory of Giving Birth to *Homer*, nor on *Alexander*, who, when he took, ſack'd, and burnt *Thebes*, ſpar'd the Houſe of *Pindar*, and fixt this Verſe over the Door.

Πινδάρου τῶ μουσοποιῶ ἢ ςέγαν μὴ κάιετε,
Burn not Pindar's *Houſe,*

the ſame reſpect was ſhew'd his Houſe by the *Lacedemonians* when they deſtroy'd *Thebes*. I'll ſay nothing of the honour paid to the Memory of *Schefitorus*, in the Octogonal Monument at the Gates of *Catana* in *Sicily*. 'Twou'd be ſuperfluous to take notice of the Value *Polycrates* had for *Anacreon*, *Archelaus* for *Euripides*, the King of *Ægypt* and *Macedon* for *Menander*; *Ptolomæus Philadelphus* for *Callimachus*; and what I have ſaid before of the *Latins* may ſuffice. But 'tis no wonder that the Politer Nations ſhou'd have this Efteem for the Divineſt of Arts, ſince the very *Danes*, look'd upon of Old as more Barbarous, have yet diſcover'd all a-long ſuch a veneration for Poets, and *Poeſie*, that on the Death of one of their Kings, they exalted a Poet to the Throne, as the moſt worthy to ſucceed the Prince, he cou'd Praiſe ſo well; as *Saxo Grammaticus*, and *Joan. Bocerus* teſtifie.

Without

Without doubt by this time 'tis sufficiently evident, That if any Art merits Esteem, either for the Antiquity of its Origine, or the Nobility of its Subject, Poetry must be granted the Prerogative of Precedence in Honor. Wherefore I shall say no more for a Proof of these two points of its Original and Subject, but now turn our Consideration to the third Branch of my Division, *viz.* The End and Profit, or advantage of *Poetry*.

The Philosophers lay down two principal kinds of Studies, which are indeed different, but not opposite; that is, the *Contemplativ* and the *Practical,* and they give the preference to the former, because Contemplation is pleasant for and in its self, and therefore more Noble ; but the Practical *quatenus* practical is so only in regard of something else, and therefore less Noble than Contemplation. But 'tis sufficiently evident, that the Study of Poetry is for the most part Contemplative : Since no Poet is capable of forming any Noble Poëm, with elaborateness and perfection, unless he first *dispose* his Speculations, and before consider, and weigh the Materials, and the peculiar Artifice that must be us'd in setting them off to their best advantage, and in the true Light, and Colours. And one thing is here to be observ'd, That a Poet through his whole performance, both whil'st he contrives, invents, and puts his Thoughts in Metre, is still at the same time contemplating, so that he's compos'd of Speculation and Action, whereas other Studies either only contemplate, or only precisely put in Execution the destin'd A-
ctions.

&ctions. First therefore, in that way *Poetry* is *Useful* in its self, and therefore admitting the former Axiom of the Philosophers, to be valu'd and persu'd, because Speculative. And Secondly, 'Tis Useful in regard of something else, because the Poetical Writings chiefly contain, the most beautiful, and inviting Doctrines, and Instructions, the best of Precepts for the happy and laudable directing of our Lives ; Noble Sayings, and Deeds, Virtues, Rights and Manners of Nations. From all which, that may be chosen for the common benefit of Mankind, that is most justly imitable, and worthy in Virtue, that avoided, that is most abominable and detested in Vice.

Contemplation and *Thinking* is peculiarly the Poet's Business, on this Depends all the Beauties of Thought, and Expression. By using much to *Think*, they come to a justness and trueness of *Thought*, they run not away by halves, with imperfect Appearances that please the Imagination ; they are not taken with all that glisters, but by much *Thinking* dive into the Nature of Things, and fix the Judgment to decide the Truth, or falsity of what is Charming, and Beautiful, and what seems so, at a sudden view. Hence proceed Justness, Proportion, and Harmony, without all which a Poet loses half his Glory, and Reputation with good Judges. From hence 'tis evident, That the End of Poetry is Noble, since it reaches the greatest Pleasure and the surest Profit, of our Minds, and of our Life. Since 'tis directed to the Praise, of the Omnipotent, the

Cele-

Celebration of Virtues, the Rewards and Glory of Noble Acts, the Punishment and Infamy of Evil : Since to it we owe all the increases of our Knowledge ; and finally, since it effects all these nobler Ends it aims at.

But methinks, Sir, I hear you say, What needs all this to prove the Excellence of a Science, that carries a Natural Worth with it, and that so clearly, that like an innate Principle 'tis confess'd by all self-evident ? for there is none, however dull, but does, or has attempted Poetry, with more or less success, whil'st other Arts, and Sciences are not so universally caress'd. All pretend not to Philosophy, Mathematics, Law, Physic, or desire to be thought Proficients in those Arts ; but ev'ry one wou'd be thought a Poet, as if without being so, he cou'd not be thought a Man, so essential to Mankind does the universal and unanimous Ambition and Aim at it of ev'ry Man make it. I grant you, Sir, this is a sufficient Argument to any sensible Man, that considers it. But how few reflect on this, when they run down what they cou'd not obtain on their Endeavour : the greatest Railer against this divine Art, wou'd be proud to Father an excellent Poem. And it must be granted by them, That the greatest Philosophers, Historians, Orators, Physicians, Divines, Princes, Kings and Emperors of all Ages have discover'd this Desire we mention, and have made it evident, That they either were, or fain wou'd be Poets.

To pass over the Hebrews we have already mention'd

tion'd among the *Roman* Emperors, how few but
have difcover'd this Ambition ? *Julius Cæfar, Auguftus, Nero, Adrian, Gratian, Theodofius, Honorius,* &c.
Thofe of *Julius Cæfar.*

> *Feltria perpetuo niviam damnata rigore*
> *Forte mihi pofthac non adeanda vale.*

Auguftus often exercis'd this Faculty, particularly
on *Virgil's* defire that his *Æneids* might be burnt ;
which begin thus :

> *Ergone fupremis potuit vox improba verba*
> *Tam dirum mandare Nefas ? Ergo ibit in ignes*
> *Magnaq; doctiloqui morietur Mufa Maronis ?* &c.

Seneca gives us this Verfe of *Nero's* compofing with
this Commendatory Introduction, 1. *De Naturæ
Quæft. Cap. 5. Quid ergo fit ? Colorem non Imaginem ducunt ; alioquin ut ait* Nero Cæfar *difer-
tiffime.*

> *Colla Cytheriacæ Splendent agitata Columbæ.*

More of his we might borrow from *Perfius,* if we
believe his Interpreters. *Adrian* returns the Poet
Florus his Complement fent him in thefe Verfes,

> *Ego nolo Florus Effe*
> *Ambulare per Tabernas*
> *Latitare per popinas*
> *Culices pati rotundas.*

Nay,

Nay, he was so very Poetical, that when he was a dying, he Versify'd on his Soul,

> *Anima vagula blandula*
> *Hospes comesq; corporis*
> *Quæ nunc abibis in loca*
> *Pallidula, rigida, nudula,*
> *Nec ut soles, dabis jocos ?*

Those that are attributed to *Gallienus*, have more of a Poet, which he repeated at the Wedding of his Nephews, as *Trebellius Pollio* has it; holding them by the Hands;

> *Ite ait, ô pueri, pariter sudate Medullis*
> *Omnibus inter vos; non murmura vestra columbæ*
> *Brachia non hederæ, non vincant Oscula conchæ.*

And to say truth, 'tis pitty *Gallienus* ever spoil'd an Emperor since he wou'd have made an excellent Poet; for as *Trebellius* confessest, *fuit enim* Gallienus, *quod negari non potest, oratione, Poemate, atq; Omnibus artibus Clarus.* For Gallienus *was,* says he, *eminent in Oratory, Poetry, and all other Arts.* And indeed his horrid Remissions proceeded from his being content with whatever fortune wou'd let him have; he wanted Ambition, and was, as *Horace* describes a Poet, *Militiæ piger & malus. Julian's* Epigrams are to be found in the Anthology; and *Ausonius* informs us, that *Theodosius* was no small pretender to Poetry in these Verses.

Bel-

Bellandi fandiq; potens Augustus, honorem
Bis meret, ut geminet titulas : qui prælia Musis
Temperat, & Geticum Moderatur Apolline Martem.
Arma inter Cimbrosq; truces, furtoq; nocentes
Sauromatas, quantum cessat de tempore belli
Indulget latiis tantùm inter castra Camænis, &c.

In short, tho' the Spirit of Poetry decay'd a-
mong the *Romans,* with their Empire, yet was
there scarce one that did not make some preten-
ces to the Muses. Nay, look among the Clergy
of former Ages, and you shall find *Popes, Bishops,*
Cardinals, &c. stand candidates for the Bays, as
well as *Socrates, Plato, Democritus, Lycurgus, Solon,*
Aristotle, among the *Philosophers* and *Legislators ;*
among the undignified Divines, *Melanchton, Beza,*
Jacomatus, Artomedes, &c. the Civilians, *Ulpian,*
Modestinus, Alciatus, Budæus, Turnebus, and a
great many others, too numerous to be here in-
serted among the Physitians, *Ansonius, Fracaste-*
rius, Cordus, Lotichius Secundus, Sinetius, Posthius,
Sambucus, &c. Nay, ev'n among the Critics, a
morose Generation, the *Scaliger's* Father and Son,
the *Dousa's* Father and Son, *Cameranus, Mycillus,*
Stigelius, &c. among the Historians, *Buchanan,*
Natales Comes, Lil. Gyraldus, Racipius, Meibonius,
Baudius, &c. Among the Rhetoritians, *Pontanus,*
Angel. Politianus, &c.

Thus much for Exotics ; but (Sir) should I
pretend to number the Poets, and Pretenders to
Poetry in our own Nation, as 'twou'd be super-
fluous, so 'twou'd be endless. Search all Ranks
and

and Degrees of Men, from the *Beau* Lord, to
the homely Swain, a keeping his Sheep, or dri-
ving his Hoggs ; and as *Cupid*, so has *Apollo* been
at work with 'em ; the *Silvia*'s and *Maria*'s, the
Jones and *Sue* have had their respective Tribute
of Rhime, and from the grave Doctor of Divinity, to the little Country Curate, with his Pro-
blematic Crambo's, and Hypothetic Propositions :
So that there can be no more doubt made of the
former Assertion of all Men's Desires and Pre-
tensions to it, than that those are a Proof of its
received Excellence.

Before I conclude this Essay, I shall obviate two
or three Objections, made by some old morose
Sparks, that have out-liv'd that little Sense their
more sprightly years afforded them, and
some Precisians, that build Piety and Godliness in
Spiritual Railings, and a mortify'd Phiz, which
are but *Feints*, or Blinds to Observers:
The first is, that 'tis a very useless and unprofitable
Study, no Estates to be got by it, at least in this
Age: That it contributes meerly to Pleasure,
not to our knowledge. To the first I answer,
that 'tis very true, that there is no hopes of rising
to be an Alderman by Poetry ; but then I must tell
them, 'tis not for those to apply themselves to't, that
place the Desires of their Souls on Mony ; for as
they'll never obtain that end by it, so will they
never reach any Excellence in the Art, as being
not destin'd by nature to it ; for to a Poet, Heaven gives a large and noble Soul, above the Narrow aim of Baggs and Hords of Treasure ; and
thus

hus far I shall grant it an unprofitable Study, as
Petronius Arbiter has witness'd long ago

> *Qui Pelago credit, magno se fænore tollit*
> *Qui Pugnas, & Castra petit, præcingitur Auro;*
> *Vilis Adulator picto jacet ebrius Ostro,*
> *Et qui sollicitat nuptas ad Præmia peccat,*
> *Sola Pruinosis horret Facundia Pannis,*
> *Atq; inopi linguâ desertas invocat Artes.*

No, there are the roaring Billows, The Camp,
the Court, and the City allotted by Fate for those
that thirst for Wealth ; the Muses love Tranquility, an Easie and Contented State, and teach
their Darlings, that

> *Nec vixit male qui Natus mori ensg; fefellit.*

The Riches the Poet gains is Fame : It termi-
nates not with this life like Money, and Estate,
nor can his Spendthrift Son lavish the mighty
Store he has laid up, as the Miser's Son does what
his Father got from Fools or Knaves. Nay, the
Usefulness of this Study is opposite to getting
Estates as they are generally got : It punishes Avarice, rewards Generosity, softens the Mind from
Barbarity to Compassion for the Miseries of others,
cleanses it from Deceit and Hypocrisie, elevates
it from little base Designs, to Noble and Open
Actions, and so through all the Ends and Uses of
this Divine Art.

D   As

As to the Second *that it contributes meerly to our Pleasure,* not Knowledge, that is evidently false, both from what has been said, and from a Consideration that it yields not only a Necessary, but Noble *Knowledge,* that is, of Men, of Manners, of Virtue, *&c.* Nor is there any Study or Art but has been attempted in Poetry, as a short view will make evident. To pass over *David* and the *Hebrew* Poets, whose Excellencies are lost by the general Ignorance, not only of the Language they wrote in, but the Custom, *&c.* on which many of the Beauties depend. *Orpheus, Homer, Pindar, Horace,* &c. have celebrated the Praises of the Divine Power, tho' under the Names of their Suppositititious Gods, and Goddesses. Among the Christians, we find *Prudentius, Juvencus, Arator, Vidas, Mauritius Sannazarius, Vulteius,* and an innumerable Company of Sacred Writers. Astrology, Astronomy, *&c.* has been treated of by *Livius, Aratus, Palingenius, Manillius, Buchanan,* &c. Physic's by *Hesiod, Macer, Lucretius, Empedocles,* and others. Husbandry by *Hesiod, Virgil,* &c. Pastoral Life and Sports, *Theocritus, Virgil, Calphurnius, Dantes,* &c. Hunting has been discours'd of by *Gratius Nemesianus, Natales Comes,* &c. Tragedy (which affords us a hundred admirable Lessons of Knowledge, and Improvement) we owe chiefly to *Æschylus, Sophocles,* and *Euripides.* Tho' I think our English Tragedians, have excell'd them, particularly Mr. *Dryden,* who in some of his Plays, I shall always think, has abundantly out done *Sophocles.* Then for the

A&s

Acts of Heroes, we have *Homer, Virgil, Pindar, Lucan, Statius, Cowly,* Sir *William D'Avenant,* &c. this is a sort of Poem which *Horace* thinks more Instructive than Philosophy, in his second Epistle of his first Book to *Lollius.*

Trojani belli scriptorem maxime Lolli,
Dum tu declamas Romæ, Præneste relegi (quidnon,
Quiquid sit Pulchrum, *quid* Turpe, *quid* Utile,
Plenius ac melius Chrysippo & Crantore dicit.

Nor are the Amorous Essays of *Anacreon, Sappho, Gallus, Catullus, Ovid, Horace, Tibullus, Propertius,* with abundance of the Moderns, to be thought ill of by the Precisians, as we shall by and by prove, but granted Improvers of our Knowledge in the Nature of the passions, the fatigues, and pleasures of Love, as well as the Dangers and Impertinences of Intrigue. *Oppian* wrote of Fishes, *Nicander* of Antidotes against the biting of Venemous Beasts, of Herbs, and Gardening. *Macer* and *Palladius,* of Plants. Mr. *Cowly,* of Medicine, *Serenus, Sammonicus,* and *Marcelius:* Of Weights, and Measures, Q. *Rhemnius Fannus Palæmon;* which Book by some is attributed to *Priscian. Phocylides,* and *Pythagoras,* writ in Verse of the Precepts of Virtue, and *Solon,* and *Tyrtæus,* of Politics or the Administration of the Common-Wealth: Wholsom, and Instructive Satyr, *Horace, Juvenal, Persius,* Mr. *Dryden,* Mr. *Wicherly* in his *Plain-dealer,* and other Poets have given us; nor are the little Epigrammatists to be forgot, having

their

their Ufe and Diverfion, tho', I confefs my felf no Admirer of that fort of Poetry, if it merit that Name.

From hence 'tis Evident, That we may not only learn all that can be advantageous to our Knowledge, and by confequence that the accufation is falfe, that it ferves only to Pleafure; but alfo that All things that are the Subjects of this Soveraign of Sciences.

There remains yet an Objection, fome Men make no fmall buftle about, *viz.* That Poetry is " too prophane in making ufe of fo many falfe " *Gods*, and *Goddeffes*, *Fanus*, *Satyrs*, and *Nymphs*, " and the reft of the gay Race of Fancy; and " that they fcatter the Seeds of Debauchery in " the Minds of Youth, by their Amorous Verfes, " their Luftful Songs, *&c.* for which Reafon " ev'n *Plato* Banifh'd them from his Common- " Wealth.

The firft part of this Objection, I'm confident, you'll think extreamly ridiculous, and that it merits not to be taken Notice of. But when you fhall remember that in the Third Century the Chriftians were fo Zealous, as to forbid the reading of all Heathen Authors, particularly Poets, on this Account, and confider, that we have fome ftill of the fame Mind here in *England*, that wou'd not have the Name of *Jupiter*, *Mars*, and *Venus* (no, not in *Propria quæ Maribus*) come into their Childrens Mouths, efpecially their Worfhips, their Lovers, *&c.* I hope you will allow that 'tis not wholly unneceffary to clear ev'n this Objection.

'Tis

'Tis true, thefe Fables cannot be condemn'd by any, but by thofe who are incapable to dive into the admirable ufe of 'em. They muft confider, that ev'ry Art, as well as ev'ry Language, has its peculiar Beauties and Proprieties of Elocution, to take which away (efpecially if, as Poets particularly do, we reprefent Antiquity) is to render it almoft infipid, and without its moft taking quality Pleafure, that beft conveys Inftruction. Rob Poetry of this Beauty of the Fables and the Gods (I mean the ancient Poems, fo full of admirable Inftruction by their means given us with Pleafure, and Delight) and you deftroy the Excellence of the beft of Poets, rendring their Poems Imperfect, and Lame ; and if any Chriftian Poets makes ufe of thefe Gods, there is no fear certainly of their paying them any Veneration, when they only employ them as the Vehicles of their Defigns. But enough on this Point.

The other of the Loofenefs of Amorous Verfes ; 'tis a part of the Knowledge of the World, to have a perfect view of all the Effects of Love, all its Ways, Manners, and Expreffions, and thofe who forbid the Reading of thefe, take away an admirable Guide to thofe that muft Live where not to be in Love, or have to do with thofe that are fo, is impoffible, and Scandalous ev'n in the Pretence. There are other advantages of the lewdeft Effays of this Nature, which a Man of Senfe will make of them, and none , indeed, fhou'd read thofe but fuch. And that *Plato* banifh'd Poets out of his Common-Wealth, yet cou'd he write things

of

of a more lewd Strain than the Worſt of 'em,
witneſs theſe Verſes on the Kiſſing of *Agatho*, done
from his Greek by *Decimus Laberius.*

> *Dum Semihulco ſavio*
> *Meum Puellum Savior*
> *Dulcemq; florem Spiritus*
> *Duco ex aperto Tramite :*
> *Anima tunc ægra & Saucia*
> *Cucurrit ad Labia mihi,*
> *Rictumq; in oris pervium*
> *Et labra pueri Mollia*
> *Rimata Itineri tranſitas*
> *Ut tranſdiret nititur.*
> *Tum ſi, moræ quid pluſcula*
> *Fuiſſet in Coitu Oſcula*
> *Amoris igni percita*
> *Tranſiſſet, & me linqueret.*
> *Et mira prorſum res foret,*
> *Ut ad me ſterem Mortuus*
> *Ad puerum ut intus Viverem.*

   Petronius himſelf has ſcarce gone beyond this
with his *Gyton,* &c. And his

> *Qualis nox fuit illa dii deæq;*
> *Quam Mollis torcus ! hæsimus calentes*
> *Et transfudimus hinc, & hinc labellis*
> *Errantes animas. Valete curæ !*
> *Mortalis ego ſic perire cæpi.*

Plato's

Plato's Republic was but a *Eutopia* at beſt, and aim'd at new ways of forming the Minds of Men by Laws, not ſo agreeable perhaps to Man's Nature, as more Politic Legiſlators have compos'd, who receiv'd this Noble Art, and honor'd its Profeſſors with Public Veneration; being ſenſible that it was the ſureſt, and beſt Inſtructrix of Mankind, but that it gave Immortality to thoſe that favour'd it with their Protection, and Generoſity.

> *O ſacer, & magnus vatum labor, omnia Fato,*
> *Eripis, & populis donas mortalibus ævum.*

Whoever wou'd raiſe his Mind above the Vulgar taſt, and form in his Breaſt noble Deſigns, muſt apply himſelf to a reading of the Poets; as *Petronius Arbiter* has it.

> *Artis ſeveræ ſiquis amat effectus*
> *Mentemq; Magnis applicat———*
> *——— Det primos verſibus annos*
> *Mæoniumq; bibat fælici pectore fontem.*

As there is a Natural Excellence in being a Poet, ſo is there in Eſteeming one and nothing, ſhews the Degeneracy of an Age more, in Honor, as well as ſenſe, than a Contempt of this Divine Science, and the true Maſters of it. So that I muſt infer that this Preſent Age is at a very low Ebb of Both; that, tho' bleſs'd with as great Poets as ever *Greece* or *Rome* produc'd has ſo very

little

little regard to them, as not to make Public Sacrifices of its Dross to the Use of *Two* such Extraordinary Men. There is a *Plebeian* Genius spread among us, and Generous and Noble Acts, are contemn'd and laugh'd at. But then, Sir, in so general a Defect to be Singular in Tast, challenges the more Honor; and this makes me asham'd to offer so unpolish'd and hasty a piece as this at your Feet, who are not only an excellent Judge of the most difficult Things, and ev'n in the first Bloom of your Youth, have Master'd the whole Circle of the Sciences, but also have a peculiar Esteem for this I plead for, and by your admirable Choice of those you converse with, shew you can let none of your Hours be lost, either with trifling Books in your Study, or Impertinent Coxcombs in your Conversation: I shou'd not have the Vanity to say this, were I so happy as to be often bless'd with your Company, I catch it but now and then unwilling to make *you* do Pennance for *my* Satisfaction; and this Consideration will oblige me to put an end to this Essay, only desiring your leave publickly to declare my self what I am; That is,

S I R,

Your real Friend and humble Servant.

To Mr. T. S. *in Vindication of Mr.* Milton's *Paradise lost.*

S I R,

YOU will pardon me, I am confident, tho in Opposition to your Thoughts, I positively declare my self extreamly well pleas'd with that part of Mr. *Milton's* most excellent Poem, to which you discover the least Inclination: Those *Antient,* and consequently *less Intelligible* Words, Phrases, and Similies, by which he frequently, and *purposedly* affects to express his Meaning, in my Opinion do well suit with the *Venerable Antiquity,* and *Sublime Grandeur* of his Subject. And how much soever some *Unthinking* have Condemn'd this his Choice. *You,* who have Maturely weigh'd, how much deeper an Impression *less us'd,* (so they be what you will grant his always are) *Significant words,* make on a *Readers* fancy, than such as are *more common* ; (you I say) must pay a vast deference to Mr. *Milton's* great *Judiciousness* in this particular, no less than to his *entire Manage* of every part of that *Charming Poem,* in which upon every Occasion he discovers himself a perfect, unimitable *Master of Language.* Here are you forc'd to give a profound Attention to the *Universal Creator,* speaking like *that Almighty,* who by the *Fiat* of his

his Mouth made all things, and yet so *Gracious* are All his *Expressions*, as if he valued himself more on his *Good Will to. Man*, than on his *Prerogative* over him : There, shall you read *Man*, addressing himself *Submissively* like a *Creature*, who owes his Being to a better, wiser, and higher power, and yet not so *Abjectly*, but you will easily perceive him to be *Lord* of the whole Creation. . *Elsewhere*, you may see an *Angel* discovering himself, not a Little *Man's Superior* by Creation, in *Place*. and *Power* more, but in *Knowledge* most of all. In *another place*, behold *Woman*, appearing *Inferiour* to both these, and yet more *Ambitious* than either, but then *softer*, much in her *Make* and *Manners*, than her *rougher Spouse*, whom *down right Sincerity*, and unaffected plainness, seem mostly to Delight. Nor can I now forget with what *vast complacency* we have oft together read the most *Natural, Lively*, yet (as their Sexes) different Descriptions, our first *Parents*, separately make of their own Apprehensions of themselves, at their *first finding* themselves *Living Creatures*. Nay, the very *fallen Angels* are much Honour'd above the best of their deserts, by the *Amazing Relation*, we there meet with of their *Ambition, Malice, Inveteracy*, and *Cunning*; and never was *Scene*, so livelily shown, as that of his *Pandæmonium* in the first Book. Once more, and you are no less astonisht at his *Description*, than he makes the *Angels*, to be at the Report of their Adversaries Thund'ring Fire-works. And yet, if his Matter requires a *Meaner Style*, how much soever

he

he speaks *Loftily* at one time, at another does, even to a *Miracle*, suit his *Speech* to his *Subject*. This (I well know) has been censur'd in him for *Servile creeping* ; but if 'tis well *consider'd*, upon what proper *Occasion* he thus *humbles* his Style, 'twill be *Accounted*, (as really it is) his *Great Commendation* : But in praise of Mr. *Milton's* admirable Dexterity in this his *Matchless Performance*, since All I can say must come exceeding short of his *due Merit*, that I bring not my self under the Correction of that known saying, *Præstat de Carthagine tacere quam pauca dicere.* I shall venture to add no more but this ; tho' the Composing such a *compleat Poem* on such a no less *Obscure*, than *weighty* Subject, was a *Task* to be perform'd by Mr. *Milton* only, yet 'tis not out of doubt, whether *himself* had ever been able so to Sing of *Unrevealed Heavenly Mysteries*, had he not been altogether depriv'd of his *Outward Sight*, and thereby made capable of such *continued Strenuous, Inward Speculations* : as he who has the use of his *Bodily Eyes*, cannot possibly become possest with. *This* however must be Granted, as indubitably true ; The *bountiful Powers* above, did more than make him amends for their taking away his Sight, by so *Illumining* his Mind, as to enable him *most compleatly* to sing of *Matchless Beings*, *Matchless Things*, before *unknown* to, and even *unthought* of by the whole Race of Men ; thus rewarding him for a *Temporary Loss*, with an *Eternal Fame*, of which *Envy* it self shall not be able ever

ever to deprive this *best of Poems*, or its moſt
Judicious Author.

In this Faith I Subſcribe my ſelf,

S I R,

Yours, &c.

To J. H. Eſq, *In Anſwer to the Queſtion, Who was the Greateſt* Engliſh-Man.

S I R,

I Am extreamly ſenſible under how many diſ-
advantages I undertake the Reſolution of
your demand, *who was the greateſt Engliſhman?*
And but that I have this Satisfaction left me, that
where the Meanneſs of my Thought is Inconſiſtent with the Eminency of his Virtues, and my
ill management of the whole, looks like a leſſen-
ing the Grandeur of his Actions, you will diſcover at once Goodneſs enough to pardon me, and
to entertain an agreeable Opinion of my *Heroe*;
(but for this I ſay) I had not dar'd thus to expoſe my own Weakneſs, and his Worthineſs.

S I R,

S I R,

I have pitch'd upon *Thomas Cromwell*, Earl of *Essex*, and Viceregent of *England*, for this *Man of Ten Thousand*: A Man, who by his Merit alone rais'd himself from the meanest Condition, to the highest Honour: A Man in nothing unhappy, so much as to have liv'd in the Reign of *Henry* the VIII. of whom it was truly said, " *That he never spar'd Woman in his Lust, or his best Favourite in the Wrath.* In whose chiefest Esteem our *Cromwell* did yet a long time remain: Admir'd by his Friends, dreaded by his Enemies, carest by all, and in one Word, invested with a more Extensive Power, than any Subject of *England* was ever before, or since possess'd of. He was born at *Putney*, in *Surrey*, where his Father liv'd, an honest *Blacksmith*. In all the little Passages of his Youth, he discover'd an Active Tow'ring Disposition, fond of Travelling, and covetous of Employments, much greater than his Descent, or Education could pretend to; tho' Nature, the better to qualifie him for the *Grandeur*, to which he was design'd, had endow'd him with an apprehensive Wit, a discerning Judgment, a prodigious Memory, a Florid Elocution, and a resolute Soul, not to be discomposed by the greatest Dangers.

By what helps he crost the Seas, I know not; but there I find him in the Year 1510. perfect in many Languages, and after a while associating himself to some Persons, deputed by the Town of *Boston*, to procure them two Pardons, for

which

which they had been long Solliciting in vain at *Rome*. *Cromwell* obferving that the Delays caus'd by the *Pope's* Minifters, proceeded only from their Griping Difpofition, refolv'd by a *Witty* Stratagem to effect that, which by Reafon and Importunity he could not: having one day prepar'd fome delicious Jellies after the *English* manner, as the *Pope* was returning from Hunting, he approach'd him with thefe, and a Song, wherewith the *Old Father Julius* being extreamly delighted; upon Enquiry after their Bufinefs and Country, he immediately ftamp'd their Pardons, and order'd 'em a Difpatch, having first learnt the Manners of preparing a Difh fo agreeable to his *Holiness's* Palate. And this little Contrivance is the more remarkable; for that the Court of *Rome*, which goes beyond all others in *Intriguing*, were hereby fairly Outwitted: He ferved afterwards in the Duke of *Bourbon's* Army at the Siege of *Rome*, and was in the *French* Camp at the Defeat of *Gatillon*; as yet he had no true Senfe of Religion, tho' after his Journey to *Rome*, in which he got the *New Testament* by Heart, he began to be better acquainted with the Principles of *Christianity*. Upon his Return into *England*, finding Cardinal *Wolsey* the only Man in Favour, he enter'd into his Service, and advanced himfelf therein confiderably, by acquitting himfelf faithfully of all things, wherewith he was intrufted; here he difcover'd fuch forwardnefs in the fuppreffing of feveral *Monasteries*, given by the *King* to the *Cardinal* his Mafter for building *Christ's Colledge*, *Oxon*; as

that

that thereby he procur'd himself such abundance
of ill Will from the *Superstitious*, as that after the
Cardinals Fall, he was represented to the *King*, as
the worst of Men; and the *King*, the more easily credited, reports against him, because with
much Zeal, and as much Ingenuity he pleaded
the *Cardinals* Cause in the House of Commons,
(of which he was then a Member) and this his Fidelity, to his declining Master, is the more worthy Praise, for that 'tis rare indeed to see any one
stand by a *Falling Favourite*.

When *Cromwell* felt the Dissolution of *Wolsey*'s
Family, he endeavour'd to get into the King's
Service; which Sir *Christopher Hales*, Master of
the Rolls, and my Lord *Russell* happily brought
about, tho' the *King* (as has been said) was pre-
possest exceedingly to his disadvantage: My Lord
(with a Goodness inseparable from his Family)
earnestly sollicited his Promotion, not only out
of Gratitude (*Cromwell* having sav'd his Life at
Bononia) but also because he found him most forward to promote a *Reformation* in Religion, to
which his *Lordship* stood well affected; and it was
one Great Argument, made use of to move the
King) to favour him, that he was the most fit of
all others to traverse the Intrigues of the *Popish*
Clergy. The *King*, after having admitted him to
his Presence, ask'd him some Questions, and
heard his Complaints against the most Eminent
Sticklers for the *Popes* Supremacys; and as a
mark of his special Favour, he gave him the
Ring from his Finger, and sent him to the *Con-*
vocation,

vocation; which he having the *King*'s Signet bold-
ly entred, and seating himself among the *Bishops*,
to their great Amazement and Confusion, taxes
them with such Crimes as had brought them into
such a Premunire, as that thereby (says he) you
have forfeited all your Goods, Chattels, Lands,
and whatever other Benefits you are possess'd of.
By this means he enrich'd the *King*'s Coffer with
118840 *l.* which the Clergy had rais'd by Subsidy,
that by Act of *Parliament* they might be quitted from the Premunire, into which *Cromwell* demonstrated they had run themselves.

By such ways he Ingratiated himself very much
with the *King*, who now conferr'd the Honour of
Knighthood upon him, made him *Master of the
King's Jewel House*, and soon after admitted him
into the *Privy Councel*; 1524 he was made *Master
of the Rolls*, and in the year 1527 he was install'd
Knight of the most Noble Order of the *Garter*,
and afterwards Created *Earl of Essex*, and *Lord
Great Chamberlain* of *England*; and as the highest Mark of the *King*'s Affection and Esteem for
him, he was constituted Vicegerent in the *King*'s
Absence. Thus being rais'd to the very Pinacle of
Honour, like a Politic and Faithful *Statesman*, he
was continually studying the Security of the *Government*, and the most proper methods for settling Peace and Tranquility throughout the whole
Kingdom ; and in order hereunto, he resolved
upon Correcting the Vices of the Age, encourage-
ing Vertue, establishing Good Orders, and reforming Corruptions : And for that was manifest,
there

there would not be wanting great Endeavours to subvert the Government: while *Monasteries* and such like Religious Houses (those Sources of vicious plotting Wretches, whose Interest it was to adhere to the *Pope*) were not destroy'd, he induc'd the *King* to suppress first *Chauntries*, then the *small Monasteries*, and afterwards the *Abbys*, till all the Religious *Fraternities* of that sort in *England* were dissolv'd. And that he might be sure of Success in his Resolution of settling the *Reformed Religion*, (of which he was a zealous Asserter, securing the Professors thereof from the *Popish Bishops* Fury and Rage) he perswades the *King* to ally himself to some *Protestant Prince*; and accordingly a Match was made with the Lady *Ann*, Sister to the Prince of *Cleve*, by whose Protection the *Protestants* were very much Emboldn'd to a more public Profession of their Religion. Thus did he fortunately carry on the *Reformation*, to the larger growth, whereof he gave an extraordinary assistance, by obtaining from the *King* a Grant for publishing the Bible in the *English* Tongue, whereby many were help'd to discern the Fallacies and Heresies of the *Romish* Faith, who before had taken up with what Trash the *Priests* had put upon 'em. Who now are importunate for a *Convocation*, which the *King* summon'd to adjust Matters of Religion; in this Assembly *Cromwell* takes place of all the *Clergy*, by the Title of *Vicar General*, and disputes strenuously for the *Protestant* Faith. But his Zeal on this Account procur'd him not a few considerable Enemies,

E

mies, of whom Bishop *Gardiner* (the most subtle and inveterate of all others) was still labouring to bring about his ruin, which at length, with a great deal of Joy he thought he saw a fit time for the accomplishment of, and herein, indeed, he was not mistaken. The *King*, by an inconstancy, natural to him, was grown weary of his *Queen*, and his Love was now plac'd upon the Lady *Katherine Howard*; this *Gardiner* observing, took the Liberty to tell the *King*, that 'twas absolutely necessary for the Quiet of the Kingdom, and Security of the Succession, to have an *English Queen*; and at same time, with abundance of Cunning, he instigates the *King* against *Cromwell*, as the sole Cause of his unhappy Marriage with Q. *Ann*; and this so wrought upon his *Majesty*, (who was ever violent in his Love and Hatred) that imagining *Cromwell* was the only Obstacle to the *Repudiation* of his Wife, and his Match with *Katherine*, he so hearkn'd to the Accusations of his *Enemies*, as to give Consent that he should be Arrested: And accordingly by the Duke of *Norfolk* he was Arrested in the *Council Chamber*, and committed to the *Tower*, where he lay not long before he was attainted of High Treason. Some of the *Articles* against him were, " That he had dispersed many Erroneous Books contrary to the Faith of the *Sacrament*; that he had Licens'd many Preachers, suspected of Heresie; that he said he would not turn to the *Pope*'s Obedience, tho' the *King* turn'd; but if the *King* did turn, he would fight in person against him; and drawing out his

Dagger,

Dagger, wish'd that might pierce him to the Heart if he shou'd not do it ; that hearing some Lords were plotting against him, he threaten'd he'd raise, great Stirs in *England*. Tho' accus'd both of *High Treason* and *Heresie*, his Enemies durst not bring him to a Tryal; but against all *Law* and *Justice* he was condemn'd, while confin'd to the *Tower* ; during his Imprisonment he requested one of the *Commissioners*, sent to treat with him, to carry from him a Letter to the *King* ; which he refusing with passion, and saying he'd carry no Letter from a *Traytor* : *Cromwell* ask'd him only to deliver a Message from him, and upon his Consent. " You shall recommend me to the " King, (says *Cromwell*) and let him understand " that by that time he hath so well try'd you, " and thoroughly prov'd you, as I have done, he " shall find you as false a Man, as ever came about " him. In all his adversity he was patient to a Miracle ; and when on the 28th of *July* he was brought to the Scaffold, and beheaded on *Tower-Hill*, he behav'd himself with all the Gallantry and Constancy of a Resolv'd *Christian*. He utter'd fervent Prayers, and made a short Speech, wherein he said he dy'd in the *Catholic Faith*, meaning thereby no more (as from his whole Life, and even at his Death, wherein he us'd no *Popish Ceremony*, it must be concluded) than that he dy'd in the true *Christian Catholic Faith*. Thus fell this *Great Man*, and with him for a long time did the *Reformation* seem to lie dead ; his Death, who was the *chief Instrument* in it, putting such a

E 2   stop

ſtop to that imperfect work, that not *Cranmer* himſelf, in that *King's* Reign, cou'd ever afterwards gain any Ground for it : Nay, rather did it decline, for ſeveral Preachers of the *Reformed Religion* were burnt in a ſhort time after; by all which it appears, how great a Loſs the *Church* ſuſtain'd, in being depriv'd of ſo able and powerful a Member, who more than any, oppos'd himſelf with *Great Zeal* againſt the Impudences and Contrivances of the *Pope's* Subtle and Malicious *Agents.*

I ſhall not tire your patience, if I recite a paſſage or two of this *Brave Man's* extraordinary Generoſity. It is but too common for thoſe, who from a low degree, are rais'd to a high Eſtate, to look with the greateſt Contempt upon ſuch, who have moſt oblig'd them; but our *Cromwell* in the full Enjoyment of all his Dignities, bore himſelf with a Moderation, peculiar to himſelf. Witneſs his taking notice of a poor Woman, who kept a Victualling-Houſe, and had formerly truſted him to the value of 40 *s.* whom eſpying, as he was riding thro' *Cheapſide,* he order'd to be call'd to him; and after having acknowledg'd the Debt, he ſent her to his Houſe, diſcharged that, and gave her an *Annual* Penſion of *Four Pound,* and a *Livery,* during Life. But what follows is much more remarkable ; As he was riding with ſome Nobles to the *King's* Palace, he ſaw one footing it in the Streets, whom he thought he knew, immediately ord'ring his whole Train to await him; he lights off his Horſe, upon Enquiry, finding him the Man he took him for, he embraces the *Mean Stranger;*

and

and to the Wonderment of all about him, invites
him to Dinner : his haft at that time prevented a
longer ftay ; and therefore he left the *amazed
Stranger*, who Enquiring his Name of my *Lord's*
Attendants, began to be troubled with the reflections which this *unexpected Accident* gave him.
Cromwell, who had ftay'd fome time with the
King, at his return home, finds him attending in
the *Court Yard*, where again Embracing him, he
takes him to his *Table*, and after fome time finding
the *Lords* who accompanied him, no lefs *furpriz'd*
at his *Condefcention* than was the *Stranger* : he makes
'em this *Relation* ; *You wonder to fee me thus Obliging;
but you will be more amaz'd when I tell you I am more
Indebted to this* Very Man, *than to the whole World
befide* ; *for after the defeat of* Gatillion, *I came to*
Florence *fo needy, that being forced to beg an Alms;
this Worthy Merchant Mr.* Francis Frefcobald *feeing
I know not what in my Face that pleas'd him upon Enquiry of what Country I was, pitying me in my Neceffity, he took me home, and gave me a Suit of Apparrel, a Horfe and* 16 *Ducats of Gold to bear my
Expences to* England ; and now turning him about
to Mr. *Frefcobald*, And *what,* Dear Friend, *(fays he)
has brought you hither ?* The *generous Merchant* after
he had recover'd himfelf out of the amaze this
happy Providence caft him into, told him, That
he was become fo Poor by his vaft Loffes, that of
all the Wealth he formerly enjoy'd, but 15000
Ducats were left him, and they were Owing him
here, and hard to be Got too : *Cromwell*, after he
he had obtain'd a Lift of his *Debtors*, fent a Servant

E 3

vant of his own, in his Name, to Demand those
Sums for the *Merchant* : After Dinner , taking his
Friend apart, he gave him first 16 *Ducats* for those
he had receiv'd, then 10 for his Apparrel, and 10
more for his Horse, and at last he Gave him *Four*
Bags, each quantity 400 *Ducats* for Interest : after
all, he passionately requested his stay in *England*,
offering to lend him 60000 *Ducats* for 4 Years to
Trade withal ; but *Frescobald* having by *Cromwell's*
Authority, obtain'd all his Money (preferring before all his *Native Country*) after a thousand Ac-
knowledgements made him, return'd for *Florence*,
with a *due Sense* of this so Extraordinary and *Generous* Entertainment.

But I am afraid, Sir, I grow too much upon
your Patience, and therefore will shut up with
the Character Archbishop *Cranmer* gave him in a
Letter to the *King* on his Behalf——— *I have found*
(says he) *that my Lord* Cromwell *has always lov'd
you above all things, and Serv'd you with such Fidelity, and Success, that I believe no* King *of* England
had Ever a better Minister, *and it is my Wish, that
your* Majesty *may find a* Counsellor *who both* can
and *will discharge his Trust as my Lord* Cromwell
hath done.

But alas, nothing could move that *Inexorable
Prince*, who rather than forego his unlawful *Lust*
to the Lady *Howard* (whom he dar'd not Marry
while *Cromwell* liv'd) Sacrificed this his *Darling
Favorite.* And tho' it adds Greatly to my Lord
Cromwell's Fame, that after his Death, he was
most passionately bewail'd by the *King*, who frequently

quently cry'd out for his *Cromwell*. Yet was not this a due Reparation to *England* for the Loſs of ſuch an *Extraordinary Man* whoſe *Virtues* were ſo *Singular*, his *Services* ſo *Signal*, both to the *Nation* in General, and to the *Reformation* in particular: whoſe *Zeal* to *God* was ſo *True*, whoſe *Temperance* ſo *Conſtant* in all Conditions; who (in one word) was poſſeſs'd of a *Courage* ſo *undaunted*, and a *Fidelity* ſo *rare*, that I make no doubt you will with me Conclude, a Man Endow'd with all theſe, and many more *Excellent Qualifications*, well deſerves the Title of the *Greateſt Engliſhman*, which therefore I affix to *Thomas Cromwell* the Great *Earl* of *Eſſex*, and ſo conclude,

S I R,

Yours, &c.

J. J.

Cloe *to* Urania, *againſt Womens being Learn'd.*

I Have, my dear *Urania*, ſo ill defended the the Cauſe you always eſpouſe, that *Lyſander* has convinc'd me that Learning is not for our Sex; but before I make an entire delivery of my Judgment to his Arguments; I thought fit to ſend them, as well as I can remember them, to *Urania*,

to

to see what influence they'll have on her; and how she'll defend the Point against an Opponent, she has often so well handl'd without one.

Lysander will have it, That *Learning* in common Prudence ought by the Men to be deny'd us; since it wou'd not only make us proud, and imperious; and aspire to the command over Men; which, as we might by such Auxiliary force easily obtain, the Charms of the Body alone giving us too great an Ascendant over Men; so we shou'd not want the desire of obtaining it, having got the means. Secondly, That since, as he will have it, we were design'd by God for Obedience, not Rule; to be instructed by our Husbands, and to study only Houshold Affairs, it wou'd be Impious to raise us from the Office Nature had allotted us, to a Nobler Station. Thirdly, That Learned Women are seldom Chast, Learning disposing 'em to Inconstancy, and Infidelity to their Husbands in longing for foreign Embraces, and that betwixt a Womans Desire and Act, there is nothing but Opportunity.

This, in short, is the Substance of what he urg'd tho' with more advantageous Circumstances of a fine turn of words, and several Examples to confirm his Assertions, which whether true or false, I cannot determine. But one thing I must not forget; that he much urg'd a Book call'd, *Advice to a Daughter*, the Authority of which was too much Establish'd for me to Condemn. I leave the whole to the Judicious, and Ingenious *Urania*, whom I, and ev'ry one must own the best

Advocate

Advocate for our Sex. But tho' I'll never difpute
that Prize with you, yet I fhall always that of
which of us is the beft Friend, and you muft confefs, that I am without referve your Sincere, and
Faithful

Cloe.

An Anfwer to the foregoing Letter in Defence of Womens being Learn'd.

URANIA to CLOE.

I Receiv'd yours; my Charming *Cloe*, the beginning of the laft Week, but the Nicenefs of
the Subject, wou'd not permit me to fend you
an immediate Anfwer, being too much, at that
time, taken up with other Affairs; but having
now got an Hour to my felf, I fhall curforily confider the weight of *Lyfander's* Objections.

Lyfander, I muft confefs, is a Man of a great
deal of Wit, and delivers his Arguments on any
Subject with that addrefs, that they appear much
ftronger from his Mouth, than in Writing; yet
I muft affure you, nothing I have yet feen of his
carries fo little weight, as what you have fent me;
which fhews how bad a Caufe he had undertaken,
fince it cou'd only furnifh him with fuch weak
Supports, as he has produc'd. And I'm confident,
your

your Love for *Lysander*, brib'd your Judgment to his side, which you have too much of to submit to such feeble Reasonings.

Learning, he tells you, will add fresh Pride to our Sex, and kindle an Ambition in us of Commanding over that of Man, which we shou'd certainly persue, assisted with so powerful an Auxiliary, since with these Charms Nature has bestow'd on our Bodies, we go so far already, and discover a desire of an absolute Mastery.

This is so Cobweb, and Vulgar a Sophism, that I'm amaz'd to hear it from the Mouth of *Lysander*. Is he Ignorant of the Nature of Learning? or, is he not very sensible that it teaches *one to know ones self?* the consequence of which must certainly, in any Woman of sense, produce Humility, not Pride: It furnishes us with Masculine, nay, Divine Thoughts, that are equally serviceable to our selves, and Husbands. It makes us contemn the designing Flatteries of Men, when they deifie that Beauty, which vanishes in a moment, and which Fools preserve with so much Care, for a Bait, and Snare to both their own and their Admirers Ruin. Learning teaches *Wisdom*, which can never render us so opposite to the Establish'd *Oeconomy* of the World, as to make us once think so wildly, as to attempt the inverting so prevalent, and inveterate a Custom as the Soveraignty of the Men. Besides, Nature has form'd us too weak, to effect a Revolution that depends on the Force, and Strength of Body, as well as Mind, since Politics are meer useless Theories,

ories, without Able Hands to put 'em in Execution. But if we muſt needs ſuppoſe this mighty Revolution effected, who wou'd not be willing to be Subject to ſo agreeable a Power, in which *Wiſdom*, and *Beauty* join'd. But, my *Cloe*, does *Lyſander* forget that a great many Women without Learning direct their Husbands, and have a very awful influence over them; but Learning wou'd qualifie that extraordinary Aſcendant, by making that *Rational*, which was before only the blind Effect of Paſſion and Fondneſs.

Lyſander's Second Objection, That *Women were by their Creator deſign'd for* **Obedience** *not* **Rule**; *to be inſtructed by their Husbands, not to inſtruct them; and to Study nothing but their Houſhold Affairs.*——— Partly depends of what has been ſaid to the firſt. Tho', by the way, *Lyſander* makes a little bold with the Secrets of the Almighty in that Aſſertion, tho' I confeſs, the Curſe that was laid on *Eve* for her Tranſgreſſion, might give him occaſion to ſay ſo, tho' it prove directly the contrary, as my *Viridomar*, has formerly obſerv'd; for if Woman was created the Subject, and Vaſſal of Man, it had been no Puniſhment to've inflicted that Subjection on her.

But, my *Cloe*, I think 'tis evident, that Learning will not leſſen that Obedience it teaches them; which will therefore make them practice it as a Duty of Reaſon, not Cuſtom, and Impoſition, two weighty and provoking Motives of Oppoſition. As to the Second Branch of this Objection, *viz. That we are to be inſtructed by our Husbands,* &c.

Learning

Learning save's a Husband that's capable, the Labor; and the Husband that is not, the *Shame* of
attempting what he's not able to perform; And
by giving him an Emulation of his Wives Virtues,
make him endeavour not to be out-done by a
Woman, in *Masculine*, and *Rational* Excellencies,
by improving his Mind with Nobler Qualifications; and not wholly devote himself to such sordid
Employments, and Diversions, which are generally the whole Business and Entertainment of
too many Gentlemen; I mean, the *Bottle*, the
Whore, the *Dice*, with *Hunting*, *Hawking*, *Cour-
sing*, and the rest of that wretched Train, as if
they were born never to think.

I come now to *Lysander*'s last Objection, which
is indeed the most infamous of all the Scandals
he endeavours to throw on Learned Women, *viz.*
*that their Knowledge makes 'em seldom Chast, and
breeds in 'em wandring Desires.*——Were this true,
I must own it a very Substantial Argument, and
I shou'd yield that all my Sex shou'd be kept from
the use of Books as cautiously, as Madmen from
Edge-Tools. But, my *Cloe*, the Assertion is too
general to be true, to which I my self cou'd bring
not a few Exceptions. The instances he produc'd,
tho' you doubt, yet to please him I'll admit, supposing therefore that such and such Learned Women have been Whores, it still remains, that he
prove this was the effect of their Learning, not
Nature, and that if they had not been Learned,
they wou'd not a' been Whores. *A Task, not so
easily perform'd.* But since a bold Assertion is no
proof

proof of any thing, it may be juftly confronted with an oppofite. I fhall therefore affirm, That thofe Women, who, tho' Learn'd, are Whores, wou'd be much more proftitute without it ; for tho' thofe Inclinations, Nature and Conftitution have given 'em, are not always entirely overcome by Learning, yet are the violence of them regulated, and reduc'd to a greater Moderation. 'Tis not to be deny'd, That Learning being very uncommon in Woman, when 'tis found in one, it draws a more Numerous Train of Addreffes from the Men ; but were it more common, 'they wou'd by being divided, be more eafily refifted : Nay, the very Motive wou'd be taken away, by the commonnefs of Learned Women, the rarity of which, is the chief bait on thefe occafions.

Having thus run through *Lyfander*'s formidable Troop of Arguments, I fhall add a pleafant Fancy of my own, which is, That the Practice of admitting Women to the Arts and Sciences, wou'd convince the Infidels of the *Jewifh* and *Turkifh* Perfwafion, that Women have Souls, fince they were not wholly taken up with the Ornament, and care of the Body only, and then we might hope an equal Share in the Paradice of *Mahomet*, with the Men, and not be fhut out of the Synagogue by the Rabbi's.

But that I may wholly obviate all your Scruples, I fhall fay one word now to that celebrated Book of the *Advice to a Daughter*, defigning at a better opportunity to give a fuller Anfwer to a Book I have very little Efteem for.

I can.

I can never admit that an implicit Faith is more excusable in our Sex, than in his; because I can by no means discover, that what he advances carries any thing of Reason with it. These are his Words.——

As to your particular Faith, keep to the Religion that is grown up with you, both as it is the best in it self, and that the Reason of staying in it on that Account, is somewhat stronger for your Sex, than it will perhaps be allow'd to be for ours, in respect of the voluminous Enquiries into Truth by reading, are less expected from you.——

Here you find a flourish of words indeed, but in my poor opinion, no very weighty Sense. The stress of the whole lyes on a false support; I mean, the corrupt Custom of the Age; *which,* he says, *will not* Expect Our reading, and search after the most Material of Truths, that this Life is given us for; if Truth be obscur'd by so many Volumes, 'tis the fault of those in whose hands it has so long been reserv'd. If it be a Truth that is also necessary for our Future Happiness to be rightly inform'd in; 'tis certainly equally our Duty to enquire into it; and they are to blame who deprive us of the fittest means, *Learning:* and if it be an incumbent Duty, 'twill be but a weak and poor Excuse for continuing in an Error, because we were bred in one; Besides, this wou'd hold on all sides, and must of Consequence be very fallacious; and I must needs add, That whatever Figure a Lady wou'd make, by the Direction of this Advice, in the Court, she wou'd make but a
very

very indifferent one in Reason. But 'tis evident, that he is not in earnest, when a little after he prescribes a quite contrary Rule —— *Let me recommend to you* (says he) *a Method of being* Rightly *inform'd, which can never fail;* 'tis in short this—— *Get* Understanding, *and practice* Virtue, &c. Now how she shou'd get this *Understanding* he leaves her, and us in the Dark; tho' I am confident it can never be obtain'd to a degree of being *Rightly inform'd* without Learning; unless he wou'd have it by Inspiration, which I humbly presume, is none of the most solid Understandings in our Age.

But my charming Friend, I have detain'd you too long this bout to say any more on this Subject, or Book, when we meet I'll give you more of my Sentiments, which nothing cou'd make me so free of imparting; but the Pleasure I have to please such a Friend; tho' I shall never yield to you in sincerity, or any other Duties that are ow'd to *Cloe*, by

Her faithful Friend,

Urania.

Some Reflections on Mr. Rymer's Short View of Tragedy, and an Attempt at a Vindication of SHAKESPEAR, *in an Essay directed to* JOHN DRYDEN *Esq*;

AS soon as Mr. *Rymer's* Book came to my Hands, I resolv'd to make some *Reflections* upon it, tho' more to shew my *Will* than my *Abilities.* But finding Mr. *Dennis* had almost promis'd the World a Vindication of the Incomparable *Shakespear*, I quitted the Design, since he had got a Champion more equal to his Worth; not doubting but Mr. *Dennis* wou'd as effectually confute our *Hypercritic* in this, as all Men must grant he has, in what he attempted in his *Impartial Critic.*

But expecting thus long, without hearing any farther of it; I concluded some other more *important*, or at least more agreeable business, had diverted him from it; or that he thought it an *unnecessary Undertaking*, to perswade the *Town* of a Truth it already receiv'd; or to give any farther Answer to a Book, that carry'd its own Condemnation in its self. However, since I find some build an Assurance on this *General Silence* of all the Friends of *Shakespear*, that Mr. *Rymer's* Objections are unanswerable; I resolv'd to bestow two or three days on an Essay to prove the contrary:

trary : Which may at least bring this advantage to the *Cause*, to convince the World how very good it is, when one of my *Inability*, in so little time, have so much to say for it, and that without going through the whole Defence.

I indeed, like the most *indifferent* Counsel, make the *Motion*, but leave more able Heads to *Plead* the Cause. One great Satisfaction, I have (however I succeed) is, that I speak before a Judge that is the best Qualify'd to decide a Controversie of this Nature, that ever *England* produc'd; for in you, Sir, The *Poet*, and The *Critic meet* in their highest Perfection; and, if the *Critic* discover the Faults of *Shakespear*, The *Poet* will also see, and admire his Beauties, and Perfections. For as you have Learning, and strong Judgment to discern his least Transgressions, so have you a Genius that can reach his Noblest Flights; and a Justice that *will* acknowledge his Deserts: And were there no other Arguments to be brought in his Vindication, it wou'd be more, than sufficient to destroy all his weak Antagonist has huddl'd together against him, that you give him your Approbation. This, Sir, is *really* my Opinion, and I'm sure the most sensible Lovers of Poetry will side with me in it: and secure me from the Imputation of being so foolishly vain, to think I Can flatter You, when I speak of your Poetry, your Judgment, and your Candor; since whatever can be said on that Subject, by any one below Mr. Dryden's Abilities, wou'd be but a very faint Shadow of the *Mighty Panegyric* of your Name alone.

F   The

The Method I shall observe in these *Reflections*
(for my time will not permit me to bring so con-
fus'd a Chaos into a more regular Form) will be
first to run over the Pages of his Book as they lye,
and give you some Animadversions in part of those
Absurdities they contain: for to examine all, wou'd
swell my Letter into a Volume, and be five hundred times as big as the Text, like a certain Reverend Dr. on *Job*. Next, I shall attempt a
Vindication of 𝔖𝔥𝔞𝔨𝔢𝔰𝔭𝔢𝔞𝔯, where he more formerly attaques him.

In the first, I hope you'll forgive me, if I use
him with no more Respect, than he does 𝔖𝔥𝔞𝔨𝔢𝔰𝔭𝔢𝔞𝔯 or 𝔜𝔬𝔲 : And in the latter, I hope you
will admit *Recriminations* on those Patterns, he
proposes to us for the Test, of 𝔖𝔥𝔞𝔨𝔢𝔰𝔭𝔢𝔞𝔯's
Faults, as a sufficient Answer to what he Magi-
sterially lays down, as *Self-Evident*, with a Scorn-
ful, tho' *Clumsy* Jest, without any other Reason
to confirm it ; if not as a *Demonstration* of that
Injur'd Poet's Excellence. And that we may
from thence conclude with Mr. *Rymer* (as he has
it in his Preface to *Rapin*) since his *Standards* of
Perfection are equally culpable, That *the greatest
Wits, both Modern, and Ancient, sometimes slip, and
are liable to Cavils* : And by consequence, that all
his Pains were needless to bring 𝔖𝔥𝔞𝔨𝔢𝔰𝔭𝔢𝔞𝔯 into that Number, since his greatest Admirers ever
confess'd he had Faults : Tho' no Man but himself,
I believe, ever *Rob'd* him of *all* Excellence ; and
I must say, That most that he produces are meer
Cavils, and convict him of being one of those
Critics,

Critics, that *like Wasps rather annoy the* Bee's, *than terrifie the* Drones.

But, indeed, the Lovers of 𝕾𝖍𝖆𝖐𝖊𝖘𝖕𝖊𝖆𝖗 may well forgive the Author of *Edgar*, and this *Short view of Tragedy*; whatever He can say against his *Excellence* and *Genius* ; since being his Opposite, 'tis no wonder his Mind's not capacious enough to Comprehend, nor his Taſt Poetical enough to relish the Noble Thoughts which the Ingenious have admir'd in 𝕾𝖍𝖆𝖐𝖊𝖘𝖕𝖊𝖆𝖗 ever ſince he Writ.

It has been the Fate of moſt Critics on Poetry, to Err in thoſe Things they Condemn in others, or to diſcover by their Writing, how ill qualify'd they are to judge of any thing, but the Regularity of the Structure of a Poem, which the *Known* Rules of Art furniſh them with, the chief formation of a Poet being wanting ; Nature denying them the *Divitem Venam.* 𝕻𝖊𝖙𝖗𝖔𝖓𝖎𝖚𝖘 𝕬𝖗𝖇𝖎𝖙𝖊𝖗, ſo ſevere on *Lucan*, and *Seneca* (for on them he reflects in his *Satyricen*) kept not clear of that unnatural Affectation he condemn'd in them. *Joſeph* and *Julius Scaliger* (as *Rapin* obſerves) had the Art, but wanted the ſupply of Nature when they attempted Poetry. But Mr. *Rymer*, in any thing he has yet publiſh'd, has not the leaſt ſhadow of pretence to the Excellence of either of theſe. 𝕻𝖊𝖙𝖗𝖔𝖓𝖎𝖚𝖘 had *Wit*, had *Fire*, a *Genius*, and *Language* ; and tho the *Scaligers* were not *Poets*, yet had they the Merits of pretty good *Critics* ; but this Gentleman has ſcarce produc'd one *Criticiſm*, that is not borrow'd from *Rapin*, *Dacier*,

F 2   or

or *Boſſu*, and miſ-apply'd to 𝕾𝖍𝖆𝖐𝖊𝖘𝖕𝖊𝖆𝖗. And for his Poetry, from the *Heroic Tragedy* of 𝕰𝖉𝖌𝖆𝖗, to the River 𝖅𝖔𝖚𝖓𝖉𝖘, he diſcovers not the leaſt Genius, nor Taſt of it; and therefore muſt be granted a very incompetent Judge of ſuch a Poet as *Shakeſpear* is.

Some of my Friends, whoſe Authority was very great with me, wou'd needs have me examine 𝕰𝖉𝖌𝖆𝖗; but there were two things that obſtruċted my complyance with them—The Firſt, That it was ſo abominably ſtor'd with Opium, that I cou'd not poſſibly keep my Eyes open to read it attentively; The other, That 'twas ſuch a Banter in it ſelf on Poetry and ſenſe, that all the pains I cou'd take about it, wou'd be only to give him the vanity of imagining it worth any Man's taking Notice of.

The Piece now under our Conſideration is in a Vein ſomething more merry, and uncommon; for tho' 'tis frequent enough to meet with a dull Poetaſter for a *Poet*, yet 'tis ſomething more rare to encounter a jolly Droll for a *Critic*. Tho', that with the abundance of *Ill Nature, Conceit,* and *Affectation* of appearing a Scholar, is the *Vehicle that carries off his Nonſence*, with as ill Juḋes of that, as he is of *Poetry*, and makes them take it for an extraordinary Thing: and this will make the better excuſe for my examining how very Monſtrous a *Fantom* 'tis, that is ſet out in ſo formidable an Equipage.

To paſs over the *Epiſtle Dedicatory*, which like *Bays* his Prologues, may ſerve as well for any other

Book

Book as this, nay —and for any other Lord too,
as well as the Noble Lord 'tis addreſs'd to (whoſe
generous Patronage of all that have any Merit
in the Republic of Letters, ought to have ſecur'd
him from ſuch a Prophanation) And what's
more, will do e'ery jot as well, for an *Advertiſe-*
ment to the Courteous Reader, as for an *Epiſtle*
Dedicatory, it being a *Medly* of Stuff without *Co-*
herence, Deſign, or *Engliſh*. But to examine all
that's *Unintelligible, falſe Engliſh*, and *abſurd*, wou'd
be an *Herculean* Labor, and extend my Conſiderations to e'ery Line. I ſhall begin with the
Work its ſelf, not leſs *abrupt*, or *inconſiſtent*.

He begins with the Neceſſity of a *Chorus*, urg-
ing, That, as 'twas the the Original, ſo 'tis the
moſt Eſſential part of a *Tragedy*, becauſe it keeps
the Poet, to the Unities of time, and place: But
'tis evident, from the *Suppliants* of *Euripides* (as
you, Sir, have formerly obſerv'd) and from *Racines*
Heſter, (as Mr. Dennis has noted) that the *Cho-*
rus does not neceſſarily do what Mr. *Rymer* pretends; nor was it at all in *Horace's* Thoughts, if
we may judge of them by the Precepts he gives
about it in his Art of Poetry.

But Mr. Dennis having evidently clear'd this
Point, I ſhall ſay no more of it ; but that if, as
our *Critic* contends, 'tis the Poet's incumbent Duty to gratifie the Eyes, as well as Ears ; this muſt
be done without offending againſt *Nature*, and
Probability , as the *Chorus* does. (which is abundantly prov'd by the Impartial Critic). But
by thoſe who have a more neceſſary Relation to

F 3   the

the Action and Fable, as the *Senators of Venice* in *Othello*, whom he reflects on ; tho', as they have a Necessary concern in the Play, so cou'd they not be introduc'd without their Habits, which afford that Gratification to the Eye he makes the Duty of e'ery Poet, without the help of so foreign, and unnatural a Thing as a *Chorus*.

The 3*d*. and 4*th*. Pages are almost unintelligible, and at cross purposes one Paragraph with another ; for he will have it, That the words of *Shake-spear* do not set off the Action, and then of a suddain he concludes the contrary, that they do. Next, *P.* 6. he has an admirable fetch, to prove that *Pronunciation* is a notable *Vehicle*, to carry off *Nonsense*, by shewing that it set off the Sense of **Demosthenes**. 'Tis granted, That a good and true *Pronunciation*, is a great help to *Sense*, because it sets it in its proper Light, as ill repeating sets it in a false one, and makes it lose its lustre ; as *Martial* sensibly observes to *Fidentinus*.

Quem recitas meus est, ô Fidentine, *libellus, Sed Male dum recitas incipit esse tuus.*

But it seems to me, That the Reason, which makes *Good Pronunciation* set off *Sense*, must make *Nonsence* more visible ; for the giving e'ery Word, and Sentence its true *Emphasis*, must make the blunder more obvious, to even those, who in the Reading wou'd perhaps over-look it. I grant, that the Pomp of the Theatre may, perhaps, dull the edge of our Judgment, but *Pronunciation* never can.

can. But were all this true, I can't find that
Shakespear falls justly under his Censure, as to
this particular; for he affirms, That *Shew, Action*,
and *Pronunciation*, lose their force under a serious
Perusal; yet after such a Perusal, Shakespear
does still maintain his Reputation with the greatest Genius's our Nation has produc'd in Poetry.
His Excellence therefore is not built on those
Supports, but *innate Worth*, and by Consequence
all his incoherent bustle is to very little purpose.

But the next Proof of the power of *Shew,
Action*, and *Pronunciation*, is extreamly merry.
P. 8. He tells us, That Cardinal *Richelieu* was by
them influenc'd in his mighty Approbation of
the Tragedy of Sir *Thomas Moor*, tho' there were
neither Poetry, nor Sense in it. Yet were not
these able to byass his nice Tast to favour the *Cid*
of *Corneil* (who had more of a Poet, than one of
our *Flecno*'s Class) which places the Cardinal in
the *Majores Numero*, of the Division of Judges
made by *Horace*, clear contrary to our *Critic*'s
intention. Well, I must say this for him, That
tho' his *Reasons* and *Observations* are far from irre-
fragable, yet his *Rambles* are *admirable* and *unaccountable* from a Comical Harangue against *Opera's, P.* 9, 10, 11, 12. he runs to *Verse burlesq*;
and how long it had been in *Italy* before it pass'd
the *Alps*, I suppose, to shew us he had read *Pe-
lisson*, quoted in the Margin, for the Devil a-bit
had it to do with the Business in hand. Thence
with another leap, he jumps back again te *Æschylus*

F 4

chylus his *Persians,* proposing it for a Model proportion'd to our English Capacities. Of which,
Page the 13th. having drawn in imitation in the
Spanish Expedition of 1588. our *Tragædo didascu-*
lus dubs it the 𝕴𝖓𝖛𝖎𝖓𝖈𝖎𝖇𝖑𝖊 𝕬𝖗𝖒𝖆𝖉𝖆. His draught
indeed is very nice and circumstantial, in the
very serious, and at the same time extreamly *Ri-*
diculous Account of all the Incidents of this
Draught to the very Beards of the *Spanish* Grandees; the Tuns of *Tar Barrels* for the *Heretics ;*
and the squabling of the *Cabinet Council,* about
Preferments not yet in their Power. And is it
not as great an Error in *Manners,* as any 𝕾𝖍𝖆𝖐𝖊𝖘𝖕𝖊𝖆𝖗 is guilty of in the worst of his Plays, to
make the greatest Politicians of that Age such
egregious Coxcombs? But what wretched
Mortal is there of so very sorrowful or morose
a temper, that must not laugh to hear him say,
That *on this* Occasion *two Competitors have juster*
Occasion *to work up, and shew the Muscles of their*
Passion, than Shakespears, Cassius, *and* Brutus?
Cou'd any Pugg in *Barbary* be so ignorant of *com-*
mon Sense and *Reason* as this? he must Pardon the
Expression, 'tis his own to a much greater Man,
than himself.

'Tis true, he tells us with his usual *Magisterial*
Assurance, That these *Spanish* Grandees of his
Creation, have a *juster* Occasion for a Passionate
Scene than 𝕾𝖍𝖆𝖐𝖊𝖘𝖕𝖊𝖆𝖗𝖘, *Brutus,* and *Cassius:*
But I must ask his Pardon if I subscribe not to his
Opinion: But to punish him sufficiently for this
gross Absurdity, and Arrogance, lay down the
matter

matter barely as 'tis, propoſing the *Occaſions* juſt as they lye in both theſe Authors, our *Hiſtoriographer*, I mean, and the inimitable *Shakeſpear*.

Firſt, Here is a Council of 15 of the greateſt, old Politic Heads that Age produc'd in *Spain*, quarrelling with one another about things out of poſſeſſion, in *Eutopia*, To be Kings of *Man* ; Duke-*Trincalos*, and Duke-*Stephanos*, &c. is there either Nature or Poſſibility of this ? ſo far is it from any probable Ground.

On the other hand : Here is *Caſſius*, a *Paſſionate*, *Ambitious* , and *Avaritious* Roman, impatient to bear a refuſal of a Requeſt he made for *Lucius Pella*, that was found guilty of *Bribery* (a Crime himſelf was guilty of) looking on himſelf of equal Power at leaſt with *Brutus*, and a Brother, if not Father of the War, being Ambitious and Choleric too, as I ſaid, cou'd not but reſent it as an infringing his Authority, and Friendſhip ; and by conſequence diſcover his Reſentment at firſt meeting. But this is not all the Ground of this Scene : Here is *Brutus* on the other hand, a ſevere follower of Virtue, to which he Sacrific'd his Friend and Father, *Cæſar*, and cou'd not therefore but reſent *Caſſius*'s deviating from Virtue, his pretence to which made him his Friend. How cou'd he bear with *Caſſius* in his *Bribery* and *Avarice*, who cou'd not with *Cæſar*'s Ambition? for in denying Money for the Payment of thoſe Legions (on whoſe Fidelity, not only their Lives, but the *Fate*, and *Liberty* of *Rome*, which was yet dearer to *Brutus*, depended) he gave them up to *Octavius* and *Anthony*.   Is

Is there any Parallel indeed betwixt thefe two Occafions? Can there be any thing more Childifh and trifling, than the firft? And can there be any thing greater, and more weighty than the latter? The Prize of Chymera's on one fide, and the Liberty, and Fate of the greateft Empire in the World; nay, Life, Honor, Virtue, and all that can or ought to be dear on the other.

Let this be a convincing proof of the *Genius* and *Judgment* of our *Hiftoriographer Royal*, who cou'd prefer his own dull Burlefque on Common Senfe to this incomparable Scene of **Shakefpear**, which is juftly admir'd by all Men of Senfe.

But to proceed, If *Defdemona*'s Character be below the dignity of *Tragedy*, what are thefe *Spanifh Segniora's*, who are to fpend a whole Act in telling of Dreams; which were likely to have fo mighty influence on the **Spanifh** *Politicians*, (always noted for their **Religion** and **Bigottry**) as to furnifh out *Diftractions and Diforders enough for an Act*. The Draught of the next Act is e'ery jot as merry: for 'tis very Natural indeed, and nicely according to *Manners*, to bring in a King *Philofophizing* on *Dreams*, and *Hobgoblins*! unlefs he were to be fuch a King as he fo much admires in the *Rehearfal*; for a King *Phiz* by his former Profeffion, might be fuppos'd to have fome *Notable*, if not *Noble* Thoughts (as our *Critic* requires) on the Matter.

The 16*th*. Page, is a brief, tho' fully as ridiculous fumming up of what he had faid at large before, tho' the Fourth Act is above meafure Comical,

mical, where the *Spaniard* is to be beaten off with a *Vanguard* of *Dreams* and *Goblins*, and the *Terrors* of the Night.

For my part, on the first reading it, I thought him absolutely out of his Wits, or what's all one, that he had a Mind to be lewdly merry extreamly out of Season, or Play the Droll, to shew how much he was better qualify'd for a *Farcewright*, than a *Critic*. But being assur'd since by several Ingenious Gentlemen, that he not only means it as a serious thing, but that the Doctors do not think him Mad enough for *Bedlam*, I will turn the Advice he has the extraordinary Assurance to give you, infinitely more justly to himself, that he wou'd undertake the Writing upon this admirable Plot; and for his Encouragement, I assure him, it shall not run the Fate of his *Edgar*, but be Acted; with a firm belief, that if it do not *Pit, box and Gallery* it with any of Shakespear; yet it may *bear the Bell* (to borrow an extraordinary Phrase from our *Historiographer Royal*) from the *Devil of a Wife*, or Dr. *Faustus*; because the very *excessive* Extravagance of the Thought might make us laugh, whereas *Edgar* cou'd provoke nothing but Sleep.

But his putting this on you, Sir, after so many Public Expressions of your Friendship for him, & private Services (as I'm inform'd) done him, shews his Morals, as faulty, as the *Manners* he has laid down for the *Heroes* of this *Anti-Tragedy*. With what Face cou'd he put so little and scurrilous an Affront on *you*, in this Book, without provocation, who

who in his Preface to *Rapin*, did preferr your Defcription of Night to all the Mafter ftroaks of the Ancients, and Moderns. If you had no other me; its certainly the *Judgment of* Virgil *animated with a more fprightly Wit*, deferv'd better from him than fo mean, and fo ungenerous an Abufe. But now to the next Chapter.

To fhew he had read *Plato*, he quotes him *P.* 18. to prove what no body yet ever deny'd that knew any thing of the Original of *Tragedy*. Nor has any one, that I ever met with, pretended that there was no Poem, that had the Name of *Tragedy* before the time of *Thefpis*. But if from hence he wou'd inferr that Tragedy was Acted before his time, he proceeds farther, than the words of *Plato*, or any other Authority will warrant him, for till *Thefpis*, it was only a Hymn to *Bacchus*, Sung and Perform'd in *Dances*, and Gefticulations by the *Chorus*. But then it had no *Epifode* or *Actor*; and therefore *Thefpis* was the Original of the *Tragedies*, that are Acted, tho' he built it on the Foundation of the *religious* 𝔊𝔬𝔞𝔱-𝔖𝔬𝔫𝔤; this, not only *Horace*, but all the Critic's, I have met with, affirm. And himfelf confeffes, *P.* 19. that when it came to be an Image of the World, it then had a *fecular* Alloy, and was by Confequence alter'd from what it was before, that is, from a *Religious Hymn*, to a *Reprefentation of Humane Life*. The End therefore and Aim of it being thus alter'd, the Mediums to that *End*, muft of Confequence, be alter'd too: The praife of *Bacchus* was no more Neceffary to forming

ming an Image of Humane Life, than the Praise
of *Hercules*, or any other of the Gods. Now,
if the *Chorus* be neceſſary, becauſe 'twas the Original of *Tragedy*, 'tis equally neceſſary the *Chorus*
ſhou'd celebrate the Praiſe of *Bacchus*, as it originally did ; but if Tragedy by the Alteration of its
end were ſet on a new bottom , we are no longer obiig'd to regulate it according to its firſt In-
ſtitution. So that I can ſee no reaſon, that becauſe *Sophocles* retain'd the *Chorus*, it was therefore
a neceſſary part of Tragedy, or if it be, why
the Dancing and Muſic that was continu'd with
it, was any more meer Religion, than the *Chorus*
its ſelf, or a leſs neceſſary part of *Tragedy*, ſince
both were of equal date, as to their Riſe, and End.
But this only *en paſſant*.

P. 20. Next, he leaps to the Care the Government had of the *Theatre*, in permitting no
Poet to preſent a Play to the Houſe till paſt
Thirty. This Obſervation might, perhaps, proceed from Self-Intereſt, hoping to perſwade us,
that, upon another Vacancy, he is qualify'd for
Poet Laureat, intimating , that the older a Man
grows, the fitter he is for a Poet, contrary to the
Judgment of his Friend *Rapin* ; from whom he
borrows the Obſervation that the *Athenians* ſpent
more of the Public Money about their *Chorus*'s,
and other *Decorations* of the *Stage*, than in all their
Wars with *Perſia*. From hence he ſoon paſſes to
his beloved *Ariſtophanes* (and to do him Juſtice,
he always expreſſes an extraordinary Paſſion for
Farces) tho' I am to ſeek in what he drives at in
all

all thofe Praifes he beftows on him , for *Running a Muc*,(as he phrafes it*) at all manner of Vice where-ever he faw it, be it in the greateft Philofophers, the greateft Poets, the Generals, or the Minifters of State.* Wou'd he have our *Poets* follow his example, and expofe our *Divines, Bifhops, Lords, Generals,* and *Minifters of State?* If this be his defire, yet either he ought not to blame them for their Defect in that, or is in Juftice bound to fecure them from the Pe-nalties, they wou'd incur by doing fo : *Scan. Mag.* and fome fuch odd things are Bug-bears, that wou'd have frighten'd his *Ariftophanes,* from his freedom, if the *Athenian* Law, like ours, had fe-cur'd Vice, and Folly in the *Great ones,* from the attaques of Poets. He ought therefore either to moderate his·Indignation at our Poets for only expofing the Common Life of Mankind, or if he wou'd have none but *Statefmen, and Generals* ri-dicul'd, let him lead the Dance ; and fear not the Succefs of *Ariftophanes,* being fo well qualify'd for a *Farce-Wright;* his Propenfity to that, influen-cing perhaps his Judgment in favour of this Greek Poet, above all thofe that fucceeded him. Tho' *Quintilian,* as good a Judge as Mr. *Rymer* fays of *Menander,* not *Ariftophanes , meo judicio diligenter lectus, ad cuncta quæ præcipimus efficienda fufficit, Ita omnium Imaginem in vitâ Expreffit. Tanta in eo inveniendi Copia, eloquendi, facultas, ita omnibus Re-bus, Perfonis, affectibus accommodatus , ut omnibus ejufdem operis Autoribus tenebras obduxerit.* But Mr. *Rymer* muft be fingular in his Opinion, or he cou'd not keep up his Character, as he is in the

meaning-

meaning of those two Verses he quotes, *Pag.* 25.

Non minimum meruere decus, vestigia Græca,
Ausi deserere, & celebrare Domestica facta.

He will have it, that *non Minimum* is but a *faint*
Commendation; tho' 'tis evident from the best
of the Latin Authors, that *non Minimum* is us'd
for *Magnum*, if not *Maximum*. 'Tis perhaps us'd
by *Horace* as a more Modest expression of their
Worth, that he might not incur the imputation of
flattering by a stronger Praise, those who were
living. But I defie him to produce *non Minimum*
in *Cicero*, or any other Author of Note, in a sense
less than *Magnum*. Nor does that Quotation out
of the Sixth Book of *Virgil's Æneids*, prove at all
that *Virgil* gave up the Cause, and yielded the
Grecians more excellent in Poetry than the Latins,
any more than *Horace* did in the Epistle by him
quoted, for thus it runs,

Excudent alii spirantia mollius æra,
Credo quidem, vivos ducent de murmore vultus:
Orabunt causas melius, cæliq; meatus,
Describent radio, & surgentia sidera dicent.
Tu Regere imperio populos Romane memento;
(Hæ tibi erunt Artes) pacisq; imponere Morem,
Parcere subjectis & debellare superbos.

From which 'tis evident that he meant only
this, that *Governing Nations*, and Justice shou'd
be their chief Care, and greatest Art, not that
he

he thought the *Romans* did not excell the *Grecians* in others too ; for, I believe, none will deny but *Cicero* was a greater Orator than *Demosthenes*, or at least as great, and that *Virgil* was as great a Poet, as *Homer*.   And for other Arts, *Pliny* was of opinion, That the *Romans* excell'd the *Grecians* ev'n in 'em, as well as that of *Governing*, when he says in the 36th Book of his *Natural History*, That he *wou'd shew the World conquer'd in the Works of Art, as well as by the Sword,* and then proceeds to *Painting, Statuary,* &c.

But, Sir, I fear, I shall tire your patience shou'd I touch upon e'ery *Page* ; I'll therefore step to P. 63. and with that and the 65th. make an end of my *Reflections*, and then examine more particularly what relates to *Shakespear*. P. 62. he expresses himself much against Rhime in Plays, by which he not only shews his Mind is much alter'd since he writ *Edgar* in Rhime ; but also makes it the distinctive mark of *Heroic* Verse in *English*, as the numbers of *Hexameters* are of Latin Heroics :   But he gives us no Reason for the Parallel, for that indeed wou'd be to break an old custom, which he's very fond of.   If therefore I cou'd produce no Argument against him in particular, yet must, a bare denial, be granted equivalent to a bare Assertion : but the matter is not so barren of Reason, as to be destitute of a very convincing proof of the contrary, *viz.* The *Numbers* or *Feet* distinguish the Latin Verse, and the *Numbers* of *Hexameters* are very different from those of *Jambics*, which is the Verse most us'd,

at

at least out of the *Chorus*, in Tragedy, so in English 'tis the Feet, or Numbers that distinguish Heroic Verse from all others, whereas the Numbers are the same in blanc Verse, as in Rhime; so that they are equally Heroic Verse, and *Milton*'s *Paradise lost*, is a sufficient proof of this; so that according to Mr. *Rymer* all Verse of ten Syllables are as improper for Tragedies in English, as Pentameters are in Latin, for that is the consequence of his Arguments,

The second Paragraph of *P.* 65, That furnishes me with the subject of my last Reflection, is a Master-piece, compos'd of his belov'd ingredients, the **unaccountable**, and the **unintelligible**; for he tells us, *that since the decay of the Roman Empire, this Island has been more fortunate in Matters of Poetry, than any of our Neighbours,* &c. I must tell him that it must be a *good-natur'd* Reader *that* (after all he has said) *shall take his word for't*; for I can't see how he can make it out, if *Shakespear* be so far from a Poet, as not to be fit to write Ballads, or what's all one, as ignorant of Nature as any Pug in *Barbary*; if *Ben Johnson* be guilty of such Stupidity; if *Milton*, as he commonly asserts, have nothing in him; and *Beaumont* and *Fletcher* are such, as he represents 'em. He wou'd do well to fix this Excellence above our Neighbours somewhere; for hitherto he has done nothing but arraign our greatest Poets. But the latter end of this Paragraph as unintelligible as 'tis, must I find pass for a Proof of this, if we will have any from him. *We find* (says he) *the British Poetry to this day:*

G   To

To confirm which, he proceeds thus. *One of our oldeſt Medals bears a harp on the Revers, with the Name* Kunobuline *around it* : But what of that good Sir? What if it had *Merlin, Gildas*, and half a ſcore more about it, what's the conſequence? I adviſe him in his next Book not to put his Friends to ſuch trouble to underſtand him ; for my part I cou'd never yet meet with an *Oedipus* to ſolve the Ridle ; for what has the oldeſt Medal to do with the proof of our having the *Britiſh* Poetry to this day, unleſs the other ſide of the Medal had furniſh'd us with ſome of it, if he draw not the odd conſequence from the Harp; that where there is Muſic, there muſt be Poetry ; as where there is Smoak, there muſt be Fire, according to the laudable Obſervation of our Matrons of Antiquity.

But there needed no Medal of *Kunobuline* to be produc'd ; for the proof of the early uſe of Potry in this Iſland, and that long before *Virgil* writ. The Britiſh *Bards* are enough to juſtifie that ; we need not wait till the decay of the *Roman Empire*, witneſs *Lucan*, Lib. 3. who writ of times that preceded *Virgil*.

Vos quoq; qui fortes animas, belloq; peremptas
Laudibus in longum vates dimittitis ævum
Plurima ſecuri fudiſtis carmina Bardi.

But what's this to the Confirmation of his Aſſertion, that next the *Romans* we excell'd in Poetry? 'Tis not the number of Years, nor Poems that will eſtabliſh our Excellence, but the Quality ; 'tis their

Per-

Perfection, that muſt give us the advantage of our Neighbours.

But to expect *Reaſon*, *Method*, (without which all is confuſion) and *Meaning* from this Author is in vain, ſince he tells us in a former Eſſay he can keep to no *Method* or *Form*, and that he is not cut out for penning any Treatiſe. But then why, in the Name of dullneſs, does he fly in the Face of Nature, and ſpight of her appear in Print, not only as an Author, but Judge, bringing to his Tribunal, thoſe who were qualified with what he extremly wants, *viz.* A *Genius* and *Judgment*: his *Judgment* being ſo weak, that he cou'd not keep Coherence through one only Page. Being thus qualify'd, no doubt his cenſure of the admirable Shakeſpear, muſt be extraordinary, which I ſhall, after I have premis'd ſome general Conſiderations examine.

To ſurvey the *Antients* with an impartial Eye 'twou'd make one wonder at thoſe *extravagant Encomiums*, and that inexpreſſible Advantage above the Moderns' ſome of our *Dogmatic* Critics give 'em, were there not an extraordinary *Vanity*, in extolling their Performances and Virtues, becauſe by that means they arrogate to themſelves the Deputation of underſtanding them better, than other Men. This makes *Rapin* tell us what an univerſal Genius *Homer* was; and that all the Arts and Sciences are to be learn'd from his Works, tho' ſome others perhaps, not leſs able to underſtand him, can not diſcover any ſuch Matter, as the Author of the *Dialogues of the Dead*, very wittily

inti-

intimates in the Dialogue betwixt *Homer* and *Æsop*. These Gentlemen wou'd cover all the Absurdities of this Poet, with the specious *Whim* of *Allegory*, never thought of by *Homer* himself. But he may thank his Fate for allotting him a time so much remote from ours, else they wou'd not be fond of him to so unreasonable an excess, since they can't allow no excuse for smaller Faults in their own Countrymen of a later date, such ill Patriots are these Partial Critics; for I defie Mr. *Rymer*, and all of his Opinion to parallel in 𝕾𝖍𝖆𝖐𝖊𝖘𝖕𝖊𝖆𝖗, the *Wounds*, the *Hatreds*, the *Battles*, and *Strifes* of the Gods. And he must confess, if he be not a sworn Enemy to all Reason, that *Homer's Juno* is a Character far beneath, and more disproportionable, than that of *Desdemona*, tho' the first be of the Queen of the Gods, *Joves* Sister and his Wife, and the other a Senators, Daughter of *Venice*, Young Innocent, and Tender. If *Desdemona* be too humble for Tragedy, and discover not Elevation of Soul enough for her *Birth* and *Fortune*: *Homer's Juno* must be much too low for an *Heroic* Poem, having no Parallel for Scolding but at *Billinsgate*. For the furious curtain Lectures of a City Wife, who is supream Lady at home, are nothing to hers. This *Jupiter* finds, when the only Remedy he has left to stop her Mouth, is to threaten to thrash her *Divine Jacket*, which makes her Son *Vulcan* something concern'd about the Shame 'twill be to have his Goddess Mother suffer the *Bastinade* before the Heavenly Crew. Where is the Nature? Where the Reason of this?

If

If the Nobleneſs of *his* Thoughts, the Majeſty of *his* Expreſſion, and Variety of *his* Numbers made the ſucceeding Ages ſo fond of *Homer*, as to find ſome Excuſe for his failures, in Conduct and Characters; is not *Shakeſpear* more ungenerouſly dealt with, whoſe Faults are made to a pretence to deny all his Beauties and Excellence?

But 'tis not theſe Inſtances in the Prince of the *Greek* Peots, (with many more, both as to the Conduct and Characters) that influence me to encline to a better Opinion of the Moderns (I mean of my own Country) than Mr. *Rymer*; and ſome of the Graver *Pedants* of the Age; the Excellence I find in *Shakeſpear* himſelf, commands a juſter Veneration; for in his Thoughts and Expreſſions he diſcovers himſelf Maſter of a very juſt Obſervation of things; ſo that if he had (which I deny) no Learning, his natural parts wou'd ſufficiently have furniſh'd him with better Ethics, than our *Hypercritic* allows him. But that which aggravates his Malice is, he extends his cenſure to Ben himſelf, whoſe skill in *Moral Philoſophy*, we ſuppoſe, at leaſt equal to his: But to give the World ſome Satisfaction, that Shakeſpear has had as great a Veneration paid his Excellence by Men of unqueſtion'd parts, as this I now expreſs for him, I ſhall give ſome Account of what I have heard from your Mouth, Sir, about the noble Triumph he gain'd over all the *Ancients*, by the Judgment of the ableſt *Critics* of that time.

The Matter of Fact (if my Memory fail me not) was this, Mr. *Hales*, of *Eaton*, affirm'd that

he

he wou'd shew all the Poets of Antiquity, out-done by 𝕾𝖍𝖆𝖐𝖊𝖘𝖕𝖊𝖆𝖗, in all the Topics, and common places made use of in Poetry. The E-nemies of *Shakespear* wou'd by no means yield him so much Excellence ; so that it came to a Resolu-tion of a trial of Skill upon that Subject; the place agreed on for the Dispute, was Mr. *Hales*'s Chamber at *Eaton* ; a great many Books were sent down by the Enemies of this Poet, and on the appointed day, my Lord *Falkland*, Sir *John Suck-ling*, and all the Persons of Quality that had Wit and Learning, and interested themselves in the Quarrel, met there, and upon a thorough Disqui-sition of the point, the Judges chose by agreement out of this Learned and Ingenious Assembly, una-nimously gave the Preference to 𝕾𝖍𝖆𝖐𝖊𝖘𝖕𝖊𝖆𝖗. And the *Greek* and *Roman* Poets were adjudg'd to Vail at least their Glory in that to the English *Here*. I cou'd wish, Sir, you wou'd give the Pub-lic a juster Account of this Affair, in Vindication of that Poet, I know you extreamly esteem, and whom none but you excels.

Shall we therefore still admire *Shakespear* with these Learned and Ingenious Gentlemen, or put him in a Class below *Sternold* or *Flecknoe*, with Mr. *Rymer*, because he has not come close to the Rules *Aristotle* drew from the Practice of the *Greek* Poets, whom nothing it seems can please, but the Antic Forms and Methods of the *Athenian* Stage, or what comes up, and sticks close to them in our Language.

I

I can see no Reason why we shou'd be so very fond of imitating them here, without better proofs than the Critical Historiographer has produc'd. 'Tis certain, the *Grecians* had not the advantage of us in *Physics*, or any other part of Philosophy, which with them chiefly consisted in words; they were a Talkative People; and being fond of the Opinion of Learning, more than the thing it self, as the most speedy way to gain that, stop'd their Enquiries on Terms, as is evident from their *Sophistry* and *Dialectic's*. There can be no dispute among the Learned, but that we excel them in these Points. Since the time of *Des Cartes*, when the Dictates of *Greece* began to be laid aside, what a Progress has been made in the discovery of Nature? and what Absurdities laid open in the School Precepts, and Terms of *Aristotle*.

But Ethics is a Study not so abstruse as the search of Natural Causes and Effects; a nice Observation of Mankind will furnish a sensible Man with them; which makes me unable to ghess how the *Greeks* shou'd have so monstrous an advantage over us in this particular, as some wou'd give them, who are so far behind us in things of greater difficulty; but it can't be otherways whilst we make that Age and Nation the Standard of Excellence without regard to the difference of Custom, Age, Climate, &c. But I question not to make it appear hereafter, that we much surpass the Greeks and Latins, at least in Dramatick Poetry. As for *Expression* (the difference of Language consider'd) the Merits of which is proportion'd to the

Idea

Idea it prefents to the Mind, and for *Thought*, as well as for Defign. And had you, Sir, but given us an *Heroic Poem*, you had put the Controverfie out of doubt as to the *Epic* too, as your *Oedipus* (for all the *Quantum mutatus*, of which a-nother time) your *All for Love*, and fome other of your Plays have in the *Dramatic*, in the efteem of impartial Judges.

Had our *Critic* entertain'd but common Juftice for the *Heroes* of his *Own Country*, he wou'd have fet *Shakefpear*'s Faults in their true Light, and di-ftinguifh'd betwixt his, and the Vices of the Age ; for as *Rapin* (a much *jufter* and more Candid *Cri-tic*) obferves, the Poet often falls into Vices by complying with the Palate of the Age he lives in ; and to this may we truly and juftly refer a great many of thefe Faults 𝕾𝖍𝖆𝖐𝖊𝖘𝖕𝖊𝖆𝖗 is guilty of. For, He not having that advantage the *Greek* Poets had, of a proper Subfiftence, or to be provided for at the Public Charge, what Fruit he was to expect of his Labors, was from the Applaufe of the Audience ; fo that his chief aim was to pleafe them ; who not being fo Skilful in *Criticifms*, as Mr. *Rymer*, wou'd not be pleas'd without fome Extravagances mingl'd in (tho' contrary to) the Characters fuch, and fuch a Player was to Act. This is the Reafon that moft of his *Tragedies* have a mixture of fomething Comical ; the *Dalilah*, of the Age muft be brought in, the Clown, and the Valet jefting with their Betters, if he refolv'd not to difoblige the Auditors. And I'm affur'd from very good hands, that the Perfon that Acted

Jago

Jago was in much esteem for a Comœdian, which made *Shakespear* put several words, and expressions into his part (perhaps not so agreeable to his Character) to make the Audience laugh, who had not yet learnt to endure to be serious a whole Play. This was the occasion of that particular place so much houted at by our *Historiographer Royal*,

Awake, what ho, Brabantio, *&c.*
An old black Ram is tupping your white Ewe,&c.

This Vice of the Age it was that perverted many of his Characters in his other Plays: Nor cou'd it be avoided if he wou'd have his Audience sit the Play out, and receive that Profit, that is the chief End of all Poets. To this same Cause may be attributed all those Quibbles, and playing upon words, so frequent in some part of him, as well as that Language that may seem too rough, and forc'd to the Ear, up, and down in some of the best of his Plays.

After all, the Head of his Accusation is, That 'tis not improbable, that *Shakespear* was ignorant of the Rules of *Aristotle's Poetics*; and was imperfect in the three Unities of Time, Place, and Action, which *Horace* in his *Art of Poetry* gives no Rules about: for that which I have heard quoted from him, has no relation to the *Dramatic Unities,*

Deniq; sit, quod vis, simplex duntaxat & unum.

as

as is evident from what goes before ; but to the
Coherence, Uniformity, and Equality of any Poem in general——

———*Amphora cœpit*
Instirui, currente Rota cur urceus exit.

'Tis only the Conclusion of what he proposes
about Seven Verses before,

Inceptis gravibus, & magna Professis, &c.

and this of *Petronius* is a just Interpretation of it
in my opinion,

*Præterea ne sententiæ emineant extra corpus ora-
tionis expressæ sed intecto vestibus colore niteant.* That
is, it gives only a Rule that all Poems be of a
Piece and Equal.

So that since he cou'd gather no Instructions
in this Point from *Horace*, we may excuse him for
transgressing against them : and this defect his
greatest Admirers confess'd before his Useless piece
of ill-natur'd censure, and cou'd have Pardon'd
Mr. *Rymer*, had he gone no farther ; But when
he Robs him of all *Genius*, and denies him the
Elevation of a *Shirly*, a *Fleckno*, or a *Jordan*, we
must modestly return his Complement, and tell
him, That never a *Blackamoor* (as he learnedly
terms a *Negro*) in the Western Plantations, but
must have a better tast of Poetry than himself;
and that 'tis evident from the Woman Judges,
whose Judgment, he assures us, seldom errs, by
their

their continual Approbation of *Othello*, *Hamlet*, &c, he is in the Wrong.

But shou'd we grant him that *Shakespear* wanted Art (tho' *Ben Johnson* denies it) can he from thence infer he was no Poet? The dispute of which confers most to the forming a Poet, (I mean, a Compleat one) Art, or Nature, was never yet agreed on; *Horace* joyns them, *Quintillian* and some others give it to *Nature* : But, till this Gentleman, never did any Man yield it wholly to *Art* ; for that all his Arguments both in this or his former Book seem to drive at.

A nice Observation of Rules, is a Confinement a great *Genius* cannot bear, which naturally covets Liberty; and tho' the *French*, whose *Genius*, as well as Language, is not strong enough to rise to the Majesty of Poetry, are easier reduc'd within the Discipline of Rules, and have perhaps of late Years, more exactly observ'd 'em. yet I never yet met with any Englishman, who wou'd preferr their Poetry to ours. All that is great of Humane things, makes a nearer approach to the *Eternal Perfection* of Greatness, and extends as much as possible its limits toward being Boundless : 'Tis not govern'd by Common Rules and Methods, but Glories in a *Noble Irregularity* ; and this not only in Writings, but Actions of some Men. *Alexander*, *Cæsar*, *Alcibiades*, &c. seem'd actuated by other Principles than the common Maxims that govern the *Rest* of Humane Kind; and in them the greatest Virtues have been mixt with great Vices, as well as the Writings of *Shake-spear* ;

spear ; yet are they granted *Heroes*, and so must He be confess'd a Poet : The *Heroes* Race are all like *Achilles*. *Jura negunt, sibi nata.*

But as I do not think that to be a *Great Man*, one must necessarily be wholly exempt from Rules, so I must grant, That *Virgil*, *Sophocles*, and *Your Self* are very *Great*, tho' generally very Regular ; But these are Rarities so uncommon, that Nature has produc'd very few of them, and like the Phœnixes of Honesty, that live up to the Precepts of Morality, ought to have public Statues erected to them. But yet the less perfect ought not to be Rob'd of their Merits, because they have defects, especially when the Number of those exceed these, as in *Shakespear*, all whose Faults have not been able to frustrate his obtaining the end of All just Poems, *Pleasure* and *Profit*. To deny this, wou'd be to fly in the Face of the known experience of so many Years. He has (I say) in most, if not all, of his Plays attain'd the full end of Poetry *Delight*, and *Profit*, by moving Terror and Pity for the Changes of Fortune, which Humane Life is subject to, by giving us a lively and just Image of them (the best Definition of a Play) for the Motion of these Passions afford us *Pleasure*, and their Purgation *Profit*. Besides, there are few or none of those many he has writ, but have their Just Moral, not only of more general Use and Advantage, but also more naturally the Effect of them, than that of the *Oedipus* of *Sophocles*, as may be soon perceiv'd by any one that will give himself the trouble of a little Thought,

and

and which will in some measure appear from what I have to say in the particular Defence I shall now make of

Othello.

To begin with the *Fable* (as our Critic has done) I must tell him, he has as falsly, as ridiculously represented it, which I shall endeavour to put in a Juster light.

Othello *a Noble* Moor, *or* Negro, *that had by long Services, and brave Acts establish'd himself in the Opinion of the* Senate *of* 𝔘𝔢𝔫𝔦𝔠𝔢, *wins the Affections of* Desdemona, *Daughter to* Brabantio *one of the* Senators, *by the moving account he gives of the imminent Dangers he had past, and hazards he had ventur'd through, a belief of which his known Virtue confirm'd, and unknown to her Father Marries her, and carries her (with the leave of the Senate) with him to* Cyprus, *his Province. He makes* Cassio *his Lieutenant, tho'* Jago, *had sollicited it by his Friends for himself, which Refusal joyn'd with a jealousie, that* Othello *had had to do with his Wife, makes him contrive the destruction of* Cassio, *and the* Moor, *to gratifie his Revenge, and Ambition. But having no way to revenge himself sufficiently on the* Moor, *from whom he suppos'd he had receiv'd a double* Wrong, *proportionable to the injury, but this, he draws him with a great deal of Cunning into a Jealousie of his Wife, and that by a chain of Circumstances contriv'd to that purpose, and urg'd with all the taking insinuations*

insinuations

insinuations imaginable; particularly by a Handker-chief, he had convey'd to Cassio *(which* Jago'*s Wife stole from* Desdemona) *to convince the* Moor *his Wife was too familiar with him, having parted with such a favour to him, which she had on her Marriage receiv'd from* Othello, *with the strictest charge of preserving, it being a Gift of his Mother of Curious Work, and secret Virtue.* Othello, *by these means, won to a belief of his own Infamy, resolves the Murder of those, he concluded guilty, viz.* Cassio, *and his Wife;* Jago *officiously undertakes, the dispatching of* Cassio, *having got his Commission already, but is disappointed of his design, employing one* Roderigo *to that purpose, who had follow'd him from* Venice, *in hopes by his means to enjoy* Desdemona; *as* Jago *had promis'd him. But the* Moor *effectually puts his Revenge in Execution on his Wife, which is no sooner done, but he's convinc'd of his Error, and in remorse kills himself, whilst* Jago, *the Cause of all this Villany, having slain his Wife for discovering it, is born away to a more ignominious* Punishment, *as more proportion'd to his* Villanies.

The *Fable* to be perfect must be *Admirable* and *Probable*, and as it approaches those two, 'tis more or less perfect in its kind. *Admirable*, is what is *uncommon*, and *extraordinary*. *Probable*; is what is agreeable to common Opinion. This must be the Test of this *Fable* of *Othello*; but then we must not take it, as given us by our Drolling Critic, who very truely confesseth in his former Book, (and in that he is no Changeling) he must be

merry

merry out of Seaſon, as he always is ; but as I have laid it down. elſe we ſhou'd do *Shakeſpear* a great deal of Injuſtice.

I ſuppoſe none will deny that it is *Admirable*: that is, compos'd of Incidents that happen not e'ery day , his Antagoniſt confeſſes as much ; there is therefore nothing but the *Probability* of it attaqu'd by him, which I queſtion not either wholly to prove, or at leaſt to ſet it on the ſame bottom with the beſt of *Sophocles*, that of his *Oedipus*.

Firſt, to ſee whether he have ſinn'd againſt Probability , let us conſider what our Caviller objects, all which may be reduc'd to two Points. Firſt, That 'tis not probable that the Senate of *Venice* (tho' it uſually employ Strangers) ſhould employ a *Moor* againſt the *Turk* : neither is it in the next place *probable* , that *Deſdemona* ſhou'd be in Love with him. On this turns all the Accuſation, this is the very Head of his offending.

All the Reaſon he gives, or rather implies, for the firſt Improbability is, That 'tis not likely the State of *Venice*, wou'd employ a *Moor*, (taking him for a *Mahometan*) againſt the *Turk*, becauſe of the mutual Bond of Religion. He, indeed ſays not ſo , but takes it for granted that *Othello* muſt be rather for the *Turkiſh* intereſt than the *Venetian*, becauſe a *Moor*. But, I think (nor does he oppoſe it with any reaſon) the Character of the *Venetian* State being to employ Strangers in their Wars, it gives ſufficient ground to

our

our Poet , to suppose a *Moor* employ'd by 'em
as well as a *German*; that is a *Christian Moor*, as
Othello is represented by our Poet, for from such
a *Moor*, there cou'd be no just fear of treachery
in favour of the *Mahometans*.   He tells us ——

I fetch my Life and Being from Men of Royal Siege.

Supposing him therefore the Son or Nephew of
the Emperor of *Monomotopa*, *Æthiopia* or *Congo*,
forc'd to leave his Country for Religion, or any
other occasion, coming to *Europe* by the conve-
nience of the *Portugueze* Ships, might after several Fortunes, serve first as a Voluntier till he had
signaliz'd himself, and prov'd himself worthy of
Command ; part of this may very reasonably be
drawn from what the Poet makes him say.   Now
upon this Supposition, it appears more rational,
and probable, the *Venetians* shou'd employ a Stranger, who wholly depended on themselves, and
whose Country was too remote, to influence him
to their prejudice , than other Strangers , whose
Princes may in some measure direct their Actions
for their own Advantage.   But that *Othello* is suppos'd to be a Christian is evident from the Second
Act, and from these words of *Jago* ; —— *And then*
for her to Win the Moor, *were't to renounce his* Bap-
tism, *&c.* Why therefore an *African* Christian
may not by the *Venetians* be suppos'd to be as zealous against the *Turks*, as an *European* Christian, I
cannot imagine.   So that this Bustle of *Littora*
littoribus Contraria, &c. is only an inconsiderate
amusement

Amusement, to shew how little the Gentleman was troubled with thought when he wrote it.

No more to the purpose, is that Heat he expresses against *Shakspears* giving a Name to his *Moor*, though *Cinthio* did not, though History did not warrant it. For this can be no more objected to our Poet, then the perverting the Character of *Dido*, and confounding the Chronology to bring her to the time of *Æneas*, is to *Virgil*; the first as 'tis not mention'd in History, so it does not contradict it; but the last is a plain opposition to express History, and Chronology. If *Virgil* be allow'd his Reason for doing that, *Shakespear* is not to seek for one for what he has done. 'Twas necessary to give his *Moor* a place of some Figure in the World, to give him the greater Authority, and to make his Actions the more Considerable, and what place more likely to fix on, than *Venice*, where Strangers are admitted to the highest Commands in Military Affairs.

'Tis granted, a *Negro* here does seldom rise above a Trumpeter, nor often perhaps higher at *Venice*. But then that proceeds from the Vice of Mankind, which is the Poets Duty as he informs us, to correct, and to represent things as they should be, not as they are. Now 'tis certain, there is no reason in the nature of things, why a *Negro* of equal Birth and Merit, should not be on any equal bottom, with a *German*, *Hollander*, *French-man*, &c. The Poet, therefore ought to do justice to Nations, as well as Persons, and

H   let

set them to rights, which the common course of things confounds. The same reason stands in force for this, as for punishing the Wicked, and making the Virtuous fortunate, which as *Rapin*, and all the Critics agree, the Poet, ought to do, though it generally happens otherways. The Poet has therefore well chosen a polite People, to cast off this customary Barbarity , of confining Nations, without regard to their Virtue , and Merits, to slavery, and contempt for the meer Accident of their Complexion.

I hope I have brought by this time as convincing proofs for the probability in this particular, as Mr. *Rymer* has against it, if I have not wholly gain'd my Point. Now therefore I shall proceed to the probability of *Desdemona*'s Love for the *Moor*, which I think is somthing more evident against him.

Whatever he aims at in his inconsistant Ramble against this, may be reduc'd to the *Person* and the *Manner*. Against the *Person* he quotes you two Verses out of *Horace*, that have no more reference to this, than——*in the Beginning God made the Heaven and the Earth*, has to the proof of the *Jus Divinum* of lay Bishops, the Verses are these,

Sed non ut placidis coeant immitia, non ut Serpentes avibus geminentur, tiegribus agni.

unless he can prove that the Colour of a Man alters his Species, and turns him into a *Beast* or *Devil.* 'Tis such a vulgar Error, so criminal a fond-

fondneſs of our Selves, to allow nothing of Humanity to any but our own Acquaintance of the fairer hew ; that I wonder a Man, that pretends to be at all remov'd from the very Dreggs of the thoughtleſs Mob, ſhould eſpouſe it in ſo public a manner a Critic too, who puts the Poet : in mind of correcting the common corruptions of Cuſtom. Any Man that has convers'd with the beſt Travels, or read any thing of the Hiſtory of thoſe parts, on the continent of *Africa*, diſcover'd by the *Portugueze*, muſt be ſo far from robbing the *Negroes* of ſome Countrys there of *Humanity*, that they muſt grant them not only greater Heroes, nicer obſervers of Honour, and and all the Moral Virtues that diſtinguiſh'd the old *Romans*, but alſo much better Chriſtians (where Chriſtianity is profeſs'd) than we of *Europe* generally are. They move by a nobler Principle, more open, free and generous, and not ſuch ſlaves to ſordid Intereſt.

After all this, *Othello* being of *Royal Blood*, and a Chriſtian, where is the diſparity of the Match If either ſide is advanc'd, 'tis *Deſdemona*. And why muſt this Prince though a Chriſtian , and of known and experienc'd *Virtue*, *Courage*, and *Conduct* , be made ſuch a Monſter, that the *Venetian* Lady can't love him without perverting Nature ? Experience tells us, that there's nothing more common than Matches of this kind, where the Whites, and Blacks cohabit, as in both the *Indies*: and Even here at home, Ladys that have not wanted white Adorers have indulg'd their A-

morous

morous Dalliances, with their Sable Lovers, without any of *Othellos's* Qualifications, which is proof enough, that Nature and Custom, have not put any such unpassable bar betwixt Creatures of the same kind, because of different colors, which I hope will remove the improbability of the Person, especially when the powerful Auxilarys of extraordinary Merit and Vertues come to plead with a generous Mind.

The probability of the *Person* being thus confirmed, I shall now consider that of the *Manner* of his obtaining her *Love.* To this end we must still keep in mind the known and experienc'd Virtue of the *Moor* which gave Credit, and Authority to what he said; and then we may easily suppose the story of his Fortunes, and Dangers, would make an impression of Pity, and admiration at least on the bosom of a Woman, of a noble and generous Nature. No *Man* of any generous Principle, but must be touch'd at suff'ring Virtue, and value the noble sufferer, whose Courage and Bravery, bears him through uncommon Trials and extraordinary Dangers. Nor would it have less force on a Woman of any principle of Honour and tenderness; she must be mov'd and pleas'd with the Narration, she must admire his constant Virtue, and Admiration is the first step to Love, which will easily gain upon those who have once entertain'd it.

Dido in *Virgil* was won by the *Trojan* stranger she never saw before, by the relation of his fortunes and Escapes; and some particulars of the Nar-

Narration of *Æneas*, carrys full as ridiculous and absurd a Face as any thing, *Othello* says; the most trifling of which is,

> *And of the Cannibals that each other eat*
> *the* Anthropophagi, *and Men whose Heads*
> *do grow beneath their Shoulders.*

for all the rest is admirably fine, though our wonderful Critic can't relish it, there is a moving Beauty in each Line, the words are well chosen, and the Image they give great, and Poetical; what an Image does *Desarts Idle* give? that very Epithet is a perfect *Hypotyposis,* and seems to place me in the midst of one, where all the active hurry of the World is lost; but all that I can say, will not reach the excellence of that Epithet so many properties of such a place meet in it. But as for the *Cannibals,* &c. *and the Men whose Heads grow beneath their Shoulders.* I have heard it condemn'd by Men whose tast I generally approve, yet must they give me leave to dissent from them here, and permit me either wholly to justifie *Shakespear,* even here, or at least to put him on an equal bottom with *Virgil,* in his most beautiful part. For the fault lyes either in the *Improbability* of those things, or their *Impertinence* to the business in Hand. First Probability we know is built on common Opinion; but 'tis certain the *Canibals* have been generally believed, and that with very good grounds of Truth; so that there can be no doubt of the probability of that.

Next

Next for the *Men whose Heads grow beneath their
Shoulders*, though that is not establish'd on so good
a Foundation as Truth ; yet the general Tradi-
tionary belief of it in those days, is sufficient to
give it a poetical probability. As this was not
Improbable, so neither was it *Impertinent*, for 'tis
certain, that whatever contributed to the raising
her Idea of his Dangers and Escapes, must conduce to his aim, but to fall into the Hands of
those, whom not only the fury of War, but that
of Custom makes Cruel, heightens the danger,
and by consequence the Concern, especially in a
young Lady possess'd with the legend of the Nur-
sery, whence she must have amazing Ideas of the
Danger of the brave *Moor* from them.

But at worst, *Shakespear* is on as good a bottom
as *Virgil*, in this particular ; the Narrative of
Æneas, that won the Heart of *Dido*, has many
things full as trifling and absurd as this, if not
far more ? For is there not as much likelyhood
that there shou'd be a People that have their
Heads grow beneath their Shoulders, as the
Race of the *Cyclops*, that have but one Eye,
just beneath their Forheads, and that *Polyphemus* his Eye was as big as a *Grecian* Shield,
or the Sun ; or that he cou'd wade through the
Sea, without being up to his middle. Can there
be invented any thing so unnatural as the Harpys
in the third Book, who had the Faces of Virgins,
Wings, Feathers , *&c.* Of Birds, and a human
Voice, as is evident from *the infælix vates*, that
foretold 'em they shou'd not build their destin'd
City,

City, till they had eaten their Tables, or Tren-
chers, (which by the way was a trivial and ridi-
lous fort of a pun, as the event fhew'd, when
Iulus found out the Jeft,) nor is *Scylla* a more
natural mixture. But let's hear the defcription of
all three, from *Virgil* himfelf, leaft I be thought
to injure his Memory, firft of the Harpys in the
Strophades:

Virginei volucrum vultus, fædiſſima ventris,
Proluvies, uncæq; Manus, & pallida femper
Ora fame. ———

The beginning of *Horace*'s Art of Poetry, *Huma-*
no Capiti, &c. feems a Copy of this; nor is *Scylla*
a more *Homogeneous* Compofition. ———

At Scyllam cæcis cohibet fpelunca latebris
Ora exfertantem & naves in faxa trahentem.
Prima hominis facies, & pulchro peƈtore virgo
Pube tenus, poſtrema immani Corpore priſtis
Delphinum Caudas utero commiſſa luporum.

Then for the Cyclop *Polyphemus*, the *Grecian* he
takes abord, tells him his Eye is

Argolici clypei, aut Phæbeæ lampadis Inſtar.

and a little after left this fhou'dbe taken as an hyperbolical magnifying it by the terror of the fear-
ful *Greek* ; in his own Perfon, he fays of him

————Graditurq; per æquor.
Jam medium, necdum fluctus latera ardua tinxit.

The Abſurdities in *Homer* are much more numerous than thoſe in *Virgil.* (I mean thoſe that
muſt paſs for ſuch, if this in *Shakeſpear* is ſo,) But
becauſe they relate not to this particular, I ſhall
ſay nothing of them here. All theſe I have
remark'd in the Narration of *Æneas,* hinder'd
not, but that it won the Heart of *Dido,* though
firmly bent againſt a ſecond Amour,

> *Ille meos primus, qui me ſibi junxit amores*
> *Abſtulit: ille habeat ſecum, ſervetq; ſepulchro.*

eſpecially one that was not like to be ſo very Honorable. *Deſdemona* had no ſuch tye, to ſteel her
Heart againſt *Othello*'s Tongue, no reaſon to curb
that Paſſion ſhe ne'er felt before, when the prevailing Virtue of the *Moor,* attaqu'd her Heart;
well may we therefore believe *Deſdemona* ſhou'd
yield to the ſame force, that conquer'd *Dido,*
with all her Reſolutions and Engagements, to the
memory of *Sichœus.* Hear how ſhe cries out
to her Siſter *Ann,*

> *Quis novus hic noſtris ſucceſſit ſedibus hoſpes*
> *Quem ſeſe ore ferens? Quam forti pectore &*
> *   Armis?*
> *Credo equidem, nec vana fides, genus eſſe deorum.*
> *Degeneres animos timor arguit, heu quibus ille*
> *Jactatur fatis, quæ bella exhauſta canebat.*

and

and at the beginning of this fourth Book,

—— *Hærent infixi pectore Vultus*
Verbaq;——

and the latter end of the first Book confirms
this

Multa super Priamo Rogitans super Hectore multa.

cou'd *Æneas* his Story not, one jot more moving or probable make a meer stranger pass for
a God, with the Carthaginian Queen at first
hearing; and must it be incredible, that the
same shall not make *Othello* pass for so much as
a Man? The Parallel is so exact, that I am apt
to think, *Shakespear* took the Copy from *Virgil*.
Nor can it justly be urg'd, that these things were
believ'd by the *Romans*, since they were so far
from believing these trifles, that *Seneca* in his E-
pistles, laughs at those Fables, that constituted
their Hell, which was of much greater consequence. But supposing they were believ'd, the
same will hold good for *Shakespear*, in this particular, I vindicate him in: for 'tis built on as
vulgar and general a tradition, as these Fables of
old were, so that the advantage is equal betwixt
these two great Poets in this particular.

By this time, I hope our *Drolling Caviller*, will
grant it no such monstrous absurdity for the *Doge*
to say,

I

I think this Tale wou'd win my Daughter too.

fince without doubt, that fhort fumming up of what was only the fubject of his tale to *Defdemona*, with only the fuppofition of the particulars, muft move any generous Breft.

But fhould all I have faid fail of clearing the *Probability* of the *Fable* from Mr. *Rymers* Objections, yet ought not that to rob *Shakefpear* of his due Character of being a *Poet*, and a great *Genius*: unlefs he will for the fame reafon deny thofe prerogatives to *Homer*, and *Sophocles*. The former has often loft the *Probable*, in the *Admirable*, as any Book of the *Iliads* and *Odyffes* will prove; and the latter, as *Rapin* juftly obferves, has not kept to probability, ev'n in his beft performance, I mean in his *Oedipus Tyrannus*; for (as *Rapin* has it) Oedipus *ought not to have been ignorant of the affaffinate of Laius, the ignorance he's in of the Murder, which makes all the Beauty of the intrigue, is not probable*; and if a Man wou'd play the Droll with this *Fable* of *Oedipus*, it would furnifh full as ridiculous a Comment, as witty Mr. *Rymer* has done from this of *Othello*; and fure I can't err in imitating fo great a Critic.

Firft, then let all Men before they defend themfelves on the High-way, think well of what they do, left not being Mathematically fure he's at home, he kill his own Father, which perhaps is fomething dangerous in this Age, where fuch boon Blades frequent the Road, and fuch good-natur'd Ladies have the difpofing of our fate.   Next

Next, let e'ry Younger Brother, that ventures to ride in another Man's Boots, be very circumspect, lest he marries his own Mother.

Thirdly and Lastly, This may be a caution to the few Fools that doat on Virtue, that they trust to a rotten Reed that will be of little use to 'em, since all is whirl'd about by an unavoidable necessity.

These are much more the consequence of this *Fable* of *Oedipus*, than those wond'rous Truths, he draws from that of *Othello*. Nay, the moral *Sophocles* concludes his *Oedipus* with, will serve as justly for *Othello*, viz. *That no Man can be call'd happy before his Death*. But the whole *Fable* of *Oedipus*, tho' so much admir'd, is so very *singular* and *improbable*, that 'tis scarce possible, it ever cou'd have happen'd; on the other hand, the fatal Jealousie of *Othello*, and the Revenge of *Jago*, are the natural Consequences of our ungovern'd Passions; which by a prospect of such Tragical effects of their being indulg'd, may be the better regulated and govern'd by us. So that tho' *Othello* ends not so formally with a moral Sentence, as *Oedipus* does, yet it sets out one of much greater Value. If it be a fault in *Shakespear*, that it end not with such a sentence, *Sophocles* is guilty of no less in his *Philoctetes*, which not only concludes without any Moral, but is also incapable of being reduc'd to any, at least of any moment. Whereas the Morals of *Hamlet*, *Macbeth*, and most of *Shakespear*'s Plays, prove a lesson of mightier consequence than any in *Sophocles*, except the *Electra*, viz. that Usurpation, tho' it thrive a while, will at last be punish'd, &c. Besides the worst, and most

irre

irregular of *Shakespear*'s Plays, contains two or three such Fables, as that of *Philoctetes*, which answers not one of the ends of Poetry; for it neither pleases or profits, it moves neither Terror nor Compassion, containing only a dry account, without any variety of the perswasions of *Pyrrhus*, to get *Philoctetes* to go with him to *Troy* with the Arrows of *Hercules*; who, after he had by Treachery gain'd 'em, as foolishly restores 'em to him again, and *Troy* might have stood long enough, if *Hercules* had not come from the Gods, to bend the stubborn Fool, that rather chose to be miserable himself; with his endless πά πα, πά πα, πά πᾶς and his Complaints of his Foot, something like the *Tumors, Chilblains, Carnosities, &c.* rak'd together by Mr. *Rymer*. And all that can be learnt from this Play of *Sophocles* is;

First, That we never send Boys of our Errand, unless we have a God at command to make up the business he has spoil'd; if we mean our business shall be thoroughly done, and not the fate of a Nation sacrific'd to a pain in the Foot.

Secondly, Not to trust Strangers we never saw before, for a fair Tale, with our Safety and Treasure, without a Mathematical Demonstration of their Fidelity and Trust.

Lastly, That all Men with sore Feet shou'd not despair of a Cure.

But I have dwelt so long on the Fable, that I have not time enough to discuss the other parts, as the *Characters, Thoughts,* and *Expressions,* so fully as I ought; especially, the *Thought* and *Expression,*

sion, for 'twou'd require a Volumn near as big as *Shakespear*, to set them off according to their worth; with all the proofs from Grammar or Rhetoric of their Truth and Justness. The Fable is look'd upon by *Rapin*, and after him by our *Gleaner of Criticisms*, as the Soul of the Play, and therefore I may be excus'd for my prolixity in its defence, and allow'd a little more time for a full Justification of the other parts of *Shakespear*, attaqu'd with less Reason and Justice: Mr. *Rymer* has taken above ten Year to digest his Accusations, and therefore it can't in reason be thought I shou'd not in half so many days be able to perform all the work he has cut out : Nor can I proceed to a particular consideration of all the Characters of this Play at this time: *Desdemona* I think is the most faulty : but since our *Antagonist* will have *Jago*, the most *intollerable*, I shall confine my self to that.

What I have said in the beginning of my Vindication of *Shakespear*, must here be recollected on *Jago*'s behalf; besides which, I have some other considerations to offer, which I hope will lighten the insupportable load of Contempt, and Ridicule cast on him by our Caviller.

First, Therefore in our Judgment of *Jago*, we must follow the Rule of *Horace*, so much stood upon by Mr. *Rymer*.

Intererit multum
Cholcus an Assyrius, Thebis nutritus, an Argis.

We

We are not only to respect the profession of the Man in our Judgment of the Character, but we must also have an Eye to his Nation, the Country he was born in, and the prevailing temper of the People, with their National Vices ; by this Rule we shall find *Jago*, an *Italian*; by Nature *Selfish*, *Jealous*, *Reserv'd*, *Revengeful* and *Proud*, nor can I see any reason to suppose his Military Profession shou'd to powerfully influence him to purge away all these Qualities, and establish contrary in their room. Nor can I believe the quotation from *Horace*, which our Caviiler produces, can justly be extended to all degrees of Soldiers.

It runs thus in *Horace.*

——*Honoratum si forte reponis Achillem*
Impiger, Jracundus, Inexcrabilis, Acer,
Jura neget sibi Nata, nihil non arroget armis.

'Tis plain from what goes before, and what follows after that *Horace* meant not this, at least for a general Character of all Soldiers, but only as a direction for the drawing *Achilles*, or such a Hero ; for he's enumerating the *Manners*, of those public Characters, that were generally made use of by the *Romans* in their Tragedies, for this follows.

Sit Medea ferox invictaq; Flebilis Ino,
Persidus Ixion, Jo *vaga, tristis Orestes.*

And a few Lines before he is giving the Characters of several Professions and Ages, from whence he
proceeds

proceeds to these particular Characters of *Achilles*, *Jno, Medea*, *&c.* drawn from the known Stories of them, and this is confirm'd by what he joyns to this;

Siquid inexpertum scenæ committis, &c.

That is, if you take known Persons, that have for so many Ages trod the Stage, this must be their Character; but if you bring some new person on it, that was never there before, then take care that your Persons preserve that Character you give 'em at first, *&c.*

I know *Rapin* gives a Soldier these qualities; *Fierce, Insolent, Surly, Inconstant*, which partly are the effects of their manner of Life, but I can't conceive these to be opposite to those other in *Jago*. The *Characters* or *Manners*, as the same *Rapin* observes, are to be drawn from Experience; and that tells us, that they differ in Soldiers according to their Nature and Discipline; that also tells us that the Camp is not free from Designs, Supplantings, and all the effects of the most criminal of Passions, and this indeed is evident from the Draught *Homer* gives us of the Grecian Camp, where *Love* was not judg'd so contrary to the Character of a General, as Mr. *Rymer* wou'd have it thought: *Achilles* and *Agamemnon* having both their admir'd Captives. And let Mr. *Rymer* say what he please, I can prove that 'twas the Love of *Briseis*, that troubl'd *Achilles*, and confirm'd his anger, as well as the meer affront of having his prize taken

ken from him, but of that in another place. In short, the *Therſites* of *Homer* differs as much from the Soldiers of Mr. *Rymers* acquaintance, as *Jago* does; nor is he the only Soldier that cou'd diſſemble. *Sinon* in *Virgil*, and *Neoptolemus* in *Sophocles*, are as guilty of it as he.

But granting that *Jago's* Character is defective ſomething in the Manners, *Homer* and *Sophocles* have been guilty (the firſt much more, the other not much leſs) of the ſame: what are the Wounds, Scuffles, Paſſions, Adulteries, *&c.* Of the Gods and Goddeſſes, obvious to the meaneſt Capacity, and beyond all diſpute? Is not the Character of *Oedipus Coloneus* of *Sophocles*, as *Rapin* remarks, extreamly unproportionable to *Oedipus Tyrannus?* And tho' Mr. *Rymer* is ſo ſevere, to deny that the Character of *Jago* is that of a Soldier, becauſe ſo different from his Military Acquaintance; yet I'm confident he wou'd take it extreamly amiſs, If I ſhou'd deny him to be a Critic, becauſe ſo contrary to all the Critics that I have met with, playing the merry Droll, inſtead of giving ſerious and ſolid Reaſons for what he advances.

The other Characters of this Play I muſt defer till another time, as well as a thorough defence of his Thoughts and Expreſſion, both which he wholly denies him; and with an extravagantly wonderful Aſſurance publicly tells us; that the Neighing of a Horſe has more *Humanity*, (for that is his Wittyciſm) than the Tragical Flights of *Shakeſpear*.

Mr.

Mr. *Rymer*'s Friend *Rapin* tells us, that the Thoughts are the expression of the Manners, as Words are of Thoughts, that is the natural result of the Manners, which being already clear'd from his Accusations, the vindication of the Thoughts are included in them, as well as their Condemnation in his Charge against the other, for he disdains to be particular in his proof. Then for the Expressions of *Shakespear*, none but Mr. *Rymer* can find fault with 'em. The excellence of expression consists in this, that it bear a proportion to the Things; that is, that it give us a full Idea of 'em; that it be *apt, clear, natural, splendid,* and *numerous*. There is scarce a serious part of *Shakespear*, but has all these qualities in the Expression.

To omit several Scenes in *Hamlet*, particularly that betwixt him, and his Fathers Ghost: I'll only instance in two or three Speeches, that are, and have been on the Stage in our Memory, which may give some sample of the Poetry, Thought, and Expression of *Shakespear*. The first is in the *Midsummer Nights Dream*, now acted under the name of the *Fairy Queen*. Act the Third, *Titania* speaks thus;

Titan : *Be kind and courteous to this Gentleman,*
    Hop in his Walks, and Gambol in his Eyes,
    Feed him with Apricocks and Dewberrys,
    With purple Grapes, green Figgs and Mulberrys,
    The Hony Baggs steal from the Humble Bees ;
    And for Night Tapers crop their waxen Thighs,

I   *And*

And light them at the fiery Glow-worms Eyes ;
To have my Love to Bed and to Arise.
And pluck the Wings from painted Butter-flyes,
To fan the Moon Beams from his sleeping Eyes.
Nod to him Elves, and do him Courtesies.

is not this extreamly poetical and fine ? The next
I shall take from the 2d. Scene of *Richard* the
Second.

York. *Then as I said the Duke (great* Bullingrbook)
Mounted upon a hot and fiery Steed,
Which his aspiring Rider seem'd to know,
With slow but stately Grace kept on his course
While all Tongues cry'd God save the Bullingbrook.
You wou'd have thought the very Windows spoke,
So many greedy looks of Young and old,
Through Casements darted their desiring Eyes
Upon his Visage, and that all the Walls
With painted Imag'ry had said at once,
Jesu *preserve thee, welcome* Bullingbrook.
Whilst He, from one side to the other turning,
Bare headed lower, than his proud Steeds Neck
Bespeak them thus ; I thank ye Countrymen.
And thus still doing thus he pass'd along,
Dutches. *Alass !* Poor Richard *where rides he the*
while ?
York. *As in a Theatre the Eyes of Men,*
After a well grac'd Actor leaves the Stage
Are idly bent on him that enters next
Thinking his prattle to be tedious

Even

Even so, or with much more contempt Mens Eyes,
Did scowl on Richard : *No Man cry'd God save*
No joyful Tongue gave Him his welcome home. (him.
But Dust was thrown upon his Sacred Head
Which with such gentle sorrow he shook off
His Face still combating with Tears and Smiles,
(The Badges of Grief and Patience)
That had not God (for some strong purpose) steel'd
The Hearts of Men, they must perforce have melted,
And Barbarism it self have pitty'd him.

Are not here all the Beautys of Thought, joyn'd
with all those of expression ? is it possible any
thing that has but the least Humanity, shou'd be
dull enough not to relish, not to be mov'd, nay
transported with this ? I must confess, it has fir'd
me, so that I think our Critic better deserves the
Arraignment *Tiberius* gave the Poet, for ill repre-
senting *Agamemnon*, whose Character at best, was
but a Child of Fancy, and therefore subject to
the Poets Will ; but to Blaspheme such a visible
Excellence, Merits the highest contempt, if not
a greater Punishment:

Shakespears Numbers carry such an Harmonious
Majesty, that what *Rapin* and some other Critics
say of *Homer*, is justly his due; they give a noble
Beauty to the meanest things. 'Tis true , the
Words he sometimes uses, by their absoleteness
renders some of his Expressions a little dark, but
then we must remember the great alteration our
Language has undergone since his time; but examine

amine well the sense of his Words, you'l seldom find him guilty of Bombast, (tho' laid to his charge by Mr. *Rymer*,) that is Words and Thoughts ill match'd. On the contrary, they are generally so well sorted, that they present us with so lively and sensible an Image of what they import, that it fixes it self in our Minds, with an extream satisfaction; and the more we view it, the more it gains upon us.

I shall hereafter step into the Scenes with Mr. *Rymer*, and also examine his Narrations, Deliberations, Didactic and Pathetic Discourses, which are all that are made use of in Tragedy, in which if he sometimes err, he has yet perform'd well; and amidst his faults you shall find some thoughts of a great Genius. I shall only now observe *en passant*, in defence of that Scene, betwixt *Jago* and *Othello*, that we ought not to be imposed on by positive assertions, or think because Mr. *Rymer* tells us so, that half words, and ambiguous Reflexions, do not naturally work up Jealousie, or that 'tis not natural, for *Othello* to catch at e'ry *blown surmise*. These Assertions of our Critic shew him to be very ignorant of the very nature of this Passion, for as 'tis reduc'd to the primitive *Desire* by the Moralists, so 'tis thus by them defin'd,

> *Jealousie is a fear of loosing a good we very much value and esteem, arising from the* least *causes of Suspicion.*

now

now 'tis evident even from the trifling, and false Objections of his enemies that *Shakespear* had this very notion of this passion. For this reason 'tis, he makes *Othello* swallow the very first bait laid by *Jago* for him. *Cassio* is found with *Desdemona*, and on *Othello*'s approach, consciously retires, which tho' he did to avoid his Anger not Jealousie; yet *Jago* improves the opportunity to his purpose, with an——*I like not that*; then to awake the *Moors* Jealousie by degrees; he takes occasion from *Cassio*'s departure to question him—— *did Cassio when you woo'd my Lady know of your Love?* Which he pursues with *half-words*, and ambiguous *Reflexions*, that plainly imply more than they barely express, in which he discover'd, fear to speak out what he desir'd *Othello* shou'd know, the natural consequence of which is the touching a jealous Nature, with curiosity in a thing, that so nearly related to his Happiness. E'ry word rous'd some surmrize; and as *Ovid* observes, *cuncta timemus Amantes*, Lovers fear any Appearance. But more of this hereafter. In the in the mean while I'm pretty confident, e'ry Mans own Sence will supply my defect of a particular defence of the working up of *Othello*'s passion of Jealousie.

And now Sir, 'tis time to turn my Thoughts from a defence of *Shakespear*, to an excuse of my own Transgression, in addressing this Essay to you without asking your Leave. I'm not for asking pardon for an Offence, before I have committed it, and then I am willing if possible, to extenuate it from all its heightning Circumstances; and Sir, I hope I have enough to say for my Self in committing this.

First, I knew your Nature so well, that tho' no Name, cou'd have given more Authority to my defence of *Shakespear* ;. yet wou'd you never have consented to the manner I thought my self oblig'd to treat his accuser in ; for tho' he has had no regard to the public Friendship you have express'd for him ; yet I know you have not resented the grosness of his public abuse of you, with indignation enough to permit me to deal with him in the same manner ; for what was said of a great Lord, is fully as true of you, *viz.* that you are

The best natur'd Man, with the worst natur'd Muse,

for tho' there is nothing so strong and so cutting as your Satire ; yet is there nothing so easie and so affable as your Temper and Conversation. Pardon me, I will speak what I know of you, and let my Enemies make the best on't, whose Malice I value not, if I can but prevail with you to forgive this boldness

THE

The Ingenious and Honourable Theocrine to Theopompus *; shewing Her the faithfullest of Lovers, and most Pious of Children.*

ALL your Letters are at last arriv'd safe, tho' it happen'd with them, as in a great many other things: what shou'd a came first, came last, by which I'm sorry to find, that one who is to judge of Souls, knows no better how to judge of Merit; else whatever your request had been, it had been granted. I wish all that can serve the generous *Theopompus*, had my sense of his deserts, then shou'd the Friend of my dear *Poliarchus* be rais'd, as far above those self Interest'd Wretches, as his Soul now is, and *Generosity* was above theirs. For most of the sordid World, neither know how to reward the living, nor how to do justice to the dead; but these are crimes unknown to all that were inspir'd with the Friendship for our dear *Poliarchus.*

There are few of the Troubles that attend us in this Life, but when we seriously examine their

I 4   cause

Cause, we shall find we our selves in one kind or other, have in some degree contributed to 'em. For who can be of a generous Temper, and not bear a part with the Afflicted? this has (as it it does with all that are good) made you sensible of my sufferings, which has by an unforeseen Consequence brought the trouble of many impertinent Letters on your self; for 'tis impossible to suffer you ever to give over that pleasing Melancholy Subject you so ingeniously entertain me with. The Death of my *Poliarchus* is as lasting in my Memory as I am: and as I am the most unfortunate of Women by his loss, so can all other Afflictions be but like drops of Water into the abyss of the Sea: Yet have I met lately with an additional Grief, that bears a much greater proportion. That dear Mother I have been in care for, is now taken from me to augment the number of the blest above ; my tender *Love*, and grateful *Duty*, was such for my unequal'd Parent, that had I not known how to live after the *Loss*, and Affliction you saw me in, I cou'd scarce have supported this ; but 𝕿𝖍𝖆𝖙 has made me know that *there is a vast difference betwixt Tears shed for those whom* 𝕯𝖊𝖆𝖙𝖍 *chooses, and* 𝕿𝖍𝖔𝖘𝖊 *who make choice of* 𝕯𝖊𝖆𝖙𝖍, rather than live without what they too much valu'd. This vast conflux of misfortunes, gives me a greater desire to be assur'd what knowledge my departed Friends will have of me at our meeting in their blest abode, for since I've committed the sacred Memory of *Poliarchus* to your care, (whichwhilst I live, can never dye.) I am eternally entertaining

all

all, I can get to listen, with my sad Story ; but you can make it from age to age endure. Time the certain cure, of all other ills can never lessen mine, so that I often resolve to seek out a solitude, where if Reason cannot overcome my *Grief*, *Grief* may overcome me, and make my wretched days short as I wish 'em, and my unhappy state requires.

I am extreamly sensible of your generous compassion, and must tell you that when I first converst in this kind with the ingenious *Theopompus*, my Esteem cou'd then be grounded on no other score, but what great value he had for what deserv'd *Love* and *Esteem* from all the World, my *best* and dearest *Poliarchus*. But now you have engag'd me the way that most prevails with Humane Nature, by a *Real. Sense* of my Pain. That is so generous a piece of good Nature, that 'tis to be admir'd wherever 'tis found ; and in return, I wou'd if I cou'd forbear tormenting you any more with my Grief. But Ah ! How can I cease my complaints to one, who so tenderly apprehends 'em, and so excellently applys the Cordial of unequal'd Advices. This makes you often troubl'd with my Melancholly Life ; for I declare I had rather read your obliging Expressions for our dead Friend, than all the finest things the greatest of Mankind can say on any other Subject, but not to tire you all at once ; I shall here conclude, that I am your Friend, and Servant.

Theocrine.

TO

84593

To ACME, *before I had seen her.*

I Ought not in Prudence (Madam) to let you know the unreasonable extent of your Charms, for fear it destroy the Happiness I aim at in your *Pitty*; Cruelty and Pride being generally the effect of so *Unlimited* a Power. Yet, since you cannot pity, without knowing the Sufferer, I must inform you, Divine Maid, that I have increas'd the number of your Slaves, without so much as the pleasure of seeing you for all the Sighs you have cost me.

Love indeed is an Off'ring that ought to be laid on the soft Altars of Beauty; But, Madam, sure never was by any, but my self, on that of an *Unknown Deity*. We keep the *Bleeding Victims* of our Hearts, as long as we can, and only yield 'em up to the *Irresistible Force* of the *present Fair One.*

This, Madam, is the common Condition of Lovers; but as my Passion has an extraordinary Object in you, so have your Beauties an uncommon Influence on me: for Charm'd by I know not what *Divine Witchery*, I Sacrifice my poor Heart to your very Name, without putting you to the expence of one killing Look, to oblige me to't; Report has often engag'd the *Curiosity*, but never till now won the *Affections.*

The first mention of you inspir'd me with all the tender Thoughts of Love; and being oblig'd to personate the Lover in Print, I had Recourse to the *Divine Idea*, I had form'd of you, Madam, to qualifie

qualifie me for it; you were the only *Heavenly Muse* that I invok'd, which abundantly furnish'd me with all the Transporting Raptures of Love. But alas! Madam, while I too much gave way to Imagination, it carry'd me to a View of those Joys, none but you can impart, at least too charming fair one, so much justice is due to the most uncommon of *Lovers*, as to permit him the Blessing of your Conversion.

Ah! Madam, excel the rest of your Sex in Perfections of Mind, as much as you do in those of Body, and let not *Pride* and *Cruelty* level you with 'em; like a lawful Prince maintain the Gloro of your Empire, by the happiness of your Vassals, and be not like a Tyrant, proud of their Destruction, at least permit the address of the greatest of

Slaves,

Septimius.

To ACME, *after I had seen her.*

WHat-ever Doubts you were pleas'd to make of my passion before I saw you, Madam, because so uncommon; yet since I have now seen you, I hope you can no longer suspect the Reality of my love, for sure you must know 'tis impossible to behold that Face with an unwounded Heart. 'Twas

'Twas not at least possible for me (who came preingag'd with strong desires) to see you, without the extremity of Love.

I sigh'd and languish'd for you before, without the pleasure of feasting my greedy Eyes with the delicious banquet of your Looks. How often did I envy those your Eyes made slaves, whilst I fell a victim to your very Name, without a sight of that Heav'n I dy'd for? How often have I said,

How blest; how more then happy must be Prove
Who from her looks drinks in full draughts of Love,
For after Pain he meets with present Joys;
With a too envy'd Fate, dissolves and Dyes,
In the vast Beatific Vision of her Eyes.

these were my thoughts then Madam, and Imagination fell short of Reality; for I wou'd not for a thousand greater torments, than the vast increase of my passion has brought me, have been without that too too fleeting pleasure of seeing you last Sunday. 'Tis true, that was not sufficient to calm all my Griefs and Sighs. An empty view of Heaven, was not the utmost bounds of my Longing: and Love took it only as an earnest of greater Satisfaction, and now makes use of it, but to aggravate my suff'rings, which nothing but your Pitty can lessen.

I wou'd not Madam, put you to too great an expence of Pitty at once, I only desire your leave to adore you, and a reviving look now and then to support my languishing Soul. I wish

I

I muſt confeſs your welcome Pitty ſhou'd extend
ſo far, as to admit the humbleſt and moſt loving
of your Slaves ſometimes to your Converſation;
I wiſh too—but ſhou'd I trouble you with all my
Wiſhes, it wou'd be endleſs, and thought perhaps
preſumptuous, for they are extravagant, and have
no limits but in you, ſoaring as my *Love*, and
Boundleſs as *your* Charms.

And cannot a Wreath thus toſs'd, thus diſtract-
ed with ſuch hopeleſs Wiſhes, merit your Compaſſion? Can nothing but Death attone for my
loving you? And oh too charming *Acme!* I wiſh
I were but as ſure of your Pity, as I am of being
the moſt miſerable of Men whilſt I live, and ſoon
a Ghoſt without it.

Give me leave Madam, to hope you will not
always deny it me——miſtake me not. This
hope is not built on an over-weening Confidence
in my own Merits, (yet if Love be ſo I have the
greateſt) but on that noble Idea, I form of your
Mind from the Beauty of your Body, for ſure Nature cannot be ſo propoſterous in the moſt *Solemn*
of her Works, as to leave ſuch outward perfection
unfiniſh'd within. And pitty Madam, is the greateſt and moſt conſummate attribute of the No-
bleſt Mind, as Beauty is of the Body.

Nay, Beauty is of no uſe nor Advantage without Pitty, and the cruelleſt of your Sex muſt at
laſt have recourſe to it, after they have fooliſhly
ſacrific'd many of the precious hours of flying,
and irrecoverable Youth to a barbarous and unaccountable Cuſtom; if they reſolve not, ſtill
more fooliſhly to fling away the greateſt, and
moſt

moſt valuable of Heav'ns Bleſſings Beauty, and Youth without making uſe of 'em.

The Miſers of Money have more Reaſon', than thoſe of Beauty: for the former have the ſtore they ſpare ſtill by them, to gratifie their Ambition or Pleaſure of viewing it; but the latter deny themſelves the enjoymeht of that Treaſure, that has no other uſe, and which they can't preſerve with all their care; and 'tis the heighth of folly to ſpare that, which tho' we uſe not, flys ſwiftly fromus without any Advantage, and which can never be recover'd.

Be not therefore, my adorable *Acme*, ſo *improvidently Provident*, of the fleeting Store, as o complement a ſenſeleſs and cuſtomary Barbarity, at the expence of your *Juſtice* and *Reaſon*; they both demand your Pitty and your Love. For *Retaliation* is the Law of Juſtice, Love for Love, and Heart for Heart, as well as Eye for Eye, and Hand for Hand. And Reaſon wou'd perſwade you to lay your coming Years out in Pleaſure, and none ſo innocent, ſo laſting, and ſo vaſt as Love.

Love's the moſt generous Paſſion of the Mind.
The ſafeſt Refuge Innocence can find.
'Tis founded in Nature, the World and all Mankind owe their beings to't.

'Tis true Madam, I am not form'd with all that nice proportion, and that curious ſhape, that Fops are ſo proud of, and Women ſo much covet; but yet my Mind (nor is it a boaſt to ſay ſo) excells them. I dreſs not like a *Beau*, nor do I
move

move by *Art*, but then, too charming *Acme*, I do not love by art as he does. My Form, my Mien, and my *Love* are of a Piece, plain and sincere, and only inform'd by Nature.

If all this merit not your Love, it must your Pitty and Friendship, and on any Terms I wou'd be admitted to the number of your Slaves.

Septimius

To the Proud Acme.

THe sending back my three last Letters, Madam, makes me suppose you can take no great Pleasure in detaining the former, and that I now do you a very grateful Office in sending for 'em. And Madam, you can't doubt but that it must be a wond'rous Satisfaction to one so infinitely enamour'd, as I am, to please you at *any Rate*. If you send 'em not, I shall conclude, that how-ever unacceptable the *Offerer* was, the *Sacrifice* was welcome; but if you return 'em, I shall have the mighty comfort amidst my *Sighs*, to kiss something that has touch'd those *Hands*, that are not us'd to bestow any Favours on Men in my Circumstances.

Well, Madam, since you are so cruel, 'tis well I've some other Balm in store for my wounded Heart; for Women to me like Scorpions, have always been their own Cure. If their *Eyes* have pierc'd my Heart, their *Vanity*, *Folly* or *Pride*, has generally restor'd it to *perfect Health*. And I am sensible that I shall never be entirely *undone* or *lost* in LOVE, 'till I meet with one as free from *affected Coyness*, as

from

from *affected Languishments*, and such pretty *arti-ficial* Tweers, *designing* Glances, betwixt *Invi-tation* and *Denyal*, as are no small Auxiliarys in *Acmes* Conquests. The only Bond, Madam, that tyes my poor Heart for ever, to the *Oar* of Love, is an *Innocent, Free, and Obliging* Kind-ness, Sense, and an *Agreeable* Conversation and Humor, with an Exemption from Defects of Constitution, and Body, that shall be name-less, for Reasons best known to my self. And 'till I meet with such an one, my Heart, I thank my Stars, has so much the command of it self, as to admit as much, or as little of *Love* as it plea-ses; else Madam, in what a *miserable* pickle shou'd I now have been d'e think? —*Sighing*, *Mourning*, and Dying; to no purpose? besides, cursing, *Fate, Stars, Planets*, and all that (as Mr. *Bays* says) for a damn'd Ingrate?

But since 'tis now over no more of that, thou wondrous fair one, lest you shou'd think me yet your Power: but as my Passion for *Acme*, had a plaguy odd *Beginning*; so shall it here have full, as *Odd* an ending. — For the Duce (or any thing, but your Eyes) take me, if I am not at this very individual Moment within ken of the *very* place, whence I set out in my Voyage of *Love*; in which since you'l not permit me to be your Fellow Tra-veller. I wish you *un bon Voyage.* Adieu,

Ma Belle Dame,

Adieu,

Septimius.

THE

To the Ingenious URANIA.

LETTER I.

I Was extreamly uneasie, Madam, to be on such unequal Terms with you, whilft you know where to direct to me, tho I don't to you ; and I confefs, I thought it as great a Grievance as Vizor Masks, by which Women have the unreafonable Advantage of walking invifibly, when Men are forc'd e'ry where to go bare-fac'd : Yet as thofe would be more tolerable, if none but the Ugly and Indifferent wore 'em, fo fhould I with the greater Eafe difpenfe with my Ignorance of a Direction to you, had you either none, or elfe lefs Wit than your Letters prove you have : For 'tis that Divine Charm that makes me defire to fettle a Correfpondence with *Urania*. Nor is this Defire oppofite to your Refolution of remaining unknown : For there fhall, upon Honour, be no further Inquiry made after you than you fhall allow ; tho *G*——perfifts in his Opinion, that you facrifice your Wit and Senfe to the Reputation of that trifling Sex you are not of ; this not only the Wit of your former, but the polite Accuracy of all your Letters perfuade him, fince you are not only free from the falfe Spelling of moft Women, but are fo entirely exempt from falfe

K   Englifh

English and Grammar, that you difcover a better Acquaintance with *Lilly*, than to've pafs'd no further, than that Caution you quote from his *Accidens*; befides fome Beauties in the meer Writing down your Thoughts, which few Men Practife or Know.

I am of the fame Opinion of you, Madam, I declared in my former; and becaufe I would fain have you a Woman, believe you firmly to be fo: And though *G*— be fo pofitive, that the Diffidence you pretend of your felf, is nothing but a cunning Subterfuge from the fureft Evidence of your Sex, your Converfation, yet am I (taking you ftill for a very Woman) both pleas'd and diffatisfy'd with it; for tho' I am pleas'd, becaufe it feems the Child of Modefty and Difcretion, which feldom join with Wit, efpecially in a Woman; Yet am I diffatisfy'd with it, fince I find 'twould deprive you of what it qualifies you for; Converfation, I mean, with Mankind, fince that, not only fecures you from the Fate which the Imprudent of your Sex, have for want of it, incurr; but alfo becaufe it renders you more defirable to Men of Senfe.

But Madam, were we fuch formidable Creatures as you feem to make us, that you cou'd not Converfe with us but you muft be Ruin'd, yet is there no Danger from me, who have none of thofe engaging Accomplifhments, that are the wondrous and bewitching Engines of your Sex's Deftruction; as Wit, Shape, Dreffing, Dancing and Singing; with the reft of the gay Train

Train that take with the Fair : For I assure you I'm Ugly enough, and Dress ill enough to be a Wit, and yet am Dull enough to be Handsome, and a Beau. I can neither Sing nor Dance, and am yet very Impertinent ; for though I talk little, yet even that is nothing to the purpose. So that, Madam, from such a Man, the most distrustfull Lady need fear no Stratagem on her Affections, since they are generally taken by the Eye or Ear ; and if neither of them be won, the Fort of your Heart is secure, and impregnable.

But referring this wholly to your self, all I shall beg, is a settl'd Correspondence with you, whether you be a real or counterfeit Woman : and shall therefore conclude with acknowledging my Error in not taking more Notice of your *Welsh* Friend ; though it may well be Pardoned, if the Wit of the Indicter disarmed all my satyric Rage, and made me rather sacrifice a just Indignation to her Praise, than forsake so pleasing a Theme, for so fruitless a Labor, as chastising those inhospitable *Britains*, who wou'd no more now have understood or improv'd the wholsom Satyre to Practice, than they did their Duty, when they made the Ingenious *Urania* their Enemy ; whom to retain my Friend, shall be the Endeavour of,

> *Madam,*
>   *Your humble Servant,*
>   Viridomar.

L E T-

LETTER II.

HAving at laſt recovered your Letter, Madam, I ſend this Anſwer to prevent your Trouble of Tranſcribing another Copy. Firſt therefore, Madam, I muſt tell you, I'm infinitely Proud that you do me the Honor to fix your Correſpondence with me; nor wou'd I for the World have the Happineſs of this entercourſe of Letters broke off on any Account, much leſs on one ſo trivial as you mention: For there's not a Line you ſend, but I eſteem it more than the whole Revenue of the *Poſt-Office*. Though I muſt confeſs I could wiſh (and that with all my Heart) that you were not leaving the Town, becauſe I find by this Letter, that there is no Danger of your Heart, if I ſhou'd be admitted to your Converſation: For I aſſure you, Madam, I am far from a Phœnix; though I may perhaps, have ſome Pretence to thoſe your darling Qualities: And I hope the Ambition I ſhall always avow to be the Friend of *Urania*, will excuſe the Vanity of being more Particular.

I hate Ingratitude where ever 'tis, and can't therefore think them Hero's, who eſpouſe the Quarrel of the Ingratefull, let their Perſonal Bravery or Courage be never ſo great. Then, Madam, for Diſſimulation, I can ſay this, that I'm far from loving it, and only practiſe it ſometimes

times on Compulfion, as a neceffary Evil; and
to fay Truth, the evident Neceffity of it, has
made it lofe the Infamy of a Vice, with almoft all, and gain'd it the Reputation of a
Vertue, with the Politick and Wife: Nor can indeed any Man be free from it, unlefs he defign
to purchafe the Name of a Mad-man, and
frighten all he knows from his Company. Confider it a little, Madam, and I'm confident you'll
allow a little Diffimulation neceffary to the Decorum of good Breeding; for you can't think it
proper to tell this fuperannuated Matron, that
all the Paint on her Face will not hide the tell-
tale Marks of Old Age; or that pretty pratling
Virgin in all the gay Bloom of her Youth, that
fhe's a Fool, and that fhe fhould be filent if fhe ha'n't
a mind to facrifice all the Trophies of her Eyes,
to the Impertinence of her Tongue: Or that
Beau of Sixty, that all his Charms are borrow-
ed from his Drefs and Garniture; or that
he's more the Creature of his Vallet, than of God
Almighty, fince the Vallet, has fo extravagantly
Transformed him from what God made him.
And fo on, to the reft of the Follies and Vices
of Mankind. This wou'd be to make one's felf
more unacceptable than a *Memento Mori* in the
midft of Joy and Pleafure. But to proceed,
Madam, I'm free from Hypocrifie: Nor can I
think any one an Hypocrite but an Athieft; nor
any one an Athieft but a Fool. As for the Two
next Endowments you require, *viz.* a Great
Soul, and a true Noblenefs of Mind, the Pra-

K 3   ctice

ctice and different Opinions of the World, have rendred the Terms so ambiguous, that the Definitions of Philosophy are of small Use : I must therefore desire you to explain in your next, what you mean by them, that so I may find how far I can pretend to 'em ; for I'd fain be qualified for the incomparable *Urania*'s Friend. Generosity (if I mistake not your Sense of the Word) has been my *Vice* and *Punishment*. In short, Madam, if by Good Humour you mean *Good Nature*, I can put in some Claim to't ; but if by't you understand a brisk Jest and jovial Air, much Talk and more Laugh ; Faith, Madam, I must own I'm not fond of making any Pretence to't.

Thus much for the Qualities both Negative and Affirmative you require in a Friend : Then as for the Follies and Vices you Abominate, I thank my Stars : I'm not very guilty of 'em, and think Affectation equally criminal in Gayety, as well as Gravity.

And now, Madam, since you have describ'd the Phœnix that must win your Heart, give me Leave to present you with a rough Sketch of her (that's almost as rare) that must make an absolute Conquest of mine, (for as for transient *Amorets*, one indifferently qualified may do.) She must be moderately Fair but no Beauty ; (and that's the reason I hinted at in my last, that I was sorry you told me you were no Beauty) or at least, if possible, only so in my Eye : She must be neither Proud, nor Affected ; as Witty as *Urania*,

nia, yet as free from Opiniature and Obstinacy as I think her. I mean not by Wit, those noisie Repartees of the Cocquets of the Town, which you with justice Condemn, but a sensible Apprehension of things, which I'm confident you can't mean, when you term Wit a Scandal. In fine, Madam, she must be Easie and Free in her Conversation, very Gratefull, very Generous, and very Loving in her Nature: And when I find one so qualified, I'm entirely her Slave.

But whilst I pursue my Thoughts, I find my Letter grow too long, which is one Fault of a whining Lover; who being much your Aversion, I'll here conclude with an humble Request that I may have Leave to hope I shall one Day be so Happy, as to be admitted to your Conversation. For that, Madam, I must own is the greatest Ambition of

Your humble Servant

Viridomar.

LETTER III.

YOur Raillery, Madam, on my Loss of your Letter, is as Just, as Witty; and I confess with a great deal of Confusion, I can make no Apology for't, unless an Assurance that I'll never trust your Letters in my Pocket again, at least with any other Papers.

I think my self extreamly Happy that I can please *Urania* in any thing; and truly, Madam, 'twas the real Value I have for you, that made me alter the Medium of our Correspondence, because my Brother had the Assurance not only to reflect upon the Direction you sent me, but also to shew your Letter to more than I desir'd shou'd have that Pleasure without your Permission. This Dealing with his Brethren of— might be Pardonable, because they have some Dependance on him; but the Respect that's due to your Merit, and the Justice that's due to me, might have curb'd his Curiosity within the Bounds of Good Manners.

I hope, Madam, you'll forgive me this Discovery and Heat, for your Letter has made me an irreconcileable Enemy to Dissimulation, who before was never any Friend to it. You have Madam, new Molded me to your own Desire; and that Vice appears now so very Ugly and Unmanly, that I'm extreamly asham'd I ever said a word in its Vindication: But above all, I shall think it a crying Sin, to dissemble with the Divine *Urania*, and for that reason, Madam, I must tell you, that my Conversation with both Sexes, has given me some reason to think I'm pretty well acquainted with the general Inclinations of Mankind; this, when I read your account of your self, makes you seem to me to describe an Angel, not a Woman: The glorious Image you give me of *Urania*, by the Vertues she doats on, and the Vices she abhors, is so extreamly

treamly uncommon, that it looks like the divine
Draught of some Inspired Poets Fancy, when he
informs us, by a great Example of his own Crea-
ting, what we shou'd be, and not like a Reality.
And your Prose has the effect of his Numbers,
conveying Instruction in its most grateful Vehicle Pleasure, and so fixes the noble Idea in my
Soul, and makes me in love with your Mind, before I see your Person : And you shall never perswade me, that Conversing with you, can ever
lessen my Esteem for you : For tho the Writings of some of the most Ingenious afford a more
agreeable Entertainment, than their Company,
yet we may lose a great deal of their Excellency
by not taking their Thoughts right ; which
made *Martial* tell *Fidentinus,* that by ill repeating
his Verses, he made 'em his own : Besides, Madam, there are a thousand Graces in the delivery
that abundantly improve the Sense, a fair
Lady speaks, which must encrease her Esteem,
and which we lose when Absent. And, Divine
Urania, since your Heart is secure in very good
hands already, I can see no reason, (forgive my
Freedom) why you shou'd deny this Favour,
since I leave to your self the management of the
Interview, and give you my Word, that you shall
have the entire government of my Discourse and
Actions.

But, Madam, tho I have a more earnest longing to Converse with *Urania,* than Slaves for
Liberty, the sick for Health, the poor for Riches, and the Ambitious for Honours ; yet Divine,
unknown,

unknown, such a respect I have, such a profound Veneration for you, that I would Sacrifice even this Content (which perhaps is not of less value than even Life it self) to your least Inconveniency, if I was sure it cou'd not be obtain'd without prejudice to *Urania*.

I have a great deal to say about the Greatness and Nobleness of Mind you describe, but that wou'd be too long for a Letter that has already exceeded its just Bounds; and I hope, I may have the liberty to deliver my Sentiments by word of Mouth; only I must say that reason, not Opinion, general or particular, ought to decide so weighty a Point. But upon the whole, Madam, by the Vices you lay down as its Opposites I may presume to make some small pretention to it.

I wou'd fain know what more than good Nature goes to the composing good Humour, since *Urania* says there is more; I take not good Nature in that general sence you hint at, but for a freedom from Malice, Envy, Moroseness, &c. but if any part of Gaity be required, I'm at a loss, for I'm naturally of a Melancholy disposition, and dull heavy Conversation, as I formerly told you; and perhaps this want of an Airy Temper, with a little foolish Modesty I've always been troubled with, is that, that has made me still so Unsuccessful with the Fair, that none cou'd ever be in Love with me, whilst others with as few Brains, more Vanity, and if possible, less agreeable Persons have prevail'd. *Waller* says, *Women stoop to the Forward and the Bold,* which

which are no ingredients in my Character, at
least in Love, and my Converse with your Sex.
So that, Madam, I hope you'll scruple no more
to give me leave to wait on you, and as I prove,
admit me into your Esteem, at least as far as
cold Friendship will allow; or discard me for
ever, a greater Curse than which cannot fall on
the Head of,

  Madam,

   Your Humble Servant,

    and (if you'll give me leave to say so)

     True Friend,

      Viridoman

LETTER IV.

May 5. 83.

COming to Town last night, and having per-
used yours, I think your Anger, Madam,
against the Bookseller, very just, since 'tis indeed a
Scandal to any Name in the opinion of the most
Sensible part of the Town, to be in these *Mercu-*
ries; and the Zeal I was told you had for 'em,
made

made me read your firſt Letters with ſome Prejudice, till ſpight of all that diſadvantage, your Wit and Addreſs raiſed my Admiration, which with each Letter encreaſing, begot this importunate deſire, you reſiſt with ſo cauſeleſs and ſevere an Obſtinacy. *Cauſeleſs*, Madam, becauſe my Opinion of a grant of a Requeſt, purſued with that ardour and importunity, wou'd be pure as your Stile, and juſt as your Thoughts ; for I'm none of thoſe cenſorious formal Hypocrites, that can receive the Favour, and yet condemn the Benefactor that beſtowed it. *Severe* to Extravagance to make the very Deſire its own Obſtacle, after our moſt reaſonable Parts have brought us acquainted. Sure, Divine *Urania*, you'll grant, that our Correſpondence is in reaſon a more honourable Introduction to Friendſhip, than a Viſit or two with a Friend ; yet after this laſt, the moſt ſcrupulous Lady will permit one to wait on her.

You muſt therefore, Madam, Pardon me, if what you have urg'd, do not reconcile me to your Denial ; nor have you by any means as good Reaſons for this, as againſt Diſſimulation ; for there you oppos'd the common Practice generally Erroneous, but here vindicate its falſeſt Principle.

The Body of good Humour I have, but want the Spirit and Life, Facetiouſneſs, which perhaps your Converſation may inſpire, as Dull as I am.

Your

Your Letters Madam, can never be too long, for as you find I can never write a short Letter to you, so I desire none from you but long ones, since their perusal is, if not the only, yet the greatest Pleasure of,

Madam,

Your Humble Servant,

and Admiring Friend,

Viridomar.

LETTER V.

ASsure your self, admired *Urania,* that this generous Compliance of yours with my repeated Importunities to see you, shall never cause any opinion but what is the natural Result of your Conduct in it; that is, that you are a Lady of Sense and Honour; and I only think you have us'd too much Caution in this tedious delay: You have sacrificed abundantly too much time to Formality and Custom, for 'tis those two, that make the Ladies more hard of access than Men. My first Letter had been sufficient to have gain'd me admission to any *Man,* nay, to *Hobbs* himself; and where our Esteem for a
Lady

Lady is of the same nature, *viz.* a Love of her Mind, bounded with a just Friendship, all delays are but needless Cautions. I only urge this, Madam, to shew you how far I'm from entertaining any ill thoughts of the dear Favour you bestowed on me in your Last ; and I'm abundantly assured, that the satisfaction of your Conversation will answer my Expectation; for whatever you may think of dull Terrestrial Conversation (true in reference to what my Alloy will give it) 'tis my opinion it cannot be dash'd with much of Earthly Dulness where *Urania* is to give it Life and Spirit.

You have reason I must confess to be something cautious in making a new Friendship with one you know not, since you have been Deceived ; so much deceived in one you thought you might so well depend on as *Asdrubal*, whose Name was well suited to his Nature, and if of his own choice, certainly his *Punick* Faith made him so fond of a *Carthaginian* Name. But since Experience can't secure you in a Friend, I fansie Madam, 'twould not be Impolitick to try what Chance will do; throw your self entirely on that, and be absolutely my Friend without any more Caution. Mr. *Dryden* says,

———— *There's a necessity in Fate Why still the brave bold Man is Fortunate.*

The Cautious sift things with a too nice and jealous Eye to be easily Happy, whereas, if we will

will really be so, we must a little contribute to
the cheating our selves into an opinion of it; for
Happiness is nothing but Opinion; and tho
this sometimes end too soon, yet it makes some
amends, by the Pleasure it gave us whilst we entertain'd the dear Amusement; whereas, the Cautious are always in pain to avoid Pain, which
is like dying for fear of Death. Let not therefore the perfidious Ingratitude of the faithless
Carthaginian influence your Judgment of *Vrida-*
mar, who is not only an irreconcileable Enemy
to Ingratitude and Infincerity, but a hater of all
Common Wealths, because they have always
fignaliz'd their Ingratitude, and indeed lie under a necessity of always being so; So that the
thing you dislike in me, ought to be your greatest satisfaction and assurance of my Fidelity and
Honour, in chusing rather to Suffer, than Triumph; for I have a Soul ambitious as any Man;
but, *Vrania* 'tis a brave Ambition governs me;
I wou'd be Great and Just, but rather Just than
Great. I wou'd be Great, to have it in my
power to do Good, to destroy those Villains
that Influence the Best of Princes, and make
them act contrary to their Natures; for I cou'd
shew a Path Princes might tread to Power,
Wealth and Honour, consistent with the Love,
the Interest, and the Glory of their Countries:
But cou'd I make my Country the Envy of
Europe and Mistress of both the *Indies*, and of a
lasting Unity at Home, I wou'd not part with
my Faith, my Honour, nor my Sincerity to effect
it.

it. Let not *Asdrubal* therefore be the Rule of your Judgment of *Viridomar*, but assure your self I wou'd not yield to you in Faith and Sincerity: And as you will atone for all the faults I have experienced in your Sex, so I'll act with such an emulation of your Vertues, that I'll force you to confess I differ from most Men. Oh! I wou'd Die before I'd make my Friend and Benefactor my Tool, my Step to pass the dirty Plashes of my Fortune, and then Regard her no more, as *Asdrubal* has done: No, let me be Just and Poor, rather than thrive by Villainy. A Woman qualified like *Urania*, ought to be valued above the World, and shall by *Viridomar*, if she admits his Friendship.

I tell you my whole Soul, *Urania*, you see it naked as *Heaven*, and void of all Disguise; I'm weary of this Villainous World, and the endless as well as bootless Impertinencies of the Conversations of my own Sex, a wretched Circle they move in, of Prophaneness, Nonsense and Hurry; I have had too large a share in this-foolish Prize, these destructive Baubles of the Town, that Men like Fools, bedeck themselves withal; proud of their very Infamy: I Long, I Sigh for a dear Refuge from them all, and nothing like the Converse of *Urania*, whose Sense, as well as Sex, affords a more reasonable and calmer Joy; the sense of it transports my Mind with such a strange Impetuosity to establish a Friendship with you, that I'm extreamly uneasie till I see you, and shall expect *Friday* with the most impatient desire, when according

cording to your appointment, I'll certainly wait on you, and with this send you the thanks of the most grateful Mind, for this Generous Condescention to the Importunity of,

Madam,

Your faithful and sincere

Friend and Humble Servant,

Viridoman

An Essay *at a Vindication of* Love *in Tragedies, against* Rapin *and* Mr. Rymer,

Directed to

Mr. *DENNIS.*

THE short yet just Account you give in your Prefatory Epistle to the *Impartial Critic,* of the Reasons that hindred the *Grecians* from bringing the tender Scenes of Love on the Stage in their Tragedies, makes me wish you had proceeded to a full Vindication of the Practice of our Poets in that particular; and indeed this Letter is design'd to provoke you to such an Undertaking, which wou'd effectually stop the Clamours of some *Cynical* Critics, that will not

L   allow

allow any thoughts of Love agreeable to the Majefty of Tragedy.

The chief Arguments indeed which thefe Gentlemen bring, are from the Practice of the Ancients, (the canfe of which, you have given in the above quoted Epiftle) whofe Authority they are of opinion fhou'd out-weigh Reafon. But fince the *Ipfe dixit* has been fo long laid afide in Philofophy, as an enemy to our Enquiries into Nature, I can fee no reafon why it fhou'd be of fo much greater force in Poetry; fince 'tis perhaps almoft as prejudicial to our imitation of Nature in *This*, as to our difcovery of it in the Other. As far as the Ancients and the Rules *Ariftotle* draws from them, agree with the Character you give thefe, of being *nothing but good fenfe and Nature reduc'd to Method*, I fhall clofe with them; but when they either deviate from this, or reach not up to what may be done, I muft think it but juft to withdraw my felf from the fubjection of the *Stagyrite*, who has had a Reign long enough o'er the Minds of Mankind, and an Empire that far exceeded the Extent and Continuance of his Royal Pupil *Alexander*.

But to deal fairly with our Opponents, I fhall firft propofe all their Objections againft this Opinion I Defend, as I find them in *Rapin*, and his Copier, Mr. *Rymer*; and then examine how far they are from being fortified by Reafon, as their Admirers boaft. I fhall begin with *Rapin*; and that he may be fure to have Juftice, I fhall Quote him as his Friend has Tranflated him. *Reflect*. 20. p. 110.

Modern

Modern Tragedy *turns on other Principles : the* Genius of our (*the French*) Nation *is not Strong* enough to *sustain an Action on the Theatre, by moving* only Terror and Pity. *These are* Machines *that will not* play *as they ought, but by great Thoughts and noble Expressions; of which we are not indeed altogether so capable as the* Greeks. *Perhaps our Nation* which is naturally Gallant, *has been oblig'd to the necessity of our Character, to frame for our selves a new System of Tragedy, to suit with our humor.* The Greeks, who were Popular Estates, *and who hated* Monarchy, took delight *in their* Spectacles, *to see* Kings Humbled, *and high Fortunes cast down because their Exaltation griev'd them.* The English, our Neighbours, love Blood *in their Sports, by the quality of their* Temperament. *These are* Insularies *sep rated from the rest of Men; we are more* Humane. Gallantry *moreover agrees with our* Manners; *and our* Poets *believ'd that they cou'd not succeed on the* Theatre, *but by sweet and tender* Sentiments; *in which perhaps they had some* Reason: For in effect, the Passions represented become Deform'd *and* Insipid, *unless they are founded on* Sentiments *conformable to those of the* Spectator. 'Tis this obliges *our* Poets *to stand up so strongly for the Privilege of* Gallantry *on the Theatre, and to bend all their Subjects to* Love *and* Tenderness; *the rather to please the* Women, *who have made themselves Judges of these Divertisements, and usurped the Right to pass Sentence.* And some besides *have suffer'd themselves to be prepossess'd, and led by the* Spaniards, *who make all their* Cavaliers Amorous.

rous. 'Tis by them that *Tragedy* began to degenerate ; and we by little and little accuſtom'd to ſee *Heroes* on the Theatre ſmitten with another Love than that of Glory ; and that by degrees, all the Great *Men* of *Antiquity* have loſt their Characters in our Hands. 'Tis likewiſe perhaps by this Gallantry that our *Age* wou'd deviſe *a* Colour to excuſe the feebleneſs of our *Wit*, not being able always to ſuſtain the ſame *Acti-*ons by the greatneſs of Words and Thoughts.

However it be, (for I am not hardy enough to declare my ſelf against the Public) 'tis to degrade *Tragedy* from that *Majeſty*, which is proper to it, to mingle it in *Love*, which is of a Character always *light*, and little ſuitable to that *Gravity* of which Tragedy *makes Profeſſion.* * *Hence* it proceeds, that theſe Tragedies *mixt with* Gallantries, *never make ſuch admirable Impreſſions on the Spirit,* as did thoſe of Sophocles *and* Euripides ; *for all the Bowels were mov'd by the great Objects of* Terror *and* Pity, *which* They *propos'd.* 'Tis likewiſe for this that the Reputation of our *Modern* Tragedies ſo ſoon Decays, *and yields but ſmall Delight at* two Years end; *whereas the* Greek *pleaſe yet to thoſe that have a good Taſte, after two Thouſand Years* ; *becauſe what is not grave and ſerious on the Theatre, tho it give Delight at preſent, after a ſhort time grows Diſtaſteful and Unpleaſant* ; *and becauſe what is not proper for great Thoughts and great Figures in* Tra-*gedy, cannot ſupport it ſelf.* The Ancients who per-cciv'd this, *did not Interweave their* Gallantry *and* Love, *ſave in* Comedy. * *For* Love *is of a Cha-*racter *that always degenerates from that Heroic Air*

of

of which Tragedy *must never divest it self. And nothing to me shews so mean and senseless, as for one to amuse himself with whining about frivolous Kindnesses, when he may be admirable by* great and noble Thoughts, *and sublime Expressions.* * *But I dare not presume so far on my own Capacity and Credit, to oppose my self of my own Head, against a Usage so Establish'd : I must be content modestly to propose my Doubts, and that may serve to exercise the Wits, in an Age that only wants* Matter. *But to end this Reflection with a touch of* Christianism, *I am perswaded, that the Innocence of the Theatre might be better preserv'd, according to the Idea of the ancient* Tragedy ; *because the New is become too Effeminate, by the Softness of later Ages ; and the Prince* de Conti, *who signaliz'd his Zeal against the Modern Tragedy, by his Treatise on that Subject, wou'd without doubt, have allow'd the* Ancient, *because that has nothing that may seem Dangerous.*

Then for Mr. *Rymer,* in his jovial way of Criticism, he condemns Love on the Stage in these Words, brought in indeed by Head and Shoulders.

After all, it is to be observ'd how much that Wild-Goose Chase of Romance runs still in their Heads, some Scenes of Love must ev'ry where be shuffled in, tho never so Unseasonable.

The Græcians *were for* Love and Music, *as mad as any Monsieur of them all, yet their Music kept within Bounds, attempted no* Metamorphosis *to turn the* Dramma *into an* Opera : *Nor did their Love come* Whining *on the Stage to* Effeminate the Majesty

jesty

jesty of Tragedy. *It was not any Love for* Briseis, *that made* Achilles *so Wroth, it was the Affront in taking his Booty from him, in the Face of the Confederate Army. This his Stomach could not Digest.*

—————————— Nec gravem
Peleidæ Stomachum cedere nescii. *Hor.*

These are the Pillars and Supports of the Gentlemen of this Opinion ; so that I hope, if I can but obviate these Objections they bring, I have gained the End propos'd to my self in the Justification of the Practice of the best of our Poets, in presenting us with the tenderest Scenes of Love in Tragedies. 'Tis true, the Charge of both these Critics, is directed against the *French* Poets, but in the excluding Love, as derogatory to the Majesty of Tragedy, it reaches our Poets, who do the same. I have Quoted *Rapin* at large, because one part of the Reflection seems to answer the other to my Hand ; for the ground of his Accusation is the deviating from the Practice of the Ancients ; for which he gives so good Reasons, that 'twould have been a madness not to have form'd a new System, since the Genius, the Character, Humour and Manners of the People, required as much. He says, that, *In effect the Passions represented become deform'd and insipid, unless they are founded on Sentiments conformable to those of the Spectator.* But before I proceed to any particular Reply, I shall draw the Objections

ons both contain, into short and positive Heads, to make their Confutation the more Evident.

The whole Charge therefore, may be reduc'd to these three Heads, the 1. Motives the Moderns (particularly the *French*) had to Introduce Love into Tragedy. 2. The Objections against it: And, 3. The Effects of it. *First*, As to the Motives, *Rapin* tells us, they were the *Necessity* of the Character, Manners, and Temperament of the People, (which, without doubt, was the Poet's Duty to regard.) *Next*, to gratify the Women Judges, (which is the Poet's Duty as a Man, both in Regard of his Profit and Sex, especially when the Interest and Power of the Women strike in with the Character, Manners, and Temperament of the People.) *Lastly*, To excuse the Feebleness of their own *Wit*. These are the Motives *Rapin* sums up of this Innovation on the Stage; which, as I have before observed, are a sufficient Justification of it, even according to himself: But for the last 'tis only a morose Caprice of his own Fancy, for certainly there is as much Wit required to the Just, and artificial Management of the Passion of Love; as those of Fear and Terror, and those other Species of Passions that are subservient to the moving of them.

I shall therefore pass to the Objections, which are four in Number, the First and Chief (in some Mens Opinion) is, That it deviates from the Practice of the Ancients; who, as the Inventors of Tragedy, challenge our Imitation.

'Tis

'Tis they muſt be our Model, and as we make more or leſs Approaches to that in the Fabrics of our Plays, we are in a greater or leſſer Degree of Perfection. I grant indeed, that the Ancients were the Inventors of Tragedy; nay, and of Comedy too; 'tis their due Glory. Nor will I pretend to rob 'em of it. I will alſo grant, that there is ſome Regard to be had to their Performances, as to their Model; but then I deny that by the Rules of Reaſon, we are oblig'd to a ſervile Obſervation of their Precepts, or Practice, without all Addition, or Improvement. Had the Practice of the Firſt Inventors been of ſuch *Inviolable* Authority, *Theſpis* had brought *Tragedy* to its Perfection, and one *Actor*, and a deal of *Chorus* (more ridiculous than an entire Opera) had been the *non plus ultra* of the Stage. But if it were lawful for *Æſchylus, Euripides, Sophocles* and others, to improve upon the Model *Theſpis* had left them, why ſhould other Poets, great as thoſe in Genius, be deprived of the ſame Liberty, provided it be for the Advancement of the Profit, and Glory of *Tragedy?* Upon this Condition I do ſuppoſe, none will deny the Moderns this Liberty to forſake the Steps of the *Greeks*. But that our Alterations are for the better, will appear from the After-proofs, as well as from what I ſhall here ſay on this Particular.

Firſt, Then 'tis evident from what you, Sir, have urged in the *Impartial Critic*, That the leaving off the *Chorus* is for the better, ſince it

frees

frees it from an unnatural Part, which took up so large a Share of the ancient *Tragedies*; and in that, delivers it from the absurdest Improbabilities in Nature, which are as destructive to the End of Tragedy as any thing that can be introduced. Next, it has enlarged the Bottom on which the ancient *Tragedy* stood, and by Consequence extended its Use and Advantage further. It has made it a more perfect Image of Humane Life, in taking in that which has so great a Share in it, LOVE; which whether it be derogatory to the *supposed* Majesty of Tragedy, I shall next examine; if not, my Assertion is evident.

This indeed is the next Objection of our Adversaries, who tell us, *That the Lightness of* Love *degrades the* Majesty *and* Gravity *of* Tragedy, *diverting it from* Great, *and* Noble Thoughts, *and* Sublime Expressions, *to whining about frivolous Kindnesses.* This I confess is the heaviest Charge in Reality, if true, and therefore I shall take the greatest Pains to remove it; for if *Love* be not guilty of this, 'tis evidently an *Improvement*, and therefore to be continued in that Possession of the Stage, it has gain'd with so universal an Approbation.

All the Arguments I shall bring to prove that it is not derogatory to the Majesty of *Tragedy* shall be drawn from — *the Consideration of their Beloved Ancients*; *the very Meaning of the Word* Majesty; *and the Nature of the Passion of* Love, *and its Place in Regard to the others.*

First,

First, 'Tis evident from the very Concessions of *Rapin*, the Agreement of all Critics, and the very Nature of the Thing, That *Tragedy* is not of greater *Majesty*, and *Dignity*, than an *Epic Poem*. In his Fourth General Reflection, he tells us, That from *Homer's* Epic Poems, Sophocles and Euripides *took the Haughty Air of the Theatre, and* Idea's *of* Tragedy; and begins the second Particular Reflection thus: *The* Epic Poem *is that which is the Greatest, and most Noble in* Poesie. To prove which he spends all that Reflection, and the magnifying of it takes up the Third and Fourth, and at the End of the Tenth particular Reflection he tells us, *That* All *ought to be* Majestic *in an Heroic Poem*. This also seems to be confess'd by Mr. *Rymer*, when he, speaking of Love's effeminating the *Majesty* of *Tragedy*, Instances an *Heroic Poem*, viz. the *Iliads* of *Homer*, foreseeing perhaps that that might be objected against his Assertion, which is still in full force notwithstanding his saying, That 'twas not the *Love* of Achilles *for* Brisais, *that made him so wroth, but the Indignity received in the Face of the Confederate Army*. But besides this Concession of our Opposers (which is indeed Argument good enough *ad Hominem*) the very Nature of the thing proves the same. *Hero's* and *Kings* are the Subjects of both, and the principal Character of an *Epic Poem*, consists in the *Narration* (as *Rapin* truly observes) in which it is only opposed to Tragedy, which consists altogether in *Action*.

The

The Majesty of an *Epic Poem* being thus demonstrated equal, if not superiour to that of Tragedy. If I can prove by the Practice of *Homer* and *Virgil* (the greatest of Heroic Poets) that they esteem'd not Love derogatory to the Majesty of their *Poems*, 'tis Proof sufficient that it cannot degrade the Majesty of *Tragedy*, which is not greater than the other.

But this is evident from the *Iliads* of *Homer*, and the *Æneids* of *Virgil*. *Homer* in his *Iliads* makes *Achilles* and *Agamemnon* in *Love*, one with his Captive *Briseis*, the other with *Chryseis*: For *Agamemnon* tells *Achilles* and the Council of the *Grecians*, that he preferrs *Chryseis* to *Clytemnestra* the Wife of his Youth; and that she is not inferiour to her in any of her Qualities or Beauties. He often calls her Beautiful *Chryseis*, and always speaks very feelingly when he mentions her. And *Achilles* his Anger had not rose to that Degree, but that he was depriv'd of his Rosie-Cheek'd *Briseis*. *Horace* was of my Opinion, in his Second Epistle Book 1.

Hunc Amor, *ira quidem urit utrumq;*

Which you very justly *English* thus,

Whose injur'd Love, in both strange Fury breeds.

For the Rise of *Agamemnon*'s Passion is evidently from his Love to *Chryseis*, as he plainly confesses in his Expressions; and that of *Achilles*

was

was not only exaggerated, but confirm'd by the
same Loss of her he Lov'd.   *Ovid* in his Amours,
lib. 2. is of the same Mind.

Theſſalus ancilla facie Briſeïdos arſit :
Serva Mycenæo Phœbus amata duci.

And in other Places he has to the same pur-
pose. Besides in the Third Book of the *Ili-*
ads, when *Hector* proclaims the Challenge of
Paris, to fight *Menelaus* in single Combat, the
Condition is, that the Victor shou'd possess *He-*
lena for his Wife. If this be not below the *Ma-*
jesty of an *Epic Poem*, certainly the Nobler
Scenes of Love cannot be below that of *Tragedy*.
But the Case is yet plainer in *Virgil*, for the
Fourth Book of his *Æneids*, is wholly on the
Intrigue of *Æneas* and *Dido*, where that Divine
Poet has given the finest Draught of that Paſſion
that Antiquity can boaſt of. But if this Crimi-
nal Paſſion of *Dido* and *Æneas*, do not degrade
the Majeſty of an *Epic Poem*, can the same, or
less Criminal, be below that of *Tragedy*? This
Book is not arraign'd by our Criticks for any
Defect in this, and by others allow'd as noble a
Piece as any of that Poet, so that *Love* is not
such an Enemy to Noble Thoughts, but that
'tis conſiſtent with them ; nor to the Majeſty of
Expreſſion, as this Fourth Book of *Virgil* evin-
ces. Besides, we find in the *Alceſtes* of *Euripides*,
an Attempt of *Love*, and something of it in the
                                              Ajax

Ajax of *Sophocles* ; nay, 'tis the Foundation and
Fable of the *Phædra* of *Euripides*.

Thus we fee the Enemy beat from one of their
beloved Holds, the Authority and Practice of the
Ancients. I fhall now therefore, proceed to the
very Meaning of the Word *Majesty*; by which
we fha!l be able to difcover how far it will contribute to the Confirmation of our Pofition.

To let alone the Grammatical Etymology of
the Word , and take it in its Poetical Sence,
where 'tis Metaphorically us'd, it means fomething that is Great and Pompous. And *Horace*
in the fourth Satyre of his Firft Book, means
this *Majesty* we talk of, when he fays,

Primum ego illorum dederim quibus esse Poetas
Excerpam Numero : Neque enim concludere versum
Dixeris esse satis; neq; siquis scribat uti nos
Sermoni propriora, *putes hunc esse Poetam*
Ingenium cui sit, cui mens divinior, atq; os
Magna sonaturum, *des. nominis hujus honorem.*

So that Majefty, is nothing elfe but an *Ele-*
vation of Thought, and Expression above the Com-
mon and Vulgar Difcourfe. By this Explanation
of it, it becomes intelligible, and we fhall fee,
that the Critics wou'd only amufe us with
Words. Now if they can prove by Reafon, that
the Thoughts and Expreffions of Love in its
feveral Effects and Emotions, cannot be exalted above the Vulgar, and Common Difcourfe,
then is *Love* of too low a Character for Tragedy.

dy. But if Love be not incapable of this Elevation, then is our Point gain'd in this Particular too, which will be evinc'd from the next Proof, drawn from the *Nature of the Passion of Love, and its Place in regard to the others.*

A Passion is more or less *Majestic*, (and by Consequence, more or less fit for Tragedy) in regard either of the Rank or Degrees of the *Passions,* of the Sentiments it inspires, the Effects it causes, the Actions that depend upon it, or in fine, the Influence it has on the Life of Mankind.

If the First, 'tis evident that *Love* has much the Preheminence above *Terror* and *Pity. Des Cartes* reduces all the Passions to Six principal Heads, *Admiration, Love, Desire,* (or rather *Concupiscence, Joy* and *Grief.*) Dr. *Moor* reduces them to Three Heads only, *Admiration, Love* and *Hate.* The first of which being plac'd in the Brain, and being but the Step to the other, he with the School-men reduces them yet to Two, the *Concupiscible* and the *Irascible*; which *Des Cartes* terms in other Words, properly *Love* and *Hate.* So that we see *Love* on all Hands, appears to be a Primitive Passion, out of several Degrees of which, and its Opposite, are the rest compounded and deriv'd. *Fear* or *Terror* is deriv'd from *Desire, Desire* from *Love, Commiseration* is deriv'd from *Grief, Grief* from *Hate*; and is compounded of *Love* and *Grief.* So that if we respect the Degrees of the Passions, *Love* is the more Excellent, as being a Primitive Passion, but *Fear* and *Pity,* only un-

der,

der-Species and Derivatives from it : So that in Nature, Love is more Noble than those. Let us therefore proceed to the *Sentiments* it *inspires*, &c. By Sentiments I mean the *Thoughts* that a *Lover* derives from the Passion he's possess'd with. But these are so different, that we must run through the several Conditions of Lovers to make any Judgment of 'em : For those Thoughts that proceed from *Anger*, *Fear*, *Jealousie*, *Hope*, *Despair* ; nay, and *Hate*, with the rest of the Passions, are to be look't for in a Lover, according to his several Circumstances. But take him in his most easie and tranquil Station, when tendrest Desires are fann'd with sure Success, his Thoughts are more or less elevated, according to the State and Degree of the Person that's affected. Those of a Shepherd might be too low, those of a *Beau* too Gay and Light, but those of a *Hero* must retain something of his Character, and must be Noble as the Object that inspires, or the Person that receives the Inspiration. The Two First indeed may be below the Dignity of Tragedy, but the latter can no more derogate from that, than from the Character of the Person. But supposing the most tender and the softest Scenes of a *Hero*'s Love are not Majestic enough for Tragedy ; yet must they be Granted as lofty as those of his *Griefs* ; and in the latter, *Horace* will have the descending from the haughty Air and Majesty of Tragedy, not only allowable, but absolutely necessary : *De Arte Poetica :*

Et

Et Tragicus plerumq; dolet sermone pedestri
Telephus & Peleus, cum pauper & exul uterq;
Projicit ampullas, & sesquipedalia verba,
Si curat cor spectantis tetigisse querelâ, &c.

There is a time therefore when the *Hero* not
only may, but ought to quit his Grandeur, in
Horace's Judgment; and that is when he's in Di-
stress and in Exile. And why is it less lawfull
to depart from this Majesty (that is, supposing
Love requires it) on the Account of the tendrest
Hours of Love? This is more natural in my poor
Opinion, than in the Case justified by *Horace*.
For to Love, is natural to all Great Souls, and
I think, as Noble and Essential to their Character, as any that make it up: But it may be
doubted whether a *Hero*, that is, a Man of
Invincible Courage, can suffer all his noble
and towring Thoughts, all his *Elation of Mind*,
to be so depress'd by Adversity, as to submit to
sordid and mean Grief and Sorrow: This may
be the Reason why some Critics have reflected
on the *Oedipus Coloneus* of *Sophocles*, as too low
and mean for the Dignity of a *Hero* furnish'd
with Resolution, Courage and Virtue in his o-
ther Play of him. 'Tis true, 'tis the general
Frailty of Mankind to be dejected in Misfortunes; but Tragedy, as our Critics contend,
shou'd be something better than the Life, something more Philosophical, affording a Draught
of what Man shou'd be: Now 'tis certain that
Philosophy will not allow Fortune any Influence on the Thoughts and Mind, at least so far
as to make 'em degenerate.   **Thus**

Thus we see if Love were what our Adversaries wou'd have it, yet is it as reasonable to
be allow'd, as what their Masters hold necessary
in *Tragedy*. But this is a Concession I am by
no means oblig'd to make; for I am not of
Opinion that there is any Necessity that the
most tender Scenes of Love, shou'd be void of
that Elevation of Thought and Expression, that
constitutes *Majesty*. or that they shou'd be deliver'd in that *Sermone pedestri*, *Horace* judges so
requisite to the Expression of Grief. This is
evident from *Virgil*'s Fourth Book, and the
All for Love of Mr. *Dryden*: Both which abound
with noble Thoughts and Language.

But the tender Scenes are the least Advantages
Love brings to *Tragedy*. There are a great
many beautifull Occasions offer'd to the Poet by
it; from the Effects of it; the other Passions
concerned in it, of Descriptions; &c. as we may
find in all the best of our Plays, particularly in
that admirable Piece of the best of Poets, which
I mentioned but now, *viz. All for Love.* 'Tis
the Love of *Anthony* and *Cleopatra*, that furnishes
the Occasion of all the admirable Scenes of that
Play: The same is to be said of the Fourth
Book of *Virgil*'s *Aeneids*.

To conclude this Point, it must be granted that
Love in its Nature, must inspire Noble and more
August Thoughts or Sentiments, than *Grief* or
Terror. For the Soul is more dilated, and exerts
its noblest Faculties more in Love, than in *Sor-
row* or *Fear*; which both contract the Soul and

M   its

its Operations. Love pushes a Generous Mind on to Great Actions, to render it self more a-greeable and taking to the Object of his Desires than others. Whereas *Grief* and *Fear* are Op-posites to all that's Great and Noble. All the Steps to Love are Great, and much a-kin to that Glory *Rapin* will have the only Object of an Hero's Passion ; for *Admiration* is the first Illu-strious Step by which a Man mounts to Love: And to acquire Admiration, a Man must perform something extraordinary: For 'tis not the Beau-ty or Manly Fabrick of the Body, that are sup-pos'd capable alone of making that Impression on an *Heroine*, (for such must the Mistress of a Hero be) 'tis his Acts that render him Admira-ble and Charming in her Eye. And indeed, common Experience will convince us, that a Per-son of Quality that has Signaliz'd himself by any Noble Deeds, shall gain the Fair much easier than a Son of the Earth unknown to Fame, and yet not born to Reputation. Love therefore, being the Spur to Noble Actions, cannot but inspire Noble Thoughts or Sentiments, and No-ble Thoughts being agreeable to the Majesty of Tragedy, Love in respect of the Sentiments it inspires, cannot derogate from that Majesty ; which is the Second Proof I propos'd in De-fence of the Nobleness of this Passion. From whence I shall pass to the Third and Fourth, which have an immediate Dependance on these, and are pretty well cleared, by what I have produc'd toward the latter end of this Second Particular.   In

In the next Place, Love is either opposite, or agreeable to the Majesty of Tragedy, by *its Effects*, or *Actions that depend upon it*. If the Noblest Actions, and the most Tragical Events be agreeable to the Majesty of Tragedy, the Effects of Love are. Witness the Performances of the Hero's in some of the best of our Modern Plays; and the *Catastrophe's* of many that depend on the Effects of Love, as that of the inimitable, and so often mention'd *All for Love*, &c. Besides, 'tis already prov'd, that Love provokes to Noble Actions, in the foregoing Paragraph; and Noble Actions are properly dignify'd for Tragedy; therefore the Actions that depend on Love, are not derogatory to the Majesty of Tragedy. Nor do the other Effects of it afford a less Noble Subject for the Poet, the many Passions that depend on them, the Jealousies, the Revenge, the Anger, the Contests of Desire, of Hope and Despair, *&c.* give unexpressible Beauty to any Poem: There is nothing so fine and moving, as the curious touching of the Passions, for those are the Engines that are to work the Effect of Tragedy, in producing *Terror* and *Compassion*. The Distractions and Disasters of those who are Sacrific'd by Love, are of a more general concern than those that are made miserable by Ambition, or other Villainies. And this brings us to the Last Test that is to try whether Love be such an Enemy to the *Majesty of Tragedy*, viz. *The Influence it has on the Life of Mankind.* And here I believe *Rapin* places the

chief

chief Diſtinction betwixt *Majeſty*, and the *Lightneſs* of *Love*. For he ſuppoſes the Influence Love has on Mankind, is of that light Nature, that it can produce nothing but ſoft whining about trifling Kindneſſes; whereas *Ambition*, which is a Love of Glory, furniſhes the Poet with Incidents as well as Thoughts, that are Noble and Surprizing; which, with the Auguſtneſs of expreſſion, compoſe what he underſtands by Majeſty. But 'tis evident from what has been ſaid, and Experience, that there are as many Noble Actions, as many extraordinary Events, and as many ſurprizing Thoughts, the Effects of *Love* of Woman, as of the Love of Glory, both which are the Ingredients that *Virgil* and *Homer*, and the other Great Poets of Antiquity compos'd their Hero's of. *Achilles* had his *Briſeis*, his *Polixena*, &c. *Pyrrhus* his *Hermione*, *Hercules* his *Omphale*, *Megara*, *Deianira*, &c. *Ajax* his *Tecmeſſa*, *Telamon* his *Heſione*, *Hector* his *Andromache*, *Æneas* his *Creuſa*, *Dido* and *Lavinia*. And none of the Hero's Race wounded the Goddeſs of Love but *Diomedes*. So Heroical a Paſſion is the Love of Woman, that I muſt think it as Majeſtical, as that of Ambition and Glory. The *Love* of *Paris* gave *Homer* the Ground of his Poem, *viz.* the *Trojan* War, founded on the Rape of *Helena*, by her *Trojan* Admirer; which ſhews that the Influence it has on Mankind, is very great, when it was ſo powerfull to prevail with the *Trojans* to keep *Helena* for the Love *Paris* bore her, at the Expence of their Peace

and

and Safety. And Dr. *Burnet* in his Anſwer to
Varillas, obſerves very truely againſt that Hiſto-
rian, that Intereſt or Ambition, are not the only
Motives of the Actions of Mankind, there is much
to be attributed to the Paſſions, and of them,
none more Violent and Sovereign, than this of
Love. Tragedy therefore wou'd not be a perfect Image of Humane Life, if it left ſo conſiderable a Share of it untouch'd, as Love Commands
or Influences.

Having thus prov'd (as I think at leaſt) that
Love does not degrade the Majeſty of Tragedy,
and that it therefore ought not, for that,
to be diſcarded by our Tragic Poets, I ſhall
now prove by the very end and deſign of this
Poem, that 'tis neceſſary to be preſerv'd by
them ; and by conſequence, that the Poſſeſſion
of the Stage the Moderns have given it, is an
Improvement of Tragedy and not a Deroga-
tion. The end of Tragedy is, as *Rapin* more than
once aſſures us, *the rectifying the Paſſions by the
Paſſions themſelves, in calming, by their Emotion,
the Troubles they wou'd excite in the Heart.* From
hence 'tis evident, that unleſs Love be taken in,
the moſt predominant and violent of Paſſions,
Tragedy cannot perfect its Cure, ſince it muſt
leave the moſt conſiderable Diſtemper (for ſo
are all the Paſſions that are not regulated by
Reaſon) without any Remedy. But in his 17*th*.
particular Reflection, where he mentions the
end of Tragedy, he ſeems to contradict himſelf, when he firſt ſays, *Pride* and *Hardneſs* of

Heart,

Heart, were the most important Faults (not most important to be cur'd if not general, by so public a Cure) to be regulated, and yet a little after he tells us, that Man is naturally timorous and compassionate: Now he that is naturally compassionate, can never be accus'd of Hardness of Heart, with any Shew of Reason and Justice. But something must be said to reduce the end of Tragedy to their Notions; whereas 'tis indeed the regulating all the most important Passions and Vices of Mankind, which contribute to the Disturbance of his Peace and Happiness, and obstruct his Progress in Vertue. Now it must be granted that Love, as well as other Passions, when it has past the Boundaries of Reason, becomes destructive to our Happiness and Vertue, and ought therefore as much to be Purg'd as Fear or Pity. In short, if the chief Aim of Tragedy be the moving of *Terror* and *Compassion*, 'tis evident, Love is extremely conducive to that end, and therefore not ill made use of by our Poets.

The next Objection that is made against Love in our Tragedy, is, that it discovers a Weakness of *Genius*. For *Rapin* tells us that it discovers a Weakness of Genius not to be able to sustain an Action on the Theatre, with moving *Terror* and *Pity* only. But he here supposes that Love does not contribute to the same end, as I have made evident already. He must be extremely out of Humor with the Moderns, else he wou'd never make this an Objection against

gainſt their Strength of Genius, which is an Argument of their Judgment; for they evidently ſaw by the Performances of the *Grecians*, that Terror and Pity, could not be mov'd always by the barren Repetition of the ſame Method to it: And it were to be wiſh'd that *Sophocles* and *Euripides* had been ſenſible of this, they wou'd then never have fail'd in keeping up the Dignity and Majeſty of the Theatre, as they have in ſome of thoſe few Plays we have of theirs. For we find a great Sterility in ſome of thoſe Seven Plays of *Sophocles*, as to the Deſign and End of Tragedy, as well as Noble Thoughts. What *Terror* or *Pity* can *Philoctetes* move, or where are the Great and Noble Thoughts to ſupport it? Where is the Majeſty of *Oedipus Coloneus*, which *Rapin* himſelf grants to be low and degenerate? Nor can I diſcover the mighty *Pity* and *Terror* that can be mov'd by the bringing in a Madman on the Stage, and a company of dead Sheep about him. I'm ſure 'twou'd make an Audience here laugh. Nay, I muſt declare (nor am I troubl'd at what Uſe the Critics will make of it) I think his Maſter-piece out-done by Mr. *Dryden* in his *All for Love*, both in the *Intrigue* and *Diſcovery*; which are built on an abundantly more probable Foundation, and not one jot leſs ſurprizing and fine. Nor will I yield that the Thought and Expreſſion of *Sophocles* at all excell our *Engliſh*.

The laſt Objection *Rapin* conjures up againſt Love, is, *That it is oppoſite to the Reformation of the*

Stage.

Stage. I can discover no such matter in any or at least in the best of our English Tragedies; and by *Corneil*'s Discourse on his *Theodora*, we find the *French* Theatre more Chast than the Pulpit. Nor can I discover any thing in ours that comes short of that Purity that becomes Ladies of the severest Honour to hear: I cannot say that for the Comedy of our Stage, which as to Tragedy I think needs no Reformation.

To pass therefore from the Objections against Love, to the prejudicial Effects, our Plays owe to it ; I find them too in Number ; 1. That it hinders those admirable Impressions those of the Ancients made on their Audience. 2. That it causes the decay of a Tragedy's Reputation, in a Year or two.

The first he builds on a Fallacy, *viz.* The wonderful Impressions the *Perseus* and *Andromeda* of *Euripides* had on the *Abderites.* This is not to be attributed to the Excellence either of the Poet or the People, who were so gross to think *Democritus* Mad, when in the most reasonable Employment of his Studies, the Dissection of Animals : Besides, the true cause of this Success of these Poems, is not to be granted to the Excellence of the Poet, but the Distemper the People of that City were Infected with at that time, being all Poetically Mad. As a Witness of the truth of this, hear the Account *Cælius,* *lib.* 3. *Cap.* 4. (as I find it Quoted) gives of it.

'*Tis*

'Tis reported, that the Abderites *in the time of* Lysimachus, *were Infected with a new and strange kind of Distemper, the progress of which was in this manner: First of all, an extream violent burning Fever seiz'd them, and rag'd through the whole Town; on the Seventh day, the Blood in great abundance, burst out at their Noses; and some of them were affected with violent Sweatings, after which the Fever ended; but still a very ridiculous Distemper possest'd all their Minds, they all ran Mad after Tragedies, thundring the* Iambics *about as loud as they could possibly bawl, but what they chiefly Sung, was the* Andromeda *of* Euripides, *and the Words of* Perseus. *This strange and uncommon Madness diffus'd it self very far, till the Winter and the severe Cold coming on, put an end to this Evil.*

Thus he: —— And can there be any thing more unfair, and absurd, than this condemning our Plays, for not making such Impressions on the Audience as the *Andromeda* of *Euripides* did on the *Abderites*, who were Distracted with a Fever, that made them Ravish'd with any Poetry; for we find, that it was not the *Andromeda* of *Euripides* only, but chiefly That they Recited.

But were it true, that these Plays of the Ancients made these wondrous Impressions on People in their Wits, I'm sure it is not our Poets fault, that ours are less Efficacious; the Passions cannot be more finely touch'd than in *All for Love*, and several other Plays of Mr. *Dryden*, Mr. *Otway*, &c. We must therefore attribute it to

another

another Cause. The Audience, at least the Major part of it, was compos'd of People not acquainted with the dismal *Catastrophe's* of Princes, which History now so abundantly furnishes us with, and so the uncommon Miseries of Princes on their Stage, influenc'd them ; as I have seen a Ballad of some Tragical Story, without any Poetry in it, draw Tears from some of the Female Mobb, and make the Male shake their Heads, and go very sorrowfully away. But our Audience that is generally compos'd of the better sort, are not so easily mov'd with these Events, they being made familiar to 'em by History and Observation ; with these the nice touching of the Passions chiefly move ; and I my self, dull as I am, have often experienced those effects in me, for which the Critics boast so much of the power of the Ancient Poets.

The other Effect is Ridiculous, *viz.* That it causes the decay of a Tradegy's Reputation in a Year or two. I know not indeed how far this may hold good against the *French* Poets ; but I'm very sure 'tis evidently false as to our Plays. Witness all Mr. *Drydens* ; the *Orphan*, and *Venice Preserv'd*, of Mr. *Otway* ; *Alexander* and Others, of Mr. *Lee's* ; which are still in Esteem, after several Years, and e'ry day encreasing their Reputation.

Finally, Since the Motives that are urg'd as the cause of this Innovation, are either falsly pretended, or sufficient to Justifie it ; since the Objections are invalid, and the Effects not so

Defective

Defective as our Adverfaries wou'd have them: We muft conclude, that Love is an Improvement of the Old *Dramma*, and ought therefore to be Continu'd.

I defire you'll excufe the length of my Letter, and hereafter confirm what my Arguments have aim'd at, both by your Practice and better of your own; fince you have both more leifure and better Penetration and Judgment, to fecure fo Noble a Caufe againft the frigid Oppofers of it. Woman is a glorious part of the Creation, therefore I wou'd willingly fee the Love of them Eftablish'd on as Noble a Foundation, as the Love of Glory, in the opinions of Men, which in Reality is fo far more Excellent and Happy. 'Tis a Caufe indeed, that deferves a greater Champion than my felf; and, I hope, 'twill find one in you.

To my Honour'd, Ingenious and Learned Friend, Dr. Midgely, about SLEEP and its Medicinal Property.

ALL your good Nature, your readinefs to ferve your Friend, as my felf have experienc'd; your Learning, Ingenuity, and the other Qualities that juftly render you dear to all that know you,

you, will not atone for one great Fault you are guilty of. That fault indeed is an excefs of an uncommon Vertue ; yet fince an enemy to your own Good, it muft be condemn'd by thofe that love you : Your *Modefty* I mean; for by this you keep your felf too much Unknown. This hinders you from pufhing forward in the World, whilft Men of abundantly lefs Parts, both Acquir'd and Natural, Shoulder one another for Prehemi-nence. Your Modefty, Doctor, does an Injury to the Public, as well as to your felf, in robbing both of the Advantages to be deriv'd to and from each other.

My felf not long ago, plaid the Phyfician with Succefs, tho I am yet to feek in the caufe of it : One complaining of fome approaches of an Ague, and Feverifh Symptoms, I gave him fomething that could have none or very little influence in his Cure ; a little Chalk fcrap'd very fine to take in a Glafs of Ale, and bid him Sleep after it, and this perfected the Cure. I am apt to believe the Sleep that he got, (for he flept hartily all that Nightand part of the next Morn-ing) was the chief Remedy ; the grounds of my Opinion I'll here give you.

Sleep, according to *Galen,* is *nothing elfe but the Quiet or Reft of the Animal Faculties.* This Definition is taken from the *Effects.* *Ariftotle* terms it, the *Impotence of the Senfes,* with a great deal of Reafon, which his Interpreters rightly obferve, is not a deftruction and lofs of the Sen-fes, but a difficult and clog'd Senfe : For, a Man

that

that is a Sleep, is not without his Senses, tho
they are with some difficulty affected: The defect of Perception in the Senses of a sleeping Man,
is attributed to their Impotence and the force of
Sleep, by which all the Senses and Animal Actions are lock'd or bound np. But *Galen* in the
above quoted Definition, does justly term *Sleep*,
the Rest or Repose of the Animal Actions, because both the *Vital*, as the *Pulses* and the *Breath-
ing*, and the *Natural Actions*, as the *Concoction of
the Ventricle*, which are very well continu'd in
Sleep, do not Cease, but are then more justly
perform'd. As for Example, The motion or
beating of the Heart is thought to be stronger
Sleeping than Waking.

But as for the *Matter of Sleep*, I find it thus in
a Modern Author Defin'd, *Somnus est vapor qua-
dam benignus Sanguinis, Spiritus, & humidioris
Arteriæ, qui per venas jugulares, & per arte-
rias carotidas fertur ad cerebrum & sensum commu-
nem vincit. Sleep is a certain friendly Vapour of
the Blood, the Spirit, and the more humid Artery,
which is convey'd by the jugular Veins and Carotid
Arteries to the Brain, and make the* Sensum commu-
nem. This must be confess'd to be some description or account of Sleep. There are therefore three requisites to a gentle and composed
Sleep; a *temperate Brain*, a *friendly Moisture*, and
a *quiet Mind*; for many tho' they sleep in all appearance, yet are disturb'd in their Minds, as
is evident from the Example of *Dido*, when in
Love with *Æneas*.

Phænissa

—————— *Phœniſſa nec unquam*
Solvitur in ſomnos oculis, nec peſtore Noſtem
Accipit. ————— ——— —

But ſhe was quite Reſtleſs, and without Sleep.

As to the efficient Cauſe of Sleep, I think it
the *Brain*, which is the firſt Senſory, tho *Ariſtotle* makes the Heart ſo. Whence I believe,
proceeded our common Saying when we are
very much diſpoſed to Sleep, that *our Heart's
a Sleep*. 'Tis therefore the Refrigeration or
Cooling of the Brain that cauſes Sleep, as the
Calefaction, or Warming of this firſt Senſific, is
the cauſe of our Awaking, and keeping Awake.
The former Author tells us—— *Somnus fit cum
ſeſe (quamvis non quieſcat) relaxat primum Senſifi-
cum, quo Spiritus animales redintegrentur. Hoc au-
ſtem evenit à blandioribus vaporibus ſublatis Sanguine
ac ſuavi pituita in cerebrum: Quibus refrigeratis, &
in roſcidum madorem coaſtis, nervorum meatus ob-
linuntur & quaſi obligantur.*

The chief *end* therefore of Sleep is, the reſto-
ring of the animal Spirits; and that the Actions of
the whole Animal acquire new Strength, and begin afreſh: As 'tis in *Ovid.*

*Quod caret alterna requie, durabile non eſt
Hoc reparat vires, feſſaq; membra levat.*

But

But besides this primary and chief end or effect of Sleep, there are others, as that the *Coction* of the *Ventricle* may be the better effected, and the Distempers and their Symptoms mitigated: For Sleep better concocts our Nourishment, mitigates the Matter of Distempers, and lessens all Symptoms. This is the reason that Children are often Cur'd of very great Sicknesses by Sleep alone.

But not to enter into a Discourse I'm so very ill qualifi'd for as this, I'll pass to a more pleasant and easie Task; I mean, the Religious use the Ancients made of Sleep, and the manner of Curing Distempers of the Priests of *Æsculapius* or *Priapus*, heretofore; to whom whilst they slept in their Chappels, those Medicinal Gods, disclos'd their Remedies for the Distemper'd that sought their help, and Advice to those who sought their Counsel. Thus *Quartilla* in *Petronius Arbiter* tells *Encolpius* and *Ascyltos*, that she had sought Help of the God *Priapus* in her Sleep, for her Ague, and *Encolpius* Comforts her in these words a little after, when she desir'd they shou'd not divulge the Secrets of the Rites of *Priapus*, which they had seen: *Nam neq; (says he) sacra quenquam evulgaturum, & si quod præterea aliud Remedium ad Tertianam Deus illi monstrâsset, adjuturos nos Divinam providentiam, vel periculo nostro.* That none of 'em wou'd divulge the Rites of her God, but on the contrary, wou'd at the expence of their own hazard endeavour to assist his divine Providence, if he shou'd reveal

veal any other Remedy for the cure of her
Ague. And *Suetonius* in the Life of *Vespasian*,
says, *Orantes opem valitudine demonstratam à Sera-*
pide per quietem restituturum oculos, si inspuisset.
This was a common thing in Antiquity to take
the *Responsa*, or Answers of the Gods by Dreams,
for *Ille incubat Jovi*, signifies, He sleeps in the *Ca-*
pitol, to receive the Oracles or Answers of that
God. Thus the Sick us'd to sleep in the Temple
of *Æsculapius*, to receive Remedies in their Sleep
from him. There was a famous and celebrated
Temple of *Æsculapius* in *Epidaurus*, to which
the Sick us'd to go on Pilgrimage from several
Places. Extraordinary Examples of this kind
of Cures one of your Profession (which has
yielded the World abundance of Learned, Ingenious and Witty Men) produces the first Chap.
and first Book *De arte Gymnastica*; I mean,
Hieron. Mercurialis. He will have it that *Hippo-*
crates form'd his Body of Medicine from these
Nocturnal Revelations of the Gods; that is from
the Tables that were hung up in the Temples,
with an account of them. *An totam* (says he)
Medicinæ partem, quæ ad sanos & victus rationem
pertinet, ex tabellulis, aliisq; donariis Æsculapii
Templo dicatis Hippocrates *conflaverit? An. vero*
totam in curandis Morbis versantem Clinecem voca-
tam, quemadmodum Varro, Strabo, *atq;* Plinius,
credidisse videntur, mihi plane compertum non est:
Nisi quod fuit mos liberatos Morbis in Templo ejus
Dei, quod auxiliatum esset scriberet. Isq; impri-
mis illis temporibus usq; ad Antonini Imperatoris *æta-*
tem,

tem, non modo in Græcia, *verum etiam in* Italia *per-
duravit. Uti præ cæteris, ex Tabella Marmorea*
Romæ *in* Æsculapii *Templo in Insula Tiberina in-
venta, & usq; in hunc diem apud Maphæos conser-
vata, intelligere licet, in qua Græce hæc· leguntur.*
I am not certain (says he) *whether* Hippocrates
*Compos'd all that part of the Medicinal Art, which
relates to the ordering of both Health and Diet, out
of the little Consecrated Tablets and other Gifts in
the Temple of* Æsculapius, *or only that part of the
Curing of Distempers which is nominated* Clinick, *as*
Varro, Strabo *and* Pliny *seem to have thought:
But that 'twas a Custom for the Sick to write in
the Temple of that God the Remedy that had Cur'd
them; which Custom continued to the time of* Antoninus, *not only in* Greece, *but also in* Italy, *as we
may above all others understand from the Marble
Table found in the Templet of* Æsculapius *in* Rome,
in the Tiberine *Island, and preserv'd till this day
by the* Maphæi, *in which this that follows is in
Greek.*

I.

Αὐταῖς ταῖς ἡμέραις, &c.

In these days he gave an Oracle to one Claudius
*that was Blind, that he should come to the Sacred
Altar, and kneel down; and then come from the
Right side to the Left, and put five Fingers on the
Altar, and lift up his Hand and put it on his own
Eyes: And he saw perfectly in the Presence of the*

People,

People, who Congratulated him, and Rejoic'd, that
such great Miracles were perform'd under our Emperor Antoninus.

2.

Λουχιω πλευρίτικῷ, χαὶ, &c.

The God gave an Oracle to Lucius, that had a
Pain in his Side, and was despair'd of by all Men,
that he should come and take Ashes from the Altar,
and mix them with Wine, and put them on his Side;
upon which he Recovered, and returned his Thanks to
the God, and the People Congratulated him.

3.

Αἷμα αναφεροντι Ἰκλίαιῷ, &c.

Julianus vomiting Blood, being despaired of by all
Men, received an Oracle from the God, that he shou'd
come and take off from the Altar Pine-Apples, and
eat them for three days with Honey, and he Recovered, and publickly in the Presence of the People gave
Thanks.

4.

Ουαλερίῳ Ἀπρῳ ρατιώτι τυφλῷ, &c.

The God gave an Oracle to Valerius Aper, a
Blind Soldier, That he should come and take the Blood
of

of a *White Cock,* and mixing it with *Honey,* compose a *Medicine* for his *Eyes,* and wear it for three days on them ; and he saw, and came and *Publickly* return'd Thanks to the God.

And I guess (continues *Mercurialis*) by these Verses of *Tibullus,* that the same us'd to be done in the Temple of *Isis.*

Nunc dea, nunc succurre mihi jam posse mederi,
Picta docet Templis multa Tabella tuis.

You may find more of this kind in *Joseph Scaliger,* in his *Indicibus Inscriptionum antiquarum, a Grutero Collectarum.* And indeed this seems to be something of the Practice of the *Jews,* to take Divine Oracles as they slept in the Temple : For thus I find it in the 3d. Chapter of the First Book of *Samuel,* ver. 3. *Samuel* slept *in the Temple of the Lord, where the Ark of God was.* 4. *Then the Lord call'd* Samuel, *and he answered and said, Here I am.* We may gather from *Geor. Fabricius,* that this Custom of sleeping in Temples or Churches, is still continued in *Italy* ; for he says he observ'd at *Padua,* young Country Fellows and Lasses, to lie in the Church of St. *Anthony* on a certain Night.

And now I think 'tis time to Wake, having rambl'd as if in a Dream, from one thing to another ; from my just Acknowledgments, to my Emperic Exploit ; from thence to the Medici-

nal

nal Power of Sleep, and thence to its Religious
Use: So that if I wou'd not have you Sleep too
in spight of the Variety, I must conclude here as
always, that I am,

S I R,

Your extreamly Obliged

Friend and Humble Servant,

Char. Gildon.

To LUCINDA.

May the 10.

I Received your's this Morning, which has put
me so much out of Humour, that it ought to
be no wonder if I write in a Stile different from
my former.   I told you in mine, the Judgment
of the Men of Sense, of your Beloved *Athenians.*
I have the Honour to know some of the greatest
Wits, and best Judges of Sense and Learning;
who unanimously agree in as contemptible an
Opinion of them, as they express of their Adversaries at all Times.

But

But after all, Madam, I fhall be very little concern'd if you put the worft Conftruction you can upon my Demeanour in this Bufinefs, fince 'tis pardonable in me, who, you know own'd my felf for a little neceffary Diffimulation, till you made me a Convert to univerfal Sincerity, which I'll always preferve for the future. But I never pretended my Life exempt from Faults or Follies — No, on the contrary, I confefs I have been more guilty of both, than moft; and among that Number, I reckon this and fome other foolifh Trifles that fhall be Namelefs: But I defign to fet a ftricter Guard on my Words and Actions for the future, and not let any Bye Refpect betray me to fay or do any thing I may repent of without the Power of retrieving. This Change I partly owe to fome Inconveniences I have drawn on my felf by Inconfideration; tho I own to you, even now, that I chiefly owe it to your well-acted Sincerity. You drew I confefs, Madam, the aimable Picture of a fine Woman (I wrong the Noble Idea you gave me of your felf, by giving it the Title of Woman) And oh! that the Lovely Piece had charm'd your Heart as it did mine; it won me fo entirely, that I hope I fhall never act contrary any more to the divine Vertue of Sincerity; from which, Madam, I muft tell you, with a great deal of Diftraction, that you extreamly deviate, who could in your laft affure me, that you made no Enquiry about me, when to my certain Knowledge, you could not

know

know me to be the Author of that Book but by
a very nice Enquiry. Woman indeed, was so
well known to me, that 'twas my Fault to be
so monſtrouſly impos'd on, as to believe there
could be any one of the Sex qualified with a
Vertue ſo oppoſite to a Woman's Nature as Sincerity. That indeed, was the golden Work,
the Chymiſtry of my Converſation has been ſo
long in Chaſe of; and oh! you made me fond-
ly believe I'd found the mighty Treaſure in
you becauſe you glitter'd: But alas! the golden Fantom vaniſh'd like thoſe deluding Hopes,
and I find a Woman of Wit and Senſe exalted
with Sincerity, is as meer a Fancy as the Philoſo-
pher's Stone. That was the Beauty that chain'd
my Soul to *Mirtilla*, and made me value her a-
bove all Sublunary Goods; that made me ſigh
for the Enjoyment of her Converſation; but
now the gay Viſion's paſt, and you have wak'd
me to find you a very, very Woman.

I have been too tedious on this Paragraph of
your Letter to give a preciſe Anſwer to the reſt,
I ſhall reſerve that till another Time, and only
now tell you, *Firſt*, That you do me but Juſtice to think no worſe of me for the Declara-
tion of a Truth, you deſired to know, with all
the Sincerity in Nature; for Madam, I muſt
always own 'twas ſuch a Veneration I had for
you, that I cou'd not but be free and ſincere with
you. *Next*, That Liberty like Religion is a
Word of a double Meaning, and equally pernicious to Human Kind. Miſtake me not, Madam,

I mean

I mean as to the villainous Use that has always been made of both ; not as to true and real Religion and Liberty, which I'm for as much as any, and am so good a Patriot, that I'd rather be tortur'd an Age for the least good of my Country, than do the least Action against the real Interest of it. *Lastly*, That tho it wou'd yet be extreamly grateful to be admitted to your Conversation, yet since you obstinately persist to have it so, I must submit to your Conditions, but I desire you wou'd put me to as little Expence of Patience as you can, because I still earnestly desire to obtain what I have with such Ardor requested, that is, the Conversation of *Mirtilla*, in Hopes to make you by my real Sincerity my Convert, as your pretended Sincerity made me your's; which wou'd be an extraordinary Happiness to

Madam,

Your Humble Servant,

and Sincere Friend,

Lycidas.

A Short View of Old Rome, in a Letter to URANIA.

NEver wonder at *Ovid*'s Trouble for being Banish'd from Old *Rome*, since we find that St. *Augustine* made it One of his Three Wishes, to have seen it in all its Glory ; as it was when *Ovid* liv'd. I'll give you but an imperfect View of it, as I can collect it from *Pliny*, and you'll confess it raises in you a most Magnificent Idea; what must then the Noble Remains that were in St. *Austin*'s Time give him?

I will begin with the *Grand Circo* built by *Julius Cesar*, a Work not of Ages, but of a few Years (for he Reign'd but five, reckoning from his first coming to *Rome* after his passing the *Rubicon*.) It was Three Furlongs in Length, and one in Breadth ; surrounded with Magnificent Buildings, able to contain two Hundred and sixty Thousand Spectators. The Palace of *Paulus*, all adorned with *Phrygian* Columns. The Temple of Peace built by *Vespasian* with all the Beauty, Art, and Expence could bestow. The *Pantheon* built by *Agrippa*, to *Jove the Avenger*, when *Valerius Ostiensis* a famous Architect, had covered that *Theatre* in which *Libo* exhibited Shews and Plays to the People of *Rome*. Can we admire the Expences of the barbarous Kings, in the raising the Pyramids, when the very Ground
for

for the Building the *Forum* cost *Cæsar* the Dictator in those Days, above Ten Thousand Sestertii; and if the Expence and dearness of things be of any Force. *Publius Clodius* who was killed by *Milo*, lived in a House that cost 1484 Sestertii, which seems to me to fall but little short of the Extragance of Kings in their Palaces; but in those Days the *Romans* were Admirers of any great Works however less beautiful, as the Vastness of the Ramparts of the *Capitol*, with its prodigious Foundations. I cannot omit the very subterraneal Magnificence of this City, even in the wondrous Conveyances of the Common-Shoars, so Spacious, that one might have Sail'd under a Pendulous City, through Rocks, which have been Penetrated to let in seven Civulets, which flow'd in with a rapid Course like a Torrent, to carry away all before them; which being increas'd and agitated by the Rains from above, beat and dasht against the sides with great Vehemency: Sometimes the River *Tyber* ran back into these Channels; where tho' the several Streams at their meeting fought and made a great deal of do, yet the firmness of the Pile and Buildings, resisted its unruly Force. These admirable Arches out-braved Ages, Earthquakes and Ruins, from the time of *Tarquinius Priscus*, to the Destruction of *Rome*; for that King it was that Built them; who when he undertook to perform a Work of that difficulty both for Length and Danger, by the Hands of the *Roman* People, put to Death all
those

those that fled from the Fatigue of the Undertaking; for the pursuance and perfecting of which,
he made use of a Remedy unheard of before or
after; which was, That all the Bodies of the
Citizens that were executed on this account,
shou'd some be fix'd on Crosses and expos'd to
the view of the People, and others in their Presence given for Food to the Wild Beasts and
Ravenous Birds; which produc'd this effect, that
they that beheld 'em, struck with a shame to be
daunted at any Undertaking, with a bold Zeal
for the Honour of the 'Roman' Name, which had
often preserv'd them at the lowest ebb of Fortune in Battles, push'd on the Work with all the
fervour imaginable; which the King observing,
took hold of the opportunity to enlarge his Im-
positions upon them, making them extend those
Subterraneal Passages to that bigness and height,
that a Cart very much loaden with Hay might
easily pass through them. But all I have already said, is inconsiderable, if we compare it to
one Miracle, which is this, When *Marcus Lepidus* and *Quintus Catulus* were *Consuls*, there
was no Nobler Structure in *Rome* than the House
of *Lepidus* himself; but within Thirty five Years
after, that was not the hundredth part as big as
innumerable Palaces that were then Raz'd. *Marcus
Scaurus*, when he was *Ædile*, with his private
Wealth and Abilities perform'd a Work beyond
all that ever was made by any before, design'd
not for time, but Eternity; and this was a *Theatre*, in which were a tripple order of Scenes

to

to the height of Three hundred and sixty Columns, the lower part was of Marble, the middle of Glass (strange kind of Luxury!) and the uppermost were adorn'd with Golden Tablets, the Brass Statues betwixt these Pillars, were in in number Three thousand; and the Pitt it self was capable of holding Fourscore thousand Spectators. To this I may add a greater Prodigy, effected by *Caius Curio*, who follow'd the part of *Julius Cæsar* in the Civil War; for when at the Funeral of his Father he saw he cou'd not surpass *Scaurus* in Pomp, Wealth, Beauty, and Nobleness of the Structure, Magnificence of the Furniture and Decorations, resolved to out-do him in Ingenuity: Therefore he caus'd two most spacious Theatres of Wood to be made near to one another, and hung them on a Versatile Ballance or Hinge; so in the Morning when the Plays were perform'd, they were Back to Back, (as I may say) but in the Evening after all the People were in them, they were whirl'd about on their Hinges, the Scenes of both descending as they met together, and Compos'd in a Moment an Amphitheatre, in which immediately were presented the Fights of the *Gladiators*. What can we most admire in this, the Invention, or the Inventor? The Artificer, or Designer? Him that durst imagin such a bold Effort, or him that could reduce it to Practice? But that which seems most strange to me, is, that the People should be so mad to venture themselves in so ticklish and uncertain a Seat. Behold, (says *Pliny*)

This

*This is that People that have Subjugated the whole
Earth, which has ftifl'd Kingdoms and Nations,
and gives Laws to far Countries, a certain Part and
Portion of the Immortal Gods, compared to the reft
of Mankind: Behold them I fay, fwinging in a pon-
derous Machine, and clapping and loudly applauding
to their own Danger. Behold all the* Roman *People
aboard two Veffels as it were, which were only fepa-
rated from Deftruction by two Hinges that fupported
them, gazing at the Combates of the* Gladiators,
*with Pleafure, tho they were fo near Perifhing them-
felves if the Machine fail'd.* What might not he
have perfwaded the *Roman* People to, who cou'd
fo eafily prevail with them to venture into a
hanging Theatre, as if he intended to Sacrifice
the whole Nation, at the Funerals of his Father,
or at leaft bid fair for it. Had *Caligula* pre-
pared fuch an Engine, he need not have been at
the expence of fo fruitlefs a Wifh, as that all the
Romans had but one Neck, that at one Blow he
might Difpatch 'em. But after the Hinges were
fo worn by Ufe that they wou'd no longer turn, he
vary'd it and left it in the form of an *Amphitheatre.*
After this, what need I tell you of the Golden
Palaces of *Nero* and *Caius,* or the Aquaducts of
the King *Quintus Martius,* or thofe Additions
which *Agrippa* made to them when he was *Ædile,*
who befides the Reparations of the Old, made
Seven Hundred Lakes, and an Hundred and Five
Fountains. Built a Hundred and Thirty Magnificent Hoftels, and Adorn'd thefe Buildings with
Three Hundred Statues of Brafs and Marble,

and

and Four Hundred Marble Pillars, and all this in the space of One Year. And for the eternal Fame of his Ædileſhip, he gave Shews to the People for near Threeſcore Days, beſides an Hundred and Seventy *Bagnio's*, as a free Gift; which Places were afterward increaſed in *Rome*, to an infinite Number. But the *Aqueducts* that were begun by *Julius Cæſar*, and finiſh'd by *Claudius*, far ſurpaſs'd the former. But if we ſhou'd nearly conſider the abundance of Water that was us'd in public, in Baths, Fiſh-Ponds, Houſes, Conduits and Gardens, in the Suburbs, and *Villa's* as well as City, the Arches that were built to convey it, the Mountains that were cut through, the Valleys that were level'd, we muſt grant that there cou'd be nothing more Admirable in the whole World. Next let me paſs to the Rareties of Art, as the Statues and Obeliſc's which were brought to *Rome* from abroad : Firſt the *Thebane* Obeliſc was made and erected by the Labour of Twenty Thouſand Men : The King himſelf when it was ſet up, fearing that the *Machines* won'd not be of ſufficient Strength to ſupport the vaſtneſs of the Weight, without an extraordinary Caution of the Workmen, to make them take the more care in erecting it, caus'd his Son to be faſtn'd to the very top of it, that their Endeavours for his Safety, ſhou'd conduce to the happy placing the Stone. The Prodigious Wonders of this Work made *Cambyſes* when he took this City of *Thebes*, and came almoſt to the Pedeſtal of this Obeliſc with Fire and Sword,

to

to command the Flames to be extinguish'd, he being struck with Astonishment at so awfull a Pile, who had no Compassion for the City its self. In *Alexandria, Ptolomæus Philadelphus* set up one of Eighty Cubits, which King *Nectabis* had caus'd to be hewn out of a Rock; but it prov'd much a greater Difficulty to carry it to its Place and erect it. Some say 'twas carried a Ship-board by the Famous Architect *Satyrus*. Others, that a Channel was cut from beyond the place where the Obelisc lay, under it, to the River *Nilus*; and then Two very broad Vessels joyn'd together, and so deeply laden, that they might when they came up the Channel, go under the Obelisc, (it reaching like a Bridge, from one side of this *Cut* to the other) And being come exactly under it, they unloading them, by degrees the Vessels rose out of the Water, and so lifted up the Obelisc from the Ground, and thus bore it down into the *Nile*. Out of this same Mountain there is a Tradition, that Six were cut of the same Magnitude, and that the Master Work-man had Fifty Talents given him for a Reward. But this Obelisc was set up in *Arsinoe* by the forementioned King, in Honour of his Wife *Arsinoe*, who was also his Sister; and from thence *Maximus* when he was Prefect in *Egypt*, Transported it, tho such a vast and unwieldy Cargo for a Ship; and plac'd it in the *Forum*, having cut off the Top of it, designing to put one of Gold in its Room, which afterwards notwithstanding he neglected. There are Two

more

more at *Alexandria*, in the Portico's of the Temple of *Cæsar* Forty Two Cubits high, which King *Mesphees* made. The chief Difficulty was to Tranfport them crofs the Sea to *Rome*, in Ships of the Firft Rate. Nor muft I omit that *Obelifc* which was plac'd in the *Grand Circo* by *Auguftus*, which was made by King *Semnefertes*, in whofe Reign *Pythagoras* was in *Egypt* : It was One Hundred Twenty Five Foot, and Three Quarters high, befides the Bafis of the fame Stone. But that which was in the Field of *Mars*, was made by *Sefoftris* : Both contain Infcriptions of the *Egyptians* Interpretations of Natural things, by their Philofophy. This laft *Auguftus* apply'd to a wonderfull Ufe, turning it to the Gnome of a Dial, receiving the Shadow of the Sun, and by it diftinguifh'd the Length of the Days, Nights and Hours, on the Pavement, which he had made to the Proportion of the Obelifc, and divided with Lines and Marks of inlaid Brafs, on which the Shadow decreas'd and increas'd by degrees, and fo artificially denoted the Motions of time. A thing fays *Pliny*, in my Opinion, worthy the Knowledge of Pofterity. There was another Obelifc in the *Vatican Circo* of *Caius* and *Nero* : And this alone amongft them all, wat broken in the making. The Son of *Sefoftris* made this, as well as another of an Hundred Cubits in height, and Confecrated to the Sun by the Order of the Oracle for the Reftoration of his Sight, after he had been Blind. There was a Statue of *Hercules* in the

Beaft-

Beaſt-Market, which was for nothing ſo remarkable, as its Antiquity and Title; for 'tis ſaid to be Conſecrated by *Evander* to him: And it obtain'd the Name of Triumphal, from being Habited in Triumphal Garments, as often as there is any Triumph. The Statue of *Janus* with his Double Face, muſt not be forgot, conſecrated to him by King *Numa*, which was Ador'd and Sacrific'd to, both for War and Peace; his Fingers being ſo contriv'd, that they denoted in Three Hundred Sixty Five Days the Year and Age. *Mummius* having Conquer'd *Achaia*, repleniſh'd the City with Statues: The *Luculli* too, brought not a few into it. Before the Burning of the *Capitol* by the Faction of *Vitellius*, there was in the Fane of *Juno*, a Dog carv'd in Braſs licking of his Wounds, which was of ſuch a noble Boldneſs, that the Value of it was beyond Purchaſe; and therefore Conſecrated to the Goddeſs. In the *Capitol* was a Statue of *Apollo*, of that prodigious Height, that it was called a *Coloſſus*; and this was brought from *Apollonia*, a City in *Pontus*, by *Marcus Lucullus*: It was Thirty Cubits high, and coſt One Hundred and Twenty Talents. Like this is that *Coloſſus* of *Jupiter*, Conſecrated by *Claudius Cæſar*. Beſides, theſe in *Rome*, were an Hundred other *Coloſſuſes* of a leſſer Magnitude.

To ſay nothing of the admirable Pictures that *Pliny* mentions, all far beyond *Raphael*, *Angelo*, *Titian*, and our Modern Artiſts, we may in ſhort, Reflect, That *Rome* muſt indeed be a

Divine

Divine Sight, whence all the Noblest pieces of Art that the Conquer'd World afforded, were Transported by the Conquerors to *Rome,* to contribute to its Majesty and Glory. Add to this the Politeness of the People *Ovid* left, and the Brutality of those he went to ; and we may well cease to admire at his Impatience, and Flattery of his Persecutor *Augustus,* for a Return. But you may see a more perfect Draught of this City in *Fabricius* his Collation of Old and New *Rome.* I am,

Madam,

>> *Your Friend and Humble Servant,*

>>> Viridomar.

To the Charming and Ingenious
URANIA.

I'll no more accuse my Fortune, *Urania,* since she has given me so generous an Antidote against all her Venomous Influence, as your *Friendship,* that furnishes me with a very *satisfactory* Retreat from all the violent Onsets of my ill Stars, where I can unload my Soul, and communicate all my Complaints. If I meet with *Villainies* and *Ingratitude,*

O

titude, the common Offspring of *Trust* and *generous Offices*; I'm fensibly pleas'd, that I can with affurance of Pity, tell my Charming Friend my Pain. This is the occafion of this Letter; for, tho I have no *Villainy* to complain of at this time, having had no *Trust* Betray'd; nor any *Ingratitude* to Refent, becaufe I have not been in a Capacity of Obliging the Perfon I addrefs'd to; yet have I ftill abundant reafon to Sigh for the continual *ill Luck* that attends my Endeavours.

I know *Urania*, you have often told me, that 'tis a very falfe Meafure to judge of others by my own Inclinations; and your Advice, I muft grant, carries a great deal of Reafon; for whether my Inclinations are juft or unjuft, I'm ten to one in the wrong, when I judge of another by them; fince Mankind differ not only in their Sentiments of the *fame thing*, by the different Apprehenfions each Man Naturally has; but the very Circumftances and ftate of our *Affairs*, give a various turn to our *Sentiments*; fo that we differ not only from one another, but even from our *Selves*, as our *Fortune* alters *our Condition*. But when I was miftaken in *Pollio*, I follow'd a more *common* and *receiv'd* tho not lefs *fallacious* Guide, than the former, that is, Report. *Pollio* has the *Reputation* of a *Generous Man*, and may be fo perhaps to others; but I'm fure he does not diftinguifh betwixt thofe who are and are not fit Objects for his *Generofity*. A *pleafant* Companion diverts and feafons our Hours of Converfation, and permits not our Judgment to weigh the Me-
rits

rits of the Perſon that affords us ſo agreeable an Entertainment. And this perhaps has miſſed *Pollio*, who has met with Ingratitude enough from ſome of that Character, whom he has highly Oblig'd ; for perhaps, even I could almoſt grant were not unpleaſant, if not witty Company. But Alas ! one of *Pollio*'s Experience ſhou'd know, that Men of that Faculty, have ſeldom any juſt Notion of things, at leaſt of 𝕮𝖊𝖗𝖙𝖚𝖊 and 𝕳𝖔𝖓𝖔𝖚𝖗 : They are their *own Gods*, and Sacrifice all to themſelves ; their very looſeſt and gayeſt Hours, that one wou'd think free from Deſign, are like the Miſer's Preſents to a young heir Apparent, only to draw ſome Advantage to themſelves in *Vanity* or *Intereſt*. And I muſt ſay, I never knew one of theſe *Witty* Companions that ever abounded much with *Sincerity*. Not that I wou'd extend this Obſervation beyond all Exceptions: But I'm ſure Prudence ſhou'd chuſe where there's leſs probability of Deceit. On the contrary I have courted his *Friendſhip* as well as *Generoſity*; *That* with a real Deſire, and *This* on no very great Matter, but have ſcarce met with a Return anſwerable to my Expectation. In ſhort, *Urania*, 'twou'd be tedious to tell you all my thoughts of *Pollio* now ; what they were when I wrote the following Verſes, theſe will let you ſee ; the effect they had, I ſhall conclude this Letter with.

To

To *POLLIO*.

The COMPLAINT.

I.

'TIs now *dead Night, and hush'd is e'ery thing*;
The *busie Cit*, and the *laborious Clown*;
The *cringing Parasite*, and *haughty Gown*;
  The *Plotting Statesman* too,
  And with his Gilded Cares the King,
  Are all at sweet Repose.
What when awake they *all* refuse;
And Sleep, Death's Image, seem'd as Death will do,
To've equall'd the poor Cottage and the Crown,
  No Wretch but me so much Unblest
  As not to be at Rest;
  Of Hope forsaken, and by Fate Opprest;   }
Despair with all its wild Anxieties,
Drives Quiet from my *Mind*, and Slumbers from
                                (my *Eyes*.

II.

Why do I Live? Why hug my *boundless Woe*,
When *Friendly* Death sets wide the Gate,
That leads to a more happy State?
    For not at all to be,
    Is better than the ills of Life to know,
  When Priestly *Barbarism* does reign
    Almost in e'ry Heart;

                                        And

And scarce one good *Samaritan* is found,
    That with one 𝔰𝔬𝔯𝔡𝔦𝔡 𝕽𝖆𝖌𝖌 will part,
To Cloath the *shuddring* Wretch, or bind his *gaping*
    Why sooth I then my present Pain, (Wound.
With the *faint* Shadow of a fansy'd Ease,
    Rather than Cure the Disease,
With *Balmy* 𝕯𝖊𝖆𝖙𝖍, its sure and lasting Remedy?

III.

When th' ills of Life too great and num'rous grow,
    They are the 𝕾𝖚𝖒𝖒𝖔𝖓𝖊𝖗𝖘 of *Fate*:
    And 'tis too foolish a Debate
    (Punish'd by present Pain)
To argue if we shou'd Obey or no.
    In tort'ring Dreams I've often found
My self with threatning Dangers compass'd round,
O'er Hills I flie, o'er Vales, o'er Shades in vain,
    The fansy'd Terror meets me when I light,
       Or close behind
    Pursues my *Imaginary* Flight :
      But when my *Lab'ring* Mind
From *near* 𝕯𝖊𝖘𝖙𝖗𝖚𝖈𝖙𝖎𝖔𝖓, can no Refuge find,
  I Wake, and all the *racking* Scene withdraws,
The Horrors past, are lost in present Joys.

IV.

So in the *gloomy* 𝕯𝖗𝖊𝖆𝖒 of Life, I see
My tatter'd Bark in 𝕱𝖔𝖗𝖙𝖚𝖓𝖊's *boistrous* Sea.
To e'ry Wind in vain I shift my Sail,
Sinister *Fate* allows no *Prosp'rous* :

                  In

In *vain* I strive to reach the *distant* Shoar,
For *all around* the angry Billows roar,
And on each side encrease th' *unequal* War.
Ten thousand Waves, each big with *certain Fate*,
On one poor sinking Bark with fury Beat :
My Sails are useless, and my Rudder lost ;
By clashing Surges to and fro I'm tost ;
Within no help ; no Succour from without,
Despair and Ruin hem me round about.
Approach then 𝕯𝖊𝖆𝖙𝖍, this *racking Scene* destroy ;
Ah ! Wake this Tempest-beaten wretch to *long-*
 (sought 𝕮𝖆𝖑𝖒𝖘 and 𝕵𝖔𝖞

V.

 (Night ! *)*
Ha ! what bright Dawn thus breaks this dismal
What *Welcome* Beams their *friendly* force unite,
To raise my drooping Soul with their *auspicious*
 (Light ! *)*

Behold the golden Glory spreads apace,
 The Heavens assume a calmer Face,
And all the loud tumultuous Billows cease !
 The threatning Storm is Over-blown,
 The scatter'd Clouds now disappear,
 And the grim Terrors of Despair
 Are all dispers'd and gone.
Whence, Ah ! whence these Rays Divine,
That with so *strong*, so *kind* a Lustre Shine ?

VI.

Lo ! now the Heavenly Cause draws near ;
See, see the mighty Goddess 𝕳𝖔𝖕𝖊 appear !
Her fluid Robes, which *subtle Threads* compose
 (From

(*From the thin Brains of* fond Projectors *Spun*)
Her naked Beauties to the Eye diſcloſe;
Beauties far brighter than the Mid-day Sun;
Fairer than Fancy e'er drew Woman-kind,
Tho' the *vain fancy* of a *Love-ſick* Mind.
Her ſpacious Front, and her inviting Eye,
Are fill'd with *humble* Majeſty.
Falſe Joys around her ſmiling Viſage Play,
　　To ſooth depending Wretches Pain,
　　　In ſpight of damn'd Delay
　　And its *long Melancholy Train.*
Her Head with *Lawrel,* and with *Myrtle's* Crown'd;
　　With her left *Hand* where e'er ſhe goes
　　　She *thinly* ſtrows
　　The Warriour's and the Lover's Wreaths;
　　But Courtiers *flat'ring Promiſes,*
With *liberal Hand* ſhe ſcatters *all around.*

VII.

Her right *Hand* boundleſs Stores does hold
　Of Liberty, of Happineſs, and Gold.
Which tho' ſhe ſeem to promiſe e'ery one
That waits about her Viſionary Throne,
　　Yet faſt ſhe graſps the wiſh'd for Treaſure,
　　And does in *ſcanty Portions* Meaſure,
　　To *Few,* and *Late,* the tardy *Pleaſure.*
A Thouſand *curling* Clouds ſhe ſits upon,
Of Colour various, and of Matter rare,
(As *Acme* Beauteous, ſubtle as the Air;
Soft as the *Downy Boſom* of that Charming Fair)
Exhal'd from the wanton *Wiſhes of Mankind,*
And all the Numerous Vanities of *his ſickly Mind.*

A

Avarice, *Ambition*, *Love*, *untasted Bliss*,
With all the *gaudy Train* of fond Desire,
The Bigots *future* Joy, and States-Man's *coming*
   That set the *foolish* World on Fire, (Happiness,
The Pompous Pageant's mighty Frame support.)
     Num'rous and vast is the Resort }
    That throng her wide Imaginary Court.)
As far as e'er her friendly Beams extend,
Rang'd in their differing Stations they attend;
All near, or distant, dart a *longing Eye*
   On this Lov'd flattering Deity.
Beyond the reach of whose enlivening day,
Beyond the Influence of **one** *kind* Ray,
Despair in tatter'd sable Weeds Array'd,
Lurks with a *gastly Troop* within the *baneful Shade*.

VIII.

Hark! hark! methinks her *melting Voice* I hear;
   Her *Voice*, that's softer far
Than happy Lovers Billing Whispers are!
   Gently methinks the Goddess Chides
   My causeless fond Despair,
While **Pollio** lives, who never Wretch deny'd
That on his bounteous Nature yet rely'd,
And spight of the effects of *black Ingratitude*
   To damp the *gen'rous Flame*,
   Bounty and he are **so** *the same* ;
To imploring Want he *must*, nay *will* do Good,
Let **Galba** *Laugh*, *Eat*, *Drink and Whore*,
And in that *thoughtless Circle* spend his Store,
And when he's Dead, be never thought on more.
So let him die like other *Sots* and *Brutes*,
Oblivion best a Life like **Galba**'s suits.

                      But

But since a more Heroic Fire
Does wiser Pollio's Breast Inspire,
And moves him to Dispense
To drooping Poesie a kind Influence;
Let him but cast one Smile on me,
   By which from Anxious *Cares* set free,
In Verse *Immortal* I'd convey his Name,
To the last *Boundaries* of *Fame*,
And *late* Posterity shou'd see him sit
Among the *Sacred Patrons* of *Almighty Wit*;
For of their Patrons, Poets have *these Odds*,
They Poets make, but Poets make them Gods;
To Mortal *Glory,* give Eternal *Date,*
And rescue Merit *from* Destructive Fate.

By this last Stanza, my dear *Urania*, you find
what I then thought of Pollio, but I must tell
you, my opinion is much alter'd by his Carriage
since. Not because he comply'd not with my
Desires, but because he has not dealt like a Gentleman by me. If Ostentation be the Motive of
his great Actions, and a present *Vain-Glory* be the
mover of his Liberality, he has a great many of
his Rank, that carry a mighty Name in the
World ; for few have learned this noble Maxim,
that *Vertue is its own Reward*. And yet methinks
the *present* Applause of *Fools* should not be grateful to a Man of Sense. But if Pollio had not
that Nobleness of Spirit to do a *private* Good,
yet methinks he should not submit to do a *little
thing*, as you know some of his Demeanour to
                          me

me was, especially in detaining what was trusted to his *Vertue*, without doing what was expected from that *Trust*. But I'll confine you no longer, *Urania*, to my Complaints, who am

Your faithful Friend,

Viridomar.

Of the MOON.

The History of the Temple of Diana *at* Ephesus, *&c. In a Letter to my Learned and Ingenious Friend, Dr.* Midgly.

I Have lately been looking over again Bishop *Wilkins* his *World in the Moon*, and cannot but agree with him, as I formerly did, that 'tis most reasonable to think that Planet capable of Inhabitants, since we know 'tis a Solid Opacous Body; that the Light it has, is only Borrow'd; and since the Discoveries made by the Telescope of *Galileus*, shew that 'tis e'ery way qualify'd for an Inhabitable World. But whether the Inhabitants be so much Wiser than us, as *Cyrano Bergerai* makes 'em, I can't tell, neither am I willing to allow them that Advantage,

vantage, since their Planet has such a dependance on our Earth, as to be oblig'd to move round us, as its Centre. I should rather agree with *Ariosto*, that makes it the *Lumber House*, or *Repository* of all things that are lost in this Earth of ours, even to the *Wits* of his *Hero* 𝔒𝔯𝔩𝔞𝔫𝔡𝔬, Bottl'd up in Bottles, like the Virtuoso's Air: But then you will answer, if I allow the *Moon* the *Receptacle* of all that is lost on our Earth, that by consequence it must be the *Juster*, *Honester*, as well as *Wiser* Abode, since *Honesty* and *Justice* have long been lost here, as well as *Wisdom*. 'Tis true, Doctor, if the Inhabitants there are one jot the better for 'em, I must yield the Cause ; but I hope our *Vertues* as well as *Wits*, are Bottl'd up from their use ; else I should wish the Bishop I mention'd but now, had perfected his Discovery, and fix'd a Correspondence betwixt us, for doubtless 'twould yield us abundance of Commodities needful for us, as well as *Wit* and *Honesty*.

However 'tis, methinks we have a greater Image of this friendly moving Light of the Heavens, than the Primitive Poetical Philosophers: They made it but a *Woman*, but we a *World*, that contains perhaps some Millions of finer Women than *Diana*: Tho 'tis probable not all so Chast, if they are not made of a much different Matter from that of our Earthly Ladies. Tho' I can't blame the Ancients for making it a Woman, from its Inconstancy, which is so natural a Folly of the Sex, that it must be thought *Characteristical*,

æteriſtical : And perhaps the Origin of this Fabu-
lous Lady *Moon*, might be from ſome *Ægyptian
Hieroglyphic* of a Woman with a Creſcent on her
Head, to denote her changable Nature and Affections.

But whence-ever it came, they had Names enough
at her Service, above an Hundred in number, too
long to inſert here. The Poets therefore gave her
a Coach too : It was but a Coach and Two ;
whereas her Brother *Phœbus* had his Coach and
Four. *Manilius, lib.* 5.

Quadrijugis & Phœbus equis, & Delia bigis.

Ovid gives her a pair of White Horſes, tho'
others differ, and will have her drawn by a Mule,
or young Heifers, or Horſes of various Colours.
They made her a Huntreſs, becauſe aſſiſting
at the Birth of her Brother *Apollo*, made her
hate all Men ; for ſhe was ſo Frighted at the
Pains her Mother underwent, that ſhe obtain'd
of *Jupiter* (for nothing but a God could ſecure
a Woman's Maidenhead) a perpetual Virginity,
as *Callimachus* tells us. And *Cicero* in his *Natura
Deorum, lib.* 2. ſays ſhe was Feign'd to aſſiſt at
the Birth of her Brother *Apollo*, tho Born at the
ſame Birth, becauſe ſhe came into the World
before him. *Jupiter* therefore according to the
ſame *Callimachus*, made her Goddeſs of *Hunting,
High-ways* and *Havens*, and beſtow'd on her
Bow, Arrows and attending Nymphs, as ſo many Maids of Honour. Hence *Horace*,

Monti-

Montium custos nemorumq; Virgo
Quæ laborantes vero puellas
Ter vocata audis, adimisq; letho,
Diva triformis.

Callimachus says, *Diana*'s Chariot is drawn by
White Hinds. She often chang'd her Habitation,
and had need therefore of some Vehicle, for now
she was above in the Heavens, now beneath,
among the Infernals. Nor is her Figure more
certain than her abode, for as a Friend of mine
has it,

Now with a full Orb she the Darkness does Chase ;
Now like Whores in the Pit, shews but half of her Face.

In *Athens*, the young Ladies that were so big
with Child, that they could not wear their usual
Girdle, or Zone, put it off in the Temple of
Diana, whence she got the Appellation of λυσίζωνος.
To her were offered the Zones or Girdles of
Women with Child, as the Garlands were to
Venus at Marriages. This Goddess also presided
over Fishers : And the Poets tell us that they us'd
to Sacrifice Bullocks to her ; but *Horace* Sacrifi-
ces a Boar to her, and *Ovid* a white Hind.

She had a most Magnificent Temple at *Ephesus*,
famous for its Building, and remarkable for its
Destruction ; of which *Natalis Comes* gives us
this Account. *Habuit* Diana *celeberrimum omnium*
Templorum, *&* Augustissimum Ephesinum, &c. *The*
most

*most Magnificent and Famous of the Temples of
Diana was at Ephesus, which was Built by the care
and Industry of all Asia, Two hundred and twenty
Years under the direction of the Architect Chesi-
phron; it was Four hundred and twenty five Feet in
Length, and Two hundred and twenty in Breadth; in
which were an hundred and twenty seven Columns,
erected by as many several Kings; and these Columns
or Pillars were wonderful in their Length as well as
Beauty, for they were sixty Foot in Heighth; thirty
six of which were very Noble, and with incredible
Art Carv'd with their several Chapiters answerable
to the Magnificence of the Pillars. Besides which, there
were an abundance of exquisite Pictures and admirable
Images or Statues, correspondent to the Grandeur
and Magnificence of the Temple: All which Herostratus an Ephesian, set on Fire and Destroyed, to
purchase to himself perpetuity of Name, since he cou'd
not effect it by his Vertues or Parts. This Combusti-
on of Diana's Temple happen'd about the Ides of
August, on the day that Alexander the Great, King
of Macedon was Born, as Plutarch says in the Life
of that Prince. But the Ephesians made a Law,
that none should mention the Name of Herostratus
for the future, under the most severe Penalties, so to deprive him of the enjoyment of that which he aimed at
the obtaining of by so great a Villainy. Thus far
Natalis.* A Description of the Ruins of this Temple, and all the Cautions us'd by the Founders of
it against Earthquakes and other Expected Causes of Ruin, *Pliny* gives us in his *Natural History*.

Among

Among other Fables of her, the Poets make
her in Love with *Endymion* sleeping on *Latmns*, a
Mountain of *Caria*, and that she Enjoy'd him according to *Catullus*.

Ut triviam furtim sub Latmia *saxa relegens*
Dulcis amor gyro devovet aerio.

So weak was the Power of a God to keep her
a Maid ! Nay, they make her very Fruitful too,
for besides Sons by this Amour with *Endymion*,
they give her fifty Daughters.

Where three Ways meet, the Ancients us'd to
perform the Rites of *Hecate*, who is call'd by
three several Names, *Luna*, *Artemis* and *Hecate*.
About the New of the Moon, the Richer sort
us'd to send a Collation to those Places where
three ways met, in the Evening, as a Supper for
Hecate ; but the Poor us'd to devour these Nocturnal Junkets of this Goddess, and give out,
that she her self had eat them, as the Priests and
their Tribe in *Daniel* ; tho' indeed these Suppers
were but very Parsimonious ; so that an ill Supper got the Proverbial Name of a Feast for *He-*
cate ; for the Poetical Divinity taught that the
Ghosts 'wou'd subsist with very little Nourishment. But that *Hecate* was the same with *Luna*,
or *Diana*, is evident from several Places, particularly from *Raphael Régius*, in his Comments on
the 7*th* Book of *Ovid's Metam.*

And

And here I think 'tis time to make an end of this Lunary Essay, lest I be thought to take so much pains about her Goddess-ship for the Influence she has on me. I wou'd not incur the Imputation of a Madman for her sake, whatever I might for the sake of some Earthly *Cynthia*, perhaps fully as Inconstant; and might deserve a greater variety of Names from her numerous Follies, than *Diana* from the several Places of her Worship. But whatever Influence the Ethereal or Terrestrial *Cynthia's* may have on me, I'm confident, that neither they, nor any other Cause can be Powerful enough to turn me to any thing that should diminish my Value and Esteem for you, or the pleasure I take in being what I shall ever Subscribe my self,

S I R,

Your Obliged and faithful

Friend and Humble Servant,

Charles Gildon.

An

An ESSAY at a Vindication of the Love-Verfes of Cowley *and* Waller, &c. *In Anfwer to the Preface of a Book Intituled,* 𝕷𝖊𝖙𝖙𝖊𝖗𝖘 𝖆𝖓𝖉 𝖁𝖊𝖗𝖘𝖊𝖘 𝕬𝖒𝖔𝖗𝖔𝖚𝖘 𝖆𝖓𝖉 𝕲𝖆𝖑𝖑𝖆𝖓𝖙.

Directed to

Mr. *CONGREVE.*

A S in my two former Critical Difcourfes of this Book againft Mr. *Rymer's* 𝖘𝖍𝖔𝖗𝖙 𝖛𝖎𝖊𝖜 𝖔𝖋 𝕿𝖗𝖆𝖌𝖊𝖉𝖞, a Zeal for the Honour of my Country in its greateft Ornaments, her Poets, Engag'd me ; fo here I cannot help challenging the fame Pretence, fince I can't fuppofe them deficient in 𝕷𝖔𝖛𝖊, without derogating from the *Juftnefs* of their Characters. But I muft confefs I have not the fame hopes of Succefs in this; for there I had to do with an *impotent Opiniator* ; but here with a Gentleman of a great deal of *Wit* and fine *Senfe.* There I addrefs'd to Parties already fenfible of the Juftice of my Caufe ; here to one who is prepoffefs'd of the contrary. But on the other hand I have the greater fatisfaction here of being Worfted by one whofe *Wit* can better defend an *Error*, than I the *Truth* ; and I'm of Opinion, that 'tis a nobler Fate to fall by the Hand of an Hero, than Conquer a *Daftard Pretender.* And tho' my Prudence might

P   be

be call'd in Question by this Attempt, yet my
generous Ambition will merit a *Magnis tamen
excidit Ausis*. One thing I must possess you of
in my favour, that my unhappy Circumstances
allow me not time to use all the Caution I ought,
or search all the Reasons might be urg'd in this
noble Cause ; so that I am not only *Viribus*, but
Opibus impar: However, I hope the Design will
gain me the Opinion of a *Good English Man*, if
my Performance shou'd not attain that of a *good
Critic*, which will sufficiently compensate my
trouble; for I shou'd be prouder to be thought
a Zealot for the Glory as well as Interest of my
Country, than the greatest Wit, and most Learned Arguer.

I shall never deny the Ancients their just Praise
of the Invention of *Arts* and *Sciences* ; but I cannot without contradicting my own Reason, allow them the Perfecters of 'em so far that they
must be our uncontroverted Patterns and Standard : For our Physicians have found the Prescripts of *Hippocrates* very Defective: And as in
Physic, so in Poetry, there must be a regard had
to the Clime, Nature, and Customs of the
People ; for the Habits of the Mind as well as
those of the Body, are influenc'd by them ; and
Love with the other Passions vary in their *Effects* as well as *Causes*, according to each Country and Age; nay, according to the very Constitution of each Person affected. This makes
me hope, that the Ingenious Author of the *Letters and Verses Amorous and Gallant*, guides himself by a fallacious Rule, when he makes the Ancients the Standard of the Excellence of the Moderns

derns (or indeed when by exalting *those*, he
wholly deprives *these* of all Honour) in Love-
Verses. His Charge is reducible to these two
Heads, *viz.* The *Occasions* and the *Performances*. He
will have it, that *the Occasions on which their Poems
are written are sought out, and that none meet with 'em
but themselves, whilst those of the Ancients are such
as happen almost to e'ry Man in Love*. Next, *That
the Verses of the Moderns, are fill'd with Thoughts
that are indeed* Surprizing *and* Glittering, *but
not* Tender, Passionate, *or* Natural *for e'ry
Man in* Love *to think*. This is the sum of his
Charge against 'em ; of which in the Order I've
plac'd 'em. First, As for the *Occasions*; I cannot remember any Subject chosen by either *Cowly*
or *Waller*, (for we've nothing to do here with
Petrarch a Foreigner) that seems to be sought
out, or unnatural for a Man in Love to choose ;
and if some of 'em do not happen to e'ry Man
in Love, they are yet on an equal Bottom with
the Ancients, many of whose *Subjects* or *Occasions*, are far from happening to all Lovers, as
none who can pretend to any knowledge of their
Writings can deny. *Corinna's* Parrot dy'd, and
Ovid writes its Funeral Elegy ; but sure none will
contend that this is an Accident common to all
Ladies who have Lovers, and those Poets too.
Catullus addresses one Copy of Verses to the very
Sparrow of *Lesbia*, and in another deplores its
Death. A great many Lovers may have Mistres-
ses who never take a Voyage during their
Amour, and yet *Ovid* has an Elegy *ad Amicam
Navigantem* ; and so may ten thousand true Lo-
vers, especially such as are Poets, never venture on

any

any other Billows, but the Frown of their Fair
ones; and yet *Propertius* tofs'd in another Storm,
Writes to *Cynthia* upon it. And indeed to reduce the *Subjects* or *Occasions* of 𝕷𝖔𝖛𝖊-𝖁𝖊𝖗𝖘𝖊𝖘
to any particular Standard, is highly Irrational,
and must only be the effect of want of Confideration, for the various Circumstances and Fortunes of the Lovers must diversifie and alter
the *Occasions* of writing to their Mistresses:
So that there is no Occasion that is General,
and that can reach all Men in Love, but
the Cruelty of their Mistresses on their first Addresses, (that is, their not immediate Compliance)
for Jealousie is not Universal, or at least to extend to the Beating of her a Man Loves; yet
Ovid Writes *ad Amicam quam verberaverat*. I
must confess, I can't see the least Reason why the
Name and *Gloves* of a Mistress, with *the Place of
her Birth*, are not as just *Occasions* to Write on
as the Ring given to a Mistress, or her Parrot
or Sparrow; or a great many more I might enu-
merate out of the Ancients. A true Lover thinks
e'ry thing that belongs to her he Loves, worthy
his Thoughts; and the more our Modern Poets
extend their Reflections beyond the Ancients in
this, so much the greater Lovers they shew themselves. But the *Place of one's Mistress's Birth* is
not only worthy a Lover's Thoughts, but even
an *Universal Occasion*, since no Lover but must
meet with that Occurrence in whatever fair one
he adores, among all the beauteous Daughters of
Eve.

By what has been said, Sir, 'tis evident that
our Moderns are not inferiour to the Ancients,

in

In their Judgment in chuſing *Occaſions* on which they write to their Miſtreſſes: Or, That this Ingenious Gentleman has either through Want of Advertence, or out of Deſign expreſſed himſelf *ambiguouſly*, or at leaſt not with that *Clearneſs* that is requiſite to a concluſive Argument; which cannot be excuſed when the Honour and Merit of ſuch great Men as *Cowley* and *Waller* is concerned; nay, the Honour of our Country.

I come now to the Second Accuſation, which is, that *the Moderns fill their Verſes with Thoughts* ſurpriſing *and* glittering, *but not natural for e'ry Man in Love to think.* This lies under the ſame Fault as the other does, of being too general to be of any Force, it either condemns all that the Moderns have wrote, it caſts off e'ry Thought in their Love-Verſes as not tender and paſſionate, or does nothing at all, for it inſtances no particular. I'm confident the ingenious Gentleman will have ſo much Candor, as to confeſs that there are a great many very tender and ſoft Thoughts, and paſſionate Expreſſions in *Cowley*'s Miſtreſs, as in this one, that now occurrs to my Mind: *Then like ſome wealthy Iſland thou ſhalt lie*, &c. but if there be ſome, nay, a great many tender, ſoft, and paſſionate thoughts in our Moderns, then is this general charge not at all concluſive againſt 'em. Beſides, *Thoughts natural to a Man in* Love, is an obſcure Expreſſion, it conveys no clear Idea of any thing to the Mind; or, what is fully as erroneous, it ſeems to level the Thoughts of all Mankind, but it cannot be doubted, but that in the very ſame

Cir-

Circumſtances the Thoughts of different Men will be various, and more or leſs Excellent and Noble, as the Wit, Judgment, Fancy, and the other Qualities of the Mind of the Perſon affected, are more or leſs Excellent and perfect: And I am confident your ingenious Friend (whom I honour for his Wit, tho I differ from his Opinion) will allow me, That one of Mr. *Cowley*'s Genius wou'd no more have the Thoughts of a Fop, a Beau, a Tinker, a Shepherd, or any other ignorant and *unelevated* Mechanic, in Love, than out of it. *Again*, Thoughts *ſurprizing*, and *glittering* without particular Inſtances of 'em, as they prove nothing, ſo can they not be well anſwer'd, for an Inſtance would have made us apprehend what he takes for *ſurprizing* and *glittering*; but without that, or any Definition, we wander in the dark, and I can at beſt but only gheſs at his meaning. If by *Thoughts ſurprizing*, and *glittering* he means *extraordinary* and *uncommon*, I'm apt to think he will allow them very natural to Mr. *Cowley* or Mr. *Waller* in any Circumſtance. A Man that is us'd to a good Habit of thinking, cannot be without extraordinary Thoughts, on what concerns him ſo near as the Heart of his Miſtreſs. *Laſtly*, As to *far-fetch'd Similes*, 'tis an Expreſſion very *obſcure* and *ambiguous*; and I muſt acknowledge my ſelf wholly to ſeek in his Meaning, if a *Simile* be juſt, and hold an exact Analogy to the thing 'tis applied to, and of the thing 'tis deſigned to heighten, I preſume it cannot come into the Number of the *far-fetch'd*, and when-ever the Gentleman will pleaſe to inſtance in Particulars in either *Cowley*

or

or *Waller*, I engage to fellow them with those
that are full as faulty, even according to his own
Definition, let that be what it will, (for I suppose it can't be much amiss from so accurate a
Pen.) And till then I may supersede any particular Defence in this. Besides, 'tis not to be supposed, that the Verses written by Lovers are the
Extempore Result of a sudden Gust of Passion,
like the Inspirations of the *Delphic* Prophetess;
for I'm confident he'll agree with me that the
Excuse of Love will not free a Poet, that lets
them pass so from the Censure of *Boileau*.

> *Un sot en ecrivant, fait tout avec plaisir*
> *I'll na point en ses vers l'ambarras de Choisir.*

A Poetizing Lover, must be allow'd not to be absolutely out of his Wits, and that 'tis possible for
him to study, and consider what he says in so
solemn a Manner to his Mistress.

After this bold Assertion without Proof, he
advances to examine which are in the right, the
Ancients or the Moderns; the Rule of our Judgment in this, he justly makes the End the Poet
aims at, *viz. The obtaining the Love of his Mistress*, tho I cannot see why he should suppose that
contrary to, or inconsistent with getting *Fame*
and *Admiration*, since Admiration is a certain
Step to Love. When I read Mr. *Dryden*'s Works,
I cannot help Loving him. If I should not
love and respect him and any other Poet that
thinks well, and expresses his Thoughts nobly,
I should sin against my Reason. *Ovid* urges his
Fame and Reputation as a Motive for his Mistress's Love, and if that can move a Man of
Sense, why should we think the Effect won'd

not

not be the same on a Woman of Sense, and Generosity? And indeed, in e'ry one but an absolute dull, insipid Fool, which no Lover can
think his Mistress.

The End of Love-Verses being the gaining
the fair ones Heart, he proceeds to the best
means of obtaining that End, *viz. The convincing her that you love her.* I must deny this Assertion too, for tho *Love* in the Severity of Justice require *Love*; yet is that an Argument that
ought not always to prevail, since 'tis a Plea that's
common to a great many, for so the fair one
ought to surrender to 'em all; a Liberty no
Lover would willingly allow his Mistriss on any
Consideration whatever. But how often does
Experience tell us, that this *best Way* fails? Or
indeed, how seldom does it hit? *Admiration* is
the only just, and unquestioneable Parent of Love;
for the Senses or the Mind must be first won with
some Perfection, either real or imaginary. Whatever therefore can ravish Fame from the envious
censorious World, may justly be suppos'd able to
give *Admiration* to a Mistress. Nor is this inconsistent with the *true and lively Representation of
the Pains, and Thoughts attending the Passion of
Love*; for sure the Advantage of *Art* in Poems
cannot destroy the *End* which is not to be obtain'd in Painting without it, *viz.* a *lively Representation of Nature. Similes,* fine *Thoughts,* and
shining Points, if they be just, and good, must certainly give a greater Idea of any Pain, than a
bare and unpolished Rhime, without Beauty or
Grace. *This* gives us a *weak,* a *faint,* an *unmo-
ving* View of the Pain; *That* sets it close to us,
magnifies

magnifies and enlarges it : *This* gives it you as the reverse end of a Prospective Glass does Objects, *That* as the right end of it ; so that if a Representation of our Pain be the Path to Success, *Art* will be no ill Help and guide in it ; unless we'll suppose that our Mistress would be more sensibly touched with a *Grubstreet* Ballad, than a Copy of Verses by a *Cowley* or a *Waller*. But indeed, the Pain a Lover feels cannot be truely, and with Life represented without *Similes*, as is evident from the very Nature of the Mind, when in Pain : For 'tis an universal Measure of our Judgment of things to compare them with something else ; and the Mind in expressing its Pains endeavours to make it known in its full Greatness: to give therefore the greater Image of it, it generally seeks out something by a Comparison of which it hopes to obtain that End ; Comparison being the only Distinction of Degrees of things. This makes it narrowly in these Circumstances, regard and observe that Train of *Ideas* that continually pass before it, to call out such as are most proper for its purpose : For *'tis evident, (as Mr. Lock remarks) to any one that will but observe what passes in his own Mind, that there is a Train of Ideas constantly succeeding one another in his Understanding, as long as he's awake.* An Assertion therefore of an Ingenious Friend of mine, to the Prejudice of the Moderns, against *Similes* in the Expression of the Passions of Love and Grief, is contrary to the very Nature of the Mind. For let any Man endeavour to retain any particular Idea firmly and without Alteration, he will find it not in his Power to do it any considerable time,

such

such a neceſſary Succeſſion and Variation of Ideas (the Origin of Similes) is there in the human Mind. But becauſe 'tis ſaid that *'tis the nature of Grief to confine the Soul, ſtraiten the Imagination, and extremely leſſen the Number of its Objects*, I ſhall only oppoſe the Aſſertion of this Gentleman (whom I have always allow'd a Man of great Wit and Senſe) with an Obſervation of Mr. *Le Clerk*, (whom I'm ſure no Man that knows his Works, will deny to be one of the beſt Philoſophers of the Age) in the 6th. *Chapter* of his *Ontologie* and the 4th. *Paragraph*, he has to this purpoſe——"This be-
"ing ſo, we obſerve that the time ſeems ſhort
"to thoſe who ſpend it in Mirth, or any Em-
"ployment they perform with Pleaſure and De-
"ſire; but on the contrary, Tedious and Irk-
"ſome to the Unfortunate, and thoſe that are
"in Pain, or to thoſe that are againſt their Wills,
"oblig'd to ſome troubleſome Buſineſs. For we
"keep the Idea that is Gratefull and Pleaſant
"to us, as long without Variation as we are
"able, and thus by the viewing of the fewer
"Ideas, the time we ſpend in Pleaſure and
"Content, ſeems the ſhorter; whilſt on the
"contrary, our Minds endeavour to drive away
"a troubleſome Idea, and ſtrive to ſubſtitute
"ſome others in its room; Turning, Winding,
"Changing, Adding and Diminiſhing it, as the
"uneaſie inquietude Prompts. Thus the time
"ſeems longer than it wou'd do elſe, by that
"vaſt and numerous Train of Ideas, which, as
"I may ſay, ſhew themſelves *en paſſant* to the
"Mind, with an incredible Rapidity and Swift-
"neſs. From this juſt and rational Obſervation
of

of Mr. *Le Clerk* 'tis evident, That Similes are
not so unnatural in expression of Grief or Pain,
as some Ingenious Gentlemen contend : For the
Mind (especially that which is us'd to an Expression of its self in Allegory and Similes) will easily
in this Number of Ideas, meet with some that will
answer the End, the Mind is born to with so
much Impatience and Desire : For 'tis here also
evident, That Grief multiplies nor lessens the
Number of the Objects of the Mind.

From what has been said 'twill appear, That
Similes cannot be an unnatural Expression of this
Passion, or any Effects of it. I shall therefore
proceed to those few particular Instances the Author of the *Preface* gives, by which he draws a
short Parallel betwixt the Ancients and the Moderns. *I am pleas'd*, says he, *with Tibullus, when
he says, he cou'd live in a Desart with his Mistress,
where never any Humane Foot-steps appear'd, because
I doubt not but he really thinks what he says : But I
confess, I can hardly forbear Laughing, when Pe-*
trarch *tells us he cou'd live without any other Suste-
nance than his Mistresses Looks.* I confess, I must
ev'n here dissent from him too; for if you go to
the Rigor or Severity of the Reason of both
Expressions, they are equally impossible, and in
Impossibilities as well as Infinites, there are no
Degrees. For I can see no greater Probability
of Living in a Desart where there were no Humane Foot-steps, than on the Looks of a Mistress
only ; unless like *Nebuchadnezzar*, he wou'd feed
on the Leaves of the Trees, and Grass of the
Ground if there were any ; which is not very kind
to hope his Mistress wou'd comply with. But supposing

poſing it impoſſible, is there any Neceſſity of a Lovers ſaying nothing that exceeds the Bounds of *Poſſibility*? eſpecially in Poetry, where Hyperbole's are juſtifiable almoſt to Extravagance. That certainly wou'd be moſt unnatural of all, for the Thoughts of a Man really in Love, are naturally Extravagant ev'n to Impoſſibilities; tho *poſſunt quia poſſe videntur.* The very Definition of this Paſſion in Ethics, ſhews it violent and exorbitant. But we may in favour of *Petrarch* and Mr. *Cowley*, (who make uſe of the ſame Thought) ſay that they mean the Dyet of their Love, is a Look of their Miſtreſs.

I muſt confeſs, I'm extremely ſurpriz'd to find your Ingenious Friend an Advocate for that which wou'd make all the Sir *Courtly*'s Compoſitions of the *Nation*, the Standard of good Verſes; when he himſelf is really ſo well qualify'd to write like *Cowley* and *Waller*, and has by his own Practice in thoſe Verſes that are Publiſh'd, better confuted his Preface, than all I can pretend to ſay.

To my Honoured and Ingenious Friend Mr. Harrington, *for the Modern Poets againſt the Ancients.*

AS the Juſtice and Generoſity of your Principle, the ſweet Agreeableneſs of your Humor, the Vivacity of your Wit, and the ſtrength and force of your Judgment and Penetration, juſtly endear you to all your Acquaintance, ſo they qualify

qualify you for a Judge of the prefent Controverfie betwixt the Moderns and the Ancients, for
the Prize of Glory in Learning and Poetry. Monfieur *Perault* (whom I have not yet had the Opportunity to Read) has given it to the Moderns,
Rapin to the Ancients: Mr. *Rymer* has with a-
bundance of Indignation appear'd on *Rapin's* fide.
I cannot determine whether Mr. *Perault* has been
too partial to his own Country-men, (an Error
on the right fide) but I'm fure Mr. *Rymer* has been
extremely injurious to his ; which has made me
perhaps, too angry with him in my former Difcourfes. But I affure my felf that you are too good
an *Englifhman*, to let Friendfhip to any Man, bribe
you to condemn thofe rough Effects of my Zeal
for the **English Nation**. I will be more juft
than my Adverfary, I will yield that *Greece* had
Great Poets, notwithftanding all thofe monftrous
Faults and Abfurdities they abound with ; tho he
will not allow the *Englifh* any Honour, becaufe
they have been guilty of Errors. Nay, I'll fay
more, that the Poetry of *Greece* was her moft
valuable Learning , for that ftill maintains its
Share of Glory and Efteem, whilft her Philofophy is now exploded by the Univerfal Reafon of
Mankind. *Homer*, *Pindar*, *Sophocles* and *Euripides*, will, as long as they are underftood, preferve their Characters of Excellent Poets, tho the
Stagyrite with all his Volumes, is now fhrunk
from his Oftentatious Title of the *Philofopher*, to
that of a good *Critic*, or *Grammarian*.

Tho I grant the *Græcians* this, yet I cannot fub-
fcribe to the reft of the Hyperbolical Praifes fome
of our Modern Critics give them. For I confefs,

I

I can difcover no fuch *Univerfal Genius* in *Homer*, as they contend for, as that all Arts and Siences may be learn't from him: *Virgil* feems to me, more generally Learned by far; and Mr. *Cowley* among our *Englifh* Poets, may without Partiality, be put up for his Rival in the Glory of Learning. As for the *Numbers* of *Homer*, *Rapin* vaftly extols their Variety, and yet confeffes that to be the Property of the *Greek* Language, which makes it the eafier Task for *Homer* to perform, and by confequence, leffens his Merit on that Account. But it cannot be deny'd that *Virgil* has as much Variety in this as the *Roman* Language wou'd allow; and as was neceffary for the Beauty of his Poem; and they are in his Defcriptions efpecially, fo well chofen, that they extremely contribute to the Image of the thing defcrib'd; as *Gemitus dedere Caverna: praruptus aqua Mons*. The found of the firft makes us as it were hear the hollow noife the Spear of *Lyacoon* made in the *Trojan* Horfe; the other Places in our View fuch a watry Mountain. Among our *Englifh* Poets, none can compare with Mr. *Dryden* for Numbers: His Defcriptions are all very perfect in all things; but his Numbers contribute not a little to the force and life of the Reprefentation, for they carry fomething in them diftinct from the Expreffion and Thought; as in his Defcription of Night, What an Image of a profound Stillnefs does this following Verfe fet before us,

The Mountains feem to Nod their droufie Heads!

I have not room nor leifure at this time to make a thorough parallel betwixt the *Ancients* and

and the *Moderns*, and shall only cursorily run over the Heads. I have touch'd the *Universality of Genius*, and the *variety of Numbers* (this last being the Prerogative of the Language more than of the Poëts.) *Judgment* I think is apparently the due of the *Moderns*, who I'm confident wou'd ne'er have been guilty of those Absurdities the Ancients abound with. They seem to have been Masters of but little Reason, when they made their Gods such *limited* and *criminal Beings*. *Homer* often digresses from the *Hero*, that is the Subject of his Poem, to entertain us with other Objects too remote from *Achilles*. You may, Sir, easily perceive that I press not so hard as I might on the *Ancients*; that I omit abundance of *Improprieties*, and *Absurdities*, ridiculous even to *Childishness*, because I won'd not be thought to rob the *Fathers* of Poetry of their just Value and Esteem ; tho I confess I am of Mr. St. *Euremont*'s Opinion, that no Name can Privilege Nonsense or ill Conduct.

The Enemies of the Moderns will not deal so Civilly with them. They deny them to be Poets because they have not strictly observed the Rules laid down by *Aristotle*, but by that they discover themselves either ignorant or negligent of the most chief and important end of Poetry, that is, Pleasure. Now, it cannot be deny'd but he is the best Poet who takes the surest means to obtain the end he aims at ; in which, regard must be had to the *Humour*, *Custom*, and *Inclination* of the Auditory ; but an *English* Audience will never be pleas'd with a dry, that Jejune and formal Method excludes Variety as the Religious observation of the Rules of *Aristotle* does. And all those that exclaim against the
Liberty

ty some of our *English* Poets have taken, must grant that a *Variety* that contributes to the main Design, cannot divide our Concern: And if so, 'tis certainly an *Excellence* the *Moderns* have gain'd above the *Ancients*. This wou'd appear plainer if I had room and time to instance in Particulars. The Plays Mr. *Dryden* has bless'd the Age with will prove this; which if compar'd (as I hereafter intend) with those of *Sophocles* and *Euripides*, either for the Plot, Thought, or Expression, will gain him the Poets Garland from those two Hero's of Old *Greece*.

The *Plagiarism* objected to our Poets is common to the Ancients too; for *Virgil* took from *Homer*, *Theocritus*, and ev'n *Ennius*; and we are assur'd *Homer* himself built upon some Predecessors: And tho' their thoughts may be something a-kin, yet they alter their Dress, and in all other things we are satisfied with the *variety* of the outward visible Form, tho' the intrinsic value be the same, as Mr. *Congreve*'s Song has it, *Nothing new besides their Faces, e'ry Woman is the same.* In all things as well as Women the meer Variety of Appearance, whets our Desire and Curiosity. I am,

S I R,

Your Humble Servant,

Charles Gildon.

TO THE
HONOURABLE
GEORGE GRANVIL Esq;

An Essay at a parallel betwixt Philosophy, *and the* Love *of* Women.

THo' I confess *Horace* has generally a very just
Apprehension of Things, yet can I never a-
gree with him in his notions of *Happiness. Lib. 1:
Epist.* 6.

> *Nil* admirari *prope res est una Numici
> Solaq; quæ possit facere, & servare* Beatum.

for 'tis certain, that *Happiness* consists in *Pleasure,*
but there can be no *Pleasure,* without a *Gentle* and
agreeable Emotion of the Passion of Admiration,
the Ground of *Love* and *Joy,* out of which all
Pleasure is compos'd. As an instance of this
Truth, it must be granted, that as Virtue is the
chief *Basis* of Humane Happiness, so 'twill never
be embrac'd by any Man, that does not admire

Q and

and esteem its *Excellence*. And in the same manner, the other parts of *Philosophy* lead us to *Pleasure*, by 𝔄𝔡𝔪𝔦𝔯𝔞𝔱𝔦𝔬𝔫. For what pleasure is there in *Physics*, which proceed not from that agreable Wonder given us, by the strange and surprizing Variety, and force, we find in the Nature of corporeal Things? What Pleasure does *Metaphysics* afford, that is not built on our *Esteem*? (and *Esteem* is the only part of *Admiration* that contributes to Pleasure, for there's a Pain attends despising, which is the other Division of it,) what Pleasure I say have we in this study, but what is built on our *Esteem* of the valuable *Certainty* it furnishes us with in what ever it proposes? For there is nothing more sure than *Abstract Ideas,* the subject of *Ontology* or *Metaphysics*. Again in *Pneumatology*, does not the Contemplation of the Purer, and Superior Beings, to the very Supream, and first cause of all that Exists, fill our Souls with excessive and amazing Delight and Wonder? Lastly, what *Pleasure* is there in *Woman*, that soft summary of Man's Happiness, which derives not its self from 𝔄𝔡𝔪𝔦𝔯𝔞𝔱𝔦𝔬𝔫? 𝔄𝔡𝔪𝔦𝔯𝔞𝔱𝔦𝔬𝔫, therefore is so far from being an Enemy to, that it is the very foundation of our *Happiness*, whether we consider it in the *Direction*, or *Aim* and *End* of our *Life*, that is in 𝔓𝔥𝔦𝔩𝔬𝔰𝔬𝔭𝔥𝔶 or 𝔚𝔬𝔪𝔞𝔫.

Some Sir, may perhaps think I have made a very strange mixture, in joyning *Philosophy* and *Woman*; tho' I'm confident, so much Wit, Youth, and all those other Accomplishments of a fine Gentleman, that render you the darling
of

of both Sexes, will not let you think I have degraded *Philosophy* in it, which will appear from a short parallel drawn betwixt them.

𝔓𝔥𝔦𝔩𝔬𝔰𝔬𝔭𝔥𝔶 is either employed in the Consideration of Bodys, as in *Physics*, of *Beings* in general, or *Abstract Ideas*, as in *Metaphysics* or *Ontology*; or of *Pure* and *Immaterial Essences*, as the *Souls*, *Angels*, *God*, as in *Pneumatology*, or lastly of 𝔙𝔦𝔯𝔱𝔲𝔢 as in Ethics.

First, the Business of Physics is extreamly uncertain, for there the Mind is employed about very *Obscure Ideas*; and though some of our Experiments, often present us with certain Effects, yet does it not always discover the absolute certainty of the Cause, nor shall we ever be able to penetrate into the inmost Nature, or all the qualitys of Matter, and till then we must be in the dark, as to the true Causes; so that *Physic*'s put us upon the chase of what we have very little probability of obtaining. On the other Hand, the 𝔏𝔬𝔳𝔢 of 𝔚𝔬𝔪𝔞𝔫 is more certain in obtaining as well as more noble in its *End*, *viz.* a perfect Enjoyment of, and a close Union with the Object desir'd, the effect of which ends not with them, but is perpetuated by their Off-Spring, who are a part of 'em, the admirable and certain *Effect*, of a known Charming, and Generous Cause.

Second-

Secondly, *Metaphysics* amuses us with meer *Abstract Ideas*, whilst the **Love** of **Woman**, puts us in a sensible Possession of a *Real*, not *Ideal Abstract* of all the Beautys and Perfections of every *Being* on this side of the Eternal. The Contemplation of whom, with the Created Spirits makes up *Pneumatology*; but we wander in too uncertain a Path, in our Contemplation of these latter, to arrive at satisfaction; for *Fancy* there directs our steps more, than *Judgment* built on *Right Reason*, and *Evidence*. And therefore that part cannot be comparable to that of the **Love** of **Woman**, which gives us by the most prevailing way, the *Senses*, a proof of the Existence of Spirits, if not distinct from, yet of a purer Make, than even the refin'd Body of Woman; for what *Lover* is there that does not feel, perfectly feel some unseen Spirits darted from the bright Eyes of the fair one he adores, which have a sensible influence on him, tho' he touch her not; and these are Spirits that chear, not shock our Natures, as those other Fantoms do.

Then for the Contemplation of the **Supream Being**, the best Philosophers form an Idea of Him by his *Wondrous Works*, of which what can give a fairer Image of him, than **Woman**, the most Beautiful, Good, and Compassionate being of the Universe? Which made St. *Austin* compare God to a fine Woman viewing her own Perfection in a Glass. 'Tis true that the Admirable Order, and Oeconomy of the Coelestial Bodys, their Glory and

and Light discover apparent Foot steps of the Eternal Mind: these shew us a powerful and a wise *Being*, but nothing has a share of his best attribute of Goodness, but the best part of Man, *Woman*, his own image. Besides, the Consideration of the Universe is as I may say a voluminous Introduction to the Contemplation of that *Being*, we are forc'd there to run through objects different, and various in their Forms and Beauty, as well as vastly distant in their situation, which all contributes to the Confusion and Imperfection of the Image they present of the *Power* and *Wisdom* of God; and the Administration of Humane Affairs is a too tedious, as well as a too controverted argument of his Goodness. But *Woman* gives us at once a Beautiful and more Compendious prospect of his *Power*, *Wisdom* and *Goodness*; for as *Pliny* says, never are the works of Nature so admirable as in small things, and *Woman* is the Minature draught of all his Attributes that are communicable to his Creatures; for in one fine *Woman* we may read the legible Characters of an Almighty Hand. From whom also had I time and room, I cou'd draw the knowledge of the Moral Attributes of the first Cause.

Lastly, Ethics teach us the Rules and Prescripts of *Virtue*, to secure us from those Inquietudes, the *Criminal* and *Vicious* Experience: but this is only subservient to, and prepares us for the enjoyment of *Woman*, in a more perfect Degree; for it contracts and calls home all our *Wandring Wishes*

and

and our *loose Desires*, and directs them all to one
Object, which like the Sun-beams contracted into a burning Glass, must be of far greater Force,
and by consequence, give a greater and more
exalted Relish of *Delight*, than when scatter'd
and dissipated.

Ethics only informs the Mind with a bare
knowledge of Vertue, without having power
to influence us to the embracing of it, for there
are a great many that with *Medea* in *Ovid* may
say,

———*Video meliora proboq;*
Deteriora sequor ———

but *Woman* can effect what Philosophy is impotent in; for whilst that proposes the meer unac-
tive Theory, the 𝕷𝖔𝖛𝖊 of 𝖂𝖔𝖒𝖆𝖓 reduces it
to Practice, for when that is necessary to please
her a Man loves, all the Facultys of the Soul u-
nite to effect the noble Work.

'Tis methinks such an Arraignment of the *first
Cause* to run down that Sex, which Heaven has
made choice of to impart to so large a share, in giving Immortality to Humane Race by the propa-
gation of our kind, that they deserve not to taste
that Pleasure that is join'd to so mighty a work.
*The greatest Pleasure in the noblest Act, with the di-
vininest of Creatures* 𝖂𝖔𝖒𝖆𝖓.

But

But whether *Philosophy* or *Woman* have the right of *Precedence*, 'tis certain they both afford us a *Noble* and *agreeable Pleasure*, without one or both, of which we can never be truly happy. But yet by the *Nil admirari* of *Horace*, they are thrown aside; for the cutting off *Admiration*, deprives us of all Pleasure in either, that in both being built on *Admiration*. And indeed, this passage seems to aim at a *Stupid*, and *Pyrrhonian Indifference*, or *Indisturbance* and *Insensibility*, which can no more be arriv'd at, than 'tis to be desir'd.

But perhaps I mistake the sense of *Horace*, who it may be, is only against that variable and wavering Admiration, that is the Mother of Ten Thousand fruitless Inquietudes and Troubles, by generating too numerous a Progeny of restless Desires for ev'ry object that presents it self. This I confess is so far an Enemy to *Happiness*, as 'tis to *Constancy* and *Resolution* its safe guard, and which are so eminently conspicuous in you.

F I N I S.

ERRATA.

PAge 17. Line. 3. read *thus*. p. 18. l. 14. r. *his*. p. 36. l. 8. dele the 2d. *that*. p. 37. l. penul. r. *tho'*. p. 41. l. 11. r. *purposely*. p. 43. l. 1. r. *he does*. l. 3. add *rashly or maliciously*. p. 44. l. 5. r. *Yours*, &c. l. 1. p. 45. l. 10. r. *his*. p. 46. l. 17. r. *was*. p. 47. l. 2. r. *and*. p. 50. l. 13. add *the* p. 54. l. 6. r. *containing*. p. 55. l. 17. dele II. p. 66. l. 11. r. *formally*. p. 72. l. 3. r. *an*. p. 83. r. *Reputation*. p. 84. l. 1. r. *can*. p. 110. l. 9. r. *so*. p. 197. l. 8. r. *Floods*. P. 195. l. 5. r. *whom* p. 125. l. 9. r. *Wretch*.

There are many false Points and Comma's, and some Faults not here mentioned, which the Reader is desir'd to excuse and correct.